kosher
ADULTERY

Seduce and Sin with Your Spouse

Shmuley Boteach

Adams Media Corporation
Avon, Massachusetts

For Debbie

Published by
Adams Media Corporation
57 Littlefield Street, Avon, MA 02322. U.S.A.
www.adamsmedia.com

ISBN: 1-58062-792-7

Printed in the United States of America.

J I H G F E D C B A

Library of Congress Cataloging-in-Publication Data
Boteach, Shmuley.
Kosher adultery : seduce and sin with your spouse / Shmuley Boteach.
p.   cm.
Includes bibliographical references.
ISBN 1-58062-792-7
1. Adultery. 2. Trust. 3. Sexual excitement. I. Title.
HQ806 .B667 2002
306.73'6--dc21
2002008430

This publication is designed to provide accurate and authoritative information
with regard to the subject matter covered. It is sold with the understanding that
the publisher is not engaged in rendering legal, accounting, or other professional advice. If legal advice or other expert assistance is required, the services
of a competent professional person should be sought.
   —From a *Declaration of Principles* jointly adopted by a Committee of the
American Bar Association and a Committee of Publishers and Associations

This book is available at quantity discounts for bulk purchases.
For information, call 1-800-872-5627.

CONTENTS

Acknowledgments v
The Raging Rapids and the Calm Currents:
The Incompatibility of "Fiery" and "Watery" Love 1

Part 1
The **Forbidden** Fruit / 5

o n e   **Trust,** the Destroyer of Marriage 7
t w o   Turning Your Spouse into Your **Lover** 19
t h r e e   **Curiosity**—The Single Most Important Ingredient . . 43
f o u r   The **Insatiable** Woman and the Male **Animal** . . . 65

Part 2
The **Pain** and **Power** of Infidelity / 87

f i v e   Adultery 101: What Makes Adultery **Hot?** 89
s i x   Monogamy and the **Sin** of Adultery 107

Part 3
The **Ten Commandments** of Kosher Adultery / 135

s e v e n   **Seducing** and **Sinning** with Your Spouse 137
e i g h t   Commandment One in Action—
Becoming a **Total** Sexual Partner 159
n i n e   Commandment Two in Action—
Erotic Obstacles That Lead to **Desire** 175
t e n   Commandments Three and Four in Action—
Creating **Friction** 189
e l e v e n   Commandment Five in Action—
Attraction to **Strangers** 217

twelve   Commandment Six in Action—
          Jealousy Is Essential 231
thirteen Commandment Seven in Action—
          Intense Focus 257
fourteen Commandment Eight in Action—
          Heightening **Attraction**, Minimizing
          Compatibility 267
fifteen   Commandment Nine in Action—
          Nourishing the **Ego** 279
sixteen   Commandment Ten in Action—
          Experiencing **Sin** 295

Part 4
The Dawning of the Kosher Adultery **Revolution** / 307

seventeen Parents Are **Lovers**, Too 309
eighteen   The Rebirth of **Lust** and **Love** in Marriage . . 323
nineteen   **Spirituality** and **Mysticism**
           As Our Erotic Guides 339

epilogue   A Final Note from the Author 351

references 355

Acknowledgments

First, I wish to thank my wife Debbie, my superior in all things related to love, for all that she has taught me about relationships through personal example. I have had to work hard throughout married life to rise to my wife's level of refinement and remain worthy of her. But she also provides the inspiration that makes the effort a joy. Still, she says, she should have jumped at the chance to marry the tall guy.

I offer humble thanks to Almighty God who has provided me with a loving spouse, who has been a great source of comfort to me since my parents' divorce, as well as my beautiful children, who are the light of my life. I am thankful to Him for the kindness of being able to write and publish books.

My kids make it difficult to write. They're always barging in just when I come up with some great idea. And it didn't help that they destroyed the only electronic copy of this book by playing with it on the computer thinking it was a video game. Only a year of work was lost. But heck, they're more fun than writing books anyway, and I want to thank them for helping me take myself far less seriously.

I wish to thank the great people of Adams Media, especially Gary M. Krebs, my editor, for believing in this project and being so patient in the arduous process of its birth. The flaws in this book are all from Adams Media, all the good stuff is mine. I hope that all the negative reviewers out there will therefore direct any criticism to the appropriate party.

I wish to thank all the men and women who have committed adultery over the years without whom this book could not have been written. If you are in an adulterous relationship even while reading this book, please call my radio show and give us all the sordid details so as to boost my ratings. If you do call in, we'll send you a free copy of my book *Moses of Oxford* (1,000 pages in length, sold fifteen copies, and even that only after my mother bought ten out of pity). And if you *don't* call in, we'll send you two.

I also wish to thank my literary agent and friend, Lois de la Haba, for all her subtle and dignified marketing of my books. (When Gary Krebs first turned this book down, she looked him squarely in the eye and said, "Look, he's got seven kids to support. Have you no mercy?") Lois is a great midwife. Without her, this and other books I have authored would still be in the gestation stage.

I offer much love and thanks to my dear friend Ronald Feiner, a consummate professional with an exemplary heart. I hope always to be there for you as you have been for me. You are like an older brother whose counsel and wisdom I seek always.

My mother is someone who is infinitely patient with me. Like a Biblical matriarch, she is kind to all whom she meets, her home is open to passersby, and she has never given up her belief in life and love amidst the trials she has experienced. She sacrificed everything for her children, and look what turned out! Okay, don't rub it in. Mom, you are a great woman and a great inspiration. It's an honor to be your son.

My father is strong, rugged, and devoted and taught me to believe in myself, even if what I had to say was controversial. Of course, after I said those things, he denied ever knowing me. But it's the thought that counts, right?

Finally, to my brothers and sisters, Sara, Bar Kochva, Chaim, and Ateret: You are the best friends I have in the entire world. I love you.

Shmuley Boteach
Englewood, New Jersey
May 2002

INTRODUCTIONINTRODUCTIONINTR
ODUCTIONINTRODUCTIONINTRODU
CTIONINTRODUCTIONINTRODUCTIO
NINTRODU introduction DUCTIONIN
TRODUCTIONINTRODUCTIONINTRO
DUCTIONINTRODUCTIONINTRODUC
TIONINTRODUCTIONINTRODUCTIO

THE RAGING RAPIDS
AND THE CALM
CURRENTS:
THE INCOMPATIBILITY OF
"Fiery" AND
"Watery"
LOVE

L ove is a spring from which two rivers flow: the river of intimate love and the river of illicit love. Just as the spring of love swells up from the underground pathways of the heart, it immediately separates into these two flows. The river of intimate love is a river of calm currents and still streams. There are few rapids on this river and little danger of being dashed against the rocks or sucked into a whirlpool. The voyage on this river is steady and predictable, and while the scenery may be lovely, you have to stay awake to see it.

Not so the river of *illicit love*. This is a river of hidden rip-tides and roller-coaster rapids. Few ever survive the tumultuous ride on this river, but wow, what a ride it is. Many are drawn to the sheer intensity of its waters, because, while they suspect that their bones will eventually be crushed against the ominous boulders, it is the only time that their heart feels totally alive, and their spirit engaged.

The river of intimate love leads to commitment and marriage. The river of illicit love leads to adultery and affairs. The river of intimate love brings pleasure and life; the river of illicit love brings pain and death. Ironically, however, the river of intimate love feels like death, while the river of illicit love makes people feel entirely alive. This is an inconstancy of existence and, indeed, one of the great tragedies of love.

A man and a woman start dating. As they spend more time in each other's company weaving the fabric of shared experience, they gradually fall in love. Their joy in each other's embrace weans them off the need for other embraces. The comfort of each other's presence makes the need for romance with others obsolete. They put each other first in their respective lives, consigning friends and even family to a secondary role. Soon they are ready to solidify their commitment to each other by being joined in wedlock. They marry, create a home, and ready themselves for the prospective pleasures of married life.

But in time—sometimes a month, sometimes ten years—they discover that married life involves "settling down." The summer of their initial passion cools into the winter of growing indifference.

Whereas in the early years of marriage they looked forward to coming home from work and telling each other everything they had experienced that day, now they come home and immediately put on the TV. Whereas in the first stages of their relationship, dates consisted of going out for drinks and talking for hours, now they go out on a Saturday night to a movie and talk only about the film. Whereas in the beginning of their relationship they made passionate love once, even twice, a day they now settle with one night a week of lovemaking—if five minutes of foreplay and a rapid denouement can even be called "lovemaking."

What has happened to this idyllic pair? How can two people with so much to share now pass entire evenings in bored silence? What was once a man and a woman in love has become a husband and wife. What used to be two lovers has become two partners. What had been a soulful connection has become two people joined by a mortgage and kids.

It is then that they eye the parallel flowing river of adultery with envy and curiosity. Its torrent is inviting. Its waves heave in an orgasmic swell. They are sucked in by its surf, invited in by its vortex, tempted by its promise of turbulence and excitement. And they are prepared to forsake all to rise and roll with its tide. Adultery is a magnet to married men and women whose lives have become like cold steel.

But the jolts and jerks of this violent river eventually exact their toll. Joints come out of socket, bones get broken, and soon the partners in the rickety raft end up washed up on shore, a motley pile of shattered hearts and battered dreams. It's at this point that they look longingly over their shoulder, back to the other river, and wonder if they could ever rejoin its tranquility. Their ardor and excitement is transformed to humility and regret as they beg their partners to take them back. Often, however, they find that their partners have continued along their steady, fixed course, leaving them behind with nary a second glance.

Most people assume that these two rivers can run only in parallel to one another, never to meet. That is what people are referring to when they talk about the tragedy of love. It is accepted as a painful reality that passion and intimacy are parallel lines that are governed by the basic rules of geometry and thus can never meet. Until now.

This book has a single purpose: to serve as a dike that causes the two opposing rivers to flow into a single stream. By sharing the intimacy of Kosher Adultery with your partner, by inviting forbiddenness, secrecy, danger, and tension into your marriage, the two rivers merge so that they may run in unison. I assert that *love and lust are truly obtainable in marriage today and that sinfulness may be brought into a legitimate union.* It is well within the power of every married couple to make the two currents coalesce and establish a union that has all the benefits of consistency and comfort, but is driven along by passion and fire.

By reading this book, you have already begun your rebirth.

part 1

The Forbidden Fruit

ONEONEONEONEONEONEONEONEO
NEONEONEONEONEONEONEONEON
EONEONEONEONEONEONEONEONE
ONEONEONEO   one   ONEONEONEO
NEONEONEONEONEONEONEONEON
EONEONEONEONEONEONEONEONE
ONEONEONEONEONEONEONEONEO

Trust,
THE DESTROYER
OF MARRIAGE

I see adultery as the soul's desire to be something other than staid and stable and the heart's desire to yield to ecstasy.

—LOUISE DESALVO, *ADULTERY*

Every good wife should commit a few infidelities to keep her husband in countenance.

—GEORGE BERNARD SHAW

There is so little difference between husbands that you might as well keep the first.

—ADELA ROGERS ST. JOHN

7

W hat if everything we thought we knew about love was dead wrong and was killing our marriages? What if husbands and wives are divorcing at alarming rates because they have all been fed a lie? What if young men and women who try to establish intimate relationships cannot achieve that simple purpose because they have been given the wrong tools? What if the entire edifice of love is collapsing because the most basic advice from relationship experts is tragically mistaken?

For decades now the leading relationship gurus have shouted their mantra from the rooftops: The twin pillars of every successful relationship are trust and respect. Famed marriage expert and author John Gottman says expressly in his book *Why Marriages Succeed or Fail* (1994) that love and respect are the two most important ingredients in a happy marriage. And because trust and respect have been established as the soul of every relationship, it follows that whatever establishes greater trust in a relationship becomes essential to a marriage. The natural tributaries of trust are communication, sharing, total openness, and respect.

Kosher Adultery is dedicated to the premise that this advice is absurd and horribly harmful. Indeed, spousal trust is the most damaging aspect of every marriage. Marriages that are based on trust become boring, routine, and predictable. Husbands who "respect" their wives usually treat them like their mothers or their sisters. They may look up to them, but they don't want to make love to them.

> *Marriages should be based not on trust, but on tension. Not on routine, but on raging emotion. Not on respect, but on jealousy. Not on confidence, but suspicion.*

Sounds crazy, right? But think of it this way: *When you trust that your spouse will never be erotically attracted to a stranger and will never be unfaithful, you start taking him or her for granted.* Isn't this really the number-one killer of marriage? Isn't growing bored and "falling out of love" the most lethal of all marital illnesses? Won't a relationship be doomed if a couple is complacent and smug to the point of not having to work at it anymore?

The Lure of a Suitor

Relationships die when two people no longer make each other's skin tingle because they've settled into a routine. Time and time again, we see people in love with each other gradually drift apart until they end up where they began—as strangers.

In the early stages of dating, a man will usually *not* take a woman for granted: He shows up on time for the date immaculately attired; he compliments her sparkling eyes and her sensuous lips; during sex he is intensely focused on his date's pleasure, rather than simply rushing to the finish line; he suppresses bad habits like his temper, or picking the wax out of his ears, until he has taken her home. Why? *Because she doesn't trust him.* He's a stranger to her, and he wants to win her over by making a favorable impression. He realizes that she is an attractive young female whom other men are interested in, and who is herself interested in other men. So he recognizes that he must be better than the other potential suitors.

Conversely, she knows that he doesn't trust her either. He doesn't immediately share his secrets with her, articulate his fears, or voice his anxieties. Why should he? They barely know each other. Indeed, he may terminate the relationship tomorrow with something as easy as a phone call. So she listens sympathetically when he talks, maintaining eye contact, showing him that she really cares. She is conscious of the fact that he is an ambitious and eligible young man who could go after another woman, if he so chooses. The dates go on, with each partner endeavoring to put his or her best foot forward and win the other over.

However, as time progresses and trust is established in the relationship and they begin to feel really comfortable around each other, they also begin taking each other for granted. He doesn't mind being late for a date. He thinks to himself, "She'll understand how hassled I am at work and sometimes I just get held up." Their sex life begins to suffer as he doesn't put as much time into kissing and hugging or giving her long sensual massages. Rather than focusing on her needs, he now does "what comes naturally," to the extreme detriment of their erotic life. With every slam-bam job—where he's finished just as she's getting started—he rationalizes to himself that she knows he's got a million responsibilities on his mind and uses sex to rid himself of pent-up anxiety and to help him sleep. He doesn't want to work at it—and feels she'll understand if he doesn't have the energy or patience for cuddling afterwards.

In short, he's behaving in a laid-back manner because he's won her over and he does not have to impress her any more. If he occasionally scratches his crotch in her presence—well, guys are guys, right? And if he belches while they're having dinner, well, they know each other, so it's ok. Yet, no matter how he acts, he doesn't think she's going anywhere.

But then a guy at her office begins to show interest in her. He suspects that she begins to reciprocate. Suddenly, the man becomes jealous and the comfort in their relationship is lost. He sees how she talks about this other man constantly, bringing him up gratuitously in their conversations. He now no longer trusts her. He conjectures that she is developing a crush on the would-be suitor. Now he cannot afford to take her for granted. He feels competitive with the other guy eyeing his woman. "Does he dress better than me?" he asks himself. "Is she more attracted to him? Maybe she likes him because he compliments her more than me." And, question of all questions, "Although she denies it, is she secretly interested in *him*? More than *me*?"

But amidst his anxiety, he suddenly starts treating her better. He doesn't want to lose her to this other man, so he realizes he better satisfy her. Now he's dressing up for her again, taking her out, and making passionate love—just like it was at the beginning of the relationship. In addition, he also feels more attracted to her: The possibility of losing her has made her seem new to him; the loss of trust has made her exciting; the act of her having become the object of forbidden desire has made her sinful; and the fact that she is a woman who is desired by another man has made her erotic. Other men giving her the eye has bestowed upon her a new beauty. All of this has been generated by the possibility of her unfaithfulness.

Ah, if only husbands fathomed the insatiability of their wife's libidos (if it's not completely killed off by their distracted spouses) and their attractiveness to other men, perhaps we would never see another divorce.

The Real Cause of Broken Marriages

In the final analysis, what is really the grim reaper of so many marriages? Is it when couples cheat on each other? Is it when they argue over money? Maybe it's when one spouse is too close to siblings or parents, making the other spouse feel secondary? Or is it the ubiquitous "irreconcilable differences" that are cited as the cause of so many celebrity divorces? Undoubtedly, all of these may serve as major factors in the unraveling of a relationship. But they are mere symptoms of a much more serious illness.

The number one cause of divorce is falling out of love. When a husband and wife lose their attraction for each other, there is nothing left, save functional things like a mortgage or kids to keep them together. As they slowly become less desirable to one another, their marriage gets sick and dies. Isn't this the source of the other four leading causes of divorce that we just mentioned?

When you no longer care what your spouse thinks of you, then you don't mind arguing with him or her over every trifling detail. If you are insufficiently attracted to your spouse, then you risk being attracted to, and cheating with, strangers. How much money you have or spend becomes more important than what you mean to each other. When there is insufficient love or attraction in your marriage, you gravitate to those with whom you share an indestructible bond, your parents and siblings. And what do you have left when the mysterious forces of attraction have so waned that they no longer draw you to one another? Of course, irreconcilable differences.

The rule is simple: As long as you are strongly attracted to each other, you can surmount any hurdle in your relationship. This is the rule which is true at the beginning of a relationship, when although you don't know each other your attraction keeps you going on dates until that knowledge is gained. And remains true throughout the life of a relationship. So long as you are strongly drawn to one another, you will do almost anything to please each other. Yet the moment the attraction and desire wanes, you will begin to drift apart no matter what else you share in common, just as surely as a tile falls off a wall once its adhesive fails even if it is the same color as the bathroom's other fixtures. In fact, attraction creates compatibility. A man who hates running will take up jogging to be next to a woman he wants to seduce. A woman who has no interest in cars will start learning about them with a boyfriend she loves in order to share his passion. Parents who love their children will spend long days at a silly amusement park in order to experience their children's smile.

And here we have the main reason for the highest divorce levels in history: Husbands and wives get married and gradually lose their attraction to each other. Men and women plan to spend sixty years together but lose the mysterious gravitational pull within four or five. Marriage today has become far too cozy and trusting. If husbands and wives were more anxious about retaining each other's faithfulness, were far more focused on the strangers that are attracted to their spouses, and confessed to each other the petty attractions they harbor toward strangers, they would become far more desirable to each other, and they would start to woo each other all over again. They usually refrain from doing so, however, for fear of undermining the relationship's trust.

In the typical scenario, a man and a woman are attracted to each other. They start dating, they fall in love, and they marry.

They marry because they want to cement their love for each other and make it permanent. Little do they know that their marriage is going to finish them off. Whatever passion they feel for each other, the routine of marriage is bound to destroy it. Whatever novelty they pose to each other, the familiarity of marriage is destined to erase it. And whatever attraction they have for each other, the predictability of marriage is bound to undercut it. Isn't it ironic that the institution that unified them—marriage—is what ultimately tears them apart?

The *Possibility* of Adultery

The purpose of *Kosher Adultery* is to establish a marriage that has all the benefits of consistency and comfort, but is driven by passion and fire. I intend to teach married couples how to have an illicit and intimate affair—with each other. I aim to teach husbands how to turn their wives into their mistresses—and wives how to turn their husbands into passionate lovers.

Husbands and wives must recapture erotic desire in their minds by bringing the forbidden into marriage, by creating erotic obstacles that heighten attraction, by noticing their spouses' irresistibility to members of the opposite sex, and by bringing voyeurism back into a long-term relationship. In short, married couples must learn how to *sin together.*

That couples sin with *strangers* rather than with *each other* is one of the great tragedies of infidelity. Studies show that adulterous sexual activities are most likely to take place in the marital bed, which begs this question: If the location could accommodate an adulterous affair, couldn't the marital relationship also have been turned into an affair? As one adulterous woman, whose infidelity led to the loss of both her husband and her lover, said, "I still love my lover *and* I love my husband. I *need,* ideally, a husband who is also a lover. I think that says it all" (*Adultery* by Annette Lawson).

The crux of this book is that the "possibility of adultery" between partners must exist in order for couples to remain attracted to each other. The fact is, adultery exists as a concept and has a powerful lesson for each of us. While people must not violate the sanctity and trust of a marriage, they must remember they are married not just to a person, but to a sexually attractive, lustful person. They must be aware of the fact that their spouse is *attracted to*, and *attractive to*, many members of the opposite sex. At any time, your spouse could choose to go outside the marriage to find sex and excitement. This very idea alone should instill a sense of urgency into always keeping the sexual attention of one's spouse. In addition, focusing on the attractiveness of our spouse to strangers makes him or her more attractive in our eyes, and brings passion and energy into a lifeless relationship.

Sex *Should* Be Out of Control

The question may be asked, if the possibility of adultery is central to marriage, and if we can never completely possess our spouse, how, then, can husbands and wives remain loyal in thought, speech, and action to each other? How can two opposites coexist? On the one hand, repressing our sexuality is unhealthy, and acknowledging our attraction and attractiveness for others to our spouse is positive and leads to excitement in marriage. On the other hand, actually committing adultery destroys in one fell swoop everything in marriage that we had hoped to achieve!

The answer is to create the most passionate relationship possible and to "have an affair" with our spouse. A man and a woman who burn with an incredible intensity toward one another are so consumed by their attraction that there is nothing left of their wick for any other flame to burn. Passion is the secret of fidelity, not repression. Intimacy is the safeguard of our virtue, not values. Contrary to popular thinking, you're no hero if you can control your sexual urge. Sexual instincts are not meant to be controlled. Really exciting sex means *losing* control, lighting a fire that is all-consuming and that burns out of control. The real passion of sex occurs only when one's senses, emotions, and libido are on autopilot. The objective is to ignite that inferno within your marriage by focusing on the sexual insatiability of your spouse and how at any moment he or she could become someone else's illicit lover.

Are Lust and Passion Kosher?

Make no mistake. *I have not written a book in favor of adultery.* Indeed, I do not in any way condone infidelity under any circumstances. Husbands and wives who cheat on their spouses are not only reckless and unfaithful, they are imbecilic. They have not lost their virtue or their values, they have lost their vision. They could easily have had a much more passionate and forbidden affair with the person they chose to marry. Doing so would have given them the best of all possible worlds: a fiery lover who is also their intimate companion. I should also point out that all sexual relations must be consensual by *both parties*. (This is quite apart from the appalling situation of date rape—or any rape for that matter. Even within a marriage there will be times when one partner wants sex and the other doesn't. Jewish law is adamant that there can be no sex in marriage unless it is undertaken willingly, even joyfully, by *both* husband and wife.) I am making a case for rising above questions of infidelity and unfaithfulness in marriage by learning to become unfaithful with one's own spouse, so that all the seductive qualities of adultery can be brought into marriage.

The title of this book is meant to emphasize the redeeming nature of adultery, how it can actually be "kosher," and how the principles behind it can be made to save rather than destroy marriages. Understanding the sizzling soul of adultery can bring life into what for many is the dead corpse of marriage. A powerful light can be extracted from the darkness of adultery and illuminate the dark alleys of a moribund marriage. Jews have always believed that everything—even that which initially seems negative—can be used in the service of

God. If adultery is indeed the most potent and intense manifestation of a male/female relationship, and jealousy is the strongest of the emotions, then we have to harness the power of these elements and carry that power over into the marital bed. That's what *kosher* means. When we say food is made "kosher," it refers to a meal previously forbidden for consumption that has been made ritually available to nourish human beings. The same can be done with adultery. Adultery, not marriage, is the most written-about theme in all of world literature. Infidelity, not faithfulness, is the most talked-about issue on all the daytime talk shows. It is time we identified the ingredients that make an affair so delectable and sprinkle them into the relationship of husband and wife so that marriage can be more savory.

I recognize that the thesis put forward in this book is potentially controversial and will likely disagree with people's sensibilities. I also recognize that its underlying premise—the centrality of sex to marriage and romantic relationships—is another contention that might rankle my readers. Religious people in particular have been conditioned to believe that, in order for sex to be sanctified, it must take place only with the intention of procreation—otherwise, engaging in sex is a sinful act. I can also imagine that many people, both religious and secular, will be outraged by some of the advice proposed in this book. Advocating, in cases of extreme urgency, that wives sit in a bar so that their husbands can see the men who want to pick them up is perhaps not the advice that people expected to garner from the author of *Kosher Sex*. I can see even my non-Jewish readers turning the pages and thinking, "Has Shmuley gone *meshugah?*" (crazy, for those of you not trained in Yiddish slang).

Yet, I offer that and other advice unapologetically. This book is driven by my belief that saving marriage from terminal decline should be the foremost responsibility of society today. No society with a 60-percent divorce rate can call itself civilized. Moreover, it is not only the institution of marriage that is crumbling, but that more women than ever before are emulating the *Sex and the City* ideal of not needing a man and finding fulfillment from their careers instead. In fact, it is heterosexuality as we know it that is currently under threat. More men than ever before are dating women and not feeling attracted to them for any other purpose than having sex.

I believe wholeheartedly in the holiness of marriage and in our responsibility to preserve its modesty and integrity. But all too often these considerations are put before the basic need to keep a married couple's sex life and mutual attraction alive and thriving. Many people actually view the sanctity of a marriage to be in conflict with the erotic side of matrimony.

The Bible relates that when the Jews came out of Egypt and God commanded Moses to build the Tabernacle, the women donated their copper mirrors to be melted down and used as the washbasin for the priests. But Moses rejected the mirrors, maintaining that since their purpose had been to arouse the lust of their husbands, their use would contradict a holy purpose. But it was God Himself who overruled Moses and insisted that the mirrors be made an integral part of the Tabernacle. God told Moses that the mirrors were particularly precious to Him because they increased love and desire between husband and wife.

Few things could have been deemed holier.

TWOTWOTWOTWOTWOTWOTWOTWO
TWOTWOTWOTWOTWOTWOTWOTW
OTWOTWOTWOTWOTWOTWOTWOT
WOTWOTWOTW two OTWOTWOTWO
TWOTWOTWOTWOTWOTWOTWOTW
OTWOTWOTWOTWOTWOTWOTWOT
WOTWOTWOTWOTWOTWOTWOTWO

TURNING YOUR
SPOUSE INTO
YOUR
Lover

There are two things a real man likes—danger and play; and he likes woman because she is the most dangerous of playthings.

—NIETZSCHE

Personally I know nothing about sex because I've always been married.

—ZSA ZSA GABOR, "SAYINGS OF THE WEEK," OBSERVER, AUGUST 16, 1987

Sometimes I wonder if men and women really suit each other. Perhaps they should live next door and just visit now and then.

—KATHARINE HEPBURN

Jeff and Tricia, married for seven years and parents of three, came to see me recently for counseling. It took tremendous effort for Tricia to get Jeff to come in; she had called and cancelled several times over a four-week period because "my husband has to be out of town on business."

She finally called one day and tried to schedule time the next morning at 9 A.M. My wife and I were leaving on a flight that afternoon, so I told her that we should meet the following Monday. "It can't wait that long. He says he's leaving me this weekend," she said, unable to hide the desperation in her voice. So I agreed to meet them that morning, fully expecting yet another cancellation. I was therefore highly surprised when they turned up on my doorstep.

With time a commodity, I sat them down on the couch and asked them to get straight to the point: "What's the problem?"

Tricia began. "I love my husband and I want my marriage to continue. But for the last year, he's been seeing another woman on and off, and now he's decided to leave me and move in with her."

"Wait a minute," Jeff interjected. "You wish it were that simple. Rabbi, the real story is that in the fourth year of our marriage, my wife had an affair with a guy that lasted for eighteen months. I never knew until she told me. When she did tell me, I thought of leaving her then, but I stayed for the kids. After six months she said she was unhappy and wasn't feeling right. She went to a doctor for extensive examinations. Then, believe it or not, she had an affair with the doctor. That lasted six months. I was left numb by all of this. So there was this woman at work whom I poured my heart out to. It was completely platonic until recently. But can you blame me? I was like a dead man, feeling nothing. My wife had killed me. And this woman brought me back to life. And now she wants me to move in."

"And what about me?" his wife cut him off. "How do you think I felt for all those years, at home with the kids, barely seeing you as you traveled around the country or lived in the office. Do you have any idea how lonely I was? I felt like I was dead, too."

"Hold it, just hold it," I said. "Everybody please calm down. I have a single question to ask both of you. It's pretty simple. Notwithstanding what happened in the past, do you still love each other?" The wife looked at her husband and responded with an immediate, "Yes." The husband, clearly confused, thought for a minute, and said, "No. I no longer love my wife. She has hurt me too deeply."

"But with all due respect," I said, "it sounds more like you are speaking out of anger than indifference. What if we allowed some time to get all the resentment out of your system? If you could cool it with this other woman, and we could give you an outlet for your pain, you and your wife might just start healing one another."

"But that still doesn't solve what I should do about the other woman," he said. "I still have to do something about the other woman."

"You will," I answered. "You will do something about the other woman. You're going to make your wife into that other woman. I'm going to teach you how to have an affair with your wife."

Marriage: A Cause Worth Saving?

Saving marriages is one of civilization's most pressing needs, and I do not say that simply because I make a living rescuing relationships. On the contrary, if the institution of marriage were to be restored to the place of honor that it held in earlier generations, I would be out of a job. I believe that saving marriages is even more important than those imperatives usually perceived as urgent—things like fighting terrorism or beefing up the global economy.

The question facing all of us is whether tomorrow's children will even entertain the idea of "true" in "true love." If one out of every two marriages ends in divorce—and by now the number is exceeding even that horrendous statistic—then why should any of today's singles continue to believe in love? And, truth be told, it seems they don't. They believe in money, they believe in hard work, they believe in weekends and pleasure and socializing—but love? So 1950s!

Sadly, today's pursuits don't make us feel special—rather, they all increase human insecurity, ultimately making us feel inadequate and unworthy. The lust for money makes us competitive and suspicious. Hard work for the sake of hard work turns us into soulless machines. The mindless pursuit of pleasure leaves us with an emptiness that can be filled only by materialism and acquisition, and the pursuit of celebrity at all costs leaves us with shallow exteriors that lack depth. Many modern celebrities have been forced to leave their dignity behind as they climbed the ladder of recognition.

The only solution to this gradual devolution is to once again believe in love. Being the object of real love makes us feel content and happy, and its validation satiates our need to constantly prove ourselves. Its warmth saves us from the bitter cold of loneliness.

Our Great Failure

Our world prides itself on the immense progress we have made in virtually every sphere—fighting disease, combating crime, and so forth. But there is one area where we've failed: the skyrocketing divorce rate.

Here is a case in point. On New Year's Eve, 2002, my wife and I were watching the festivities in Times Square and the swearing-in ceremony of Mayor Michael Bloomberg by outgoing Mayor Rudy Giuliani. My wife pointed out that there wasn't a single wife in attendance at the momentous ceremony. Mayor Giuliani was accompanied by his "friend," Judith Nathan, while Mayor Bloomberg was accompanied by his daughter, Emma. One divorced mayor was passing off to another divorced mayor. My intention here is not to judge these men or women—not at all. But I am noting how marriage—once the hallmark of an aspiring politician—has fallen by the wayside.

Here are some other startling figures:

- Since 1990, more than 65 percent of all marriages in the United States have ended in divorce. Some put the figure even higher.
- In 2000 alone, the National Center for Health Statistics reported almost a million divorces, or approximately four divorces per every 1,000 people in the population.
- The situation is not limited to the United States. The director general of Israel's rabbinical courts recently announced a 38-percent divorce rate, and is concerned that if the trend continues, it will reach 50 percent within a few years.
- In March 2002, the *New York Times* reported that in Scandinavia less than 23 percent of the population are married and 65 percent of all births are outside of marriage, with most people opting to live together as a permanent goal, rather than marry.
- According to an October 2000 *Time*/CNN poll, 43 percent of American women claim that they don't even need a man for happiness anymore, which is another way of saying that they don't believe in love.
- The 2000 census found that singles constitute more than 40 percent of the adult population. Even more worrisome, 10 percent of all adults will never marry.
- The National Marriage Project has found that in the past thirty years the marriage rate has dropped by over a third.

With marriage plummeting and divorce skyrocketing, you might think a lack of passion is the reason. Not so. The passion is still there, but it is just happening more and more outside of marriage. Around the world illegitimate births are reaching astonishing numbers: 44 percent in France; 39 percent in Great Britain; and one third in the United States. On January 23, 2001, the *Times* reported a finding from paternity testing centers indicating that as many as one in seven children is not really his or her father's child. What is happening to marriage that so many people are finding their needed passion outside rather than within?

The Silent War Against Marriage

So, who fired the first shot against marriage? We might start by looking at the checkout aisle of our local grocery store. There we find rack after rack of tantalizingly placed tabloids with their incessant stories of Hollywood heartbreak and divorce caused by "irreconcilable differences." Every divorcing Hollywood couple inevitably issues a statement with those two words. The problem here is that if you take any two men and women on the planet—even the most compatible—there are bound to be differences and tough issues that divide them. No two people are going to agree on everything. So, how do couples get together in the first place if there are always things that get in between them?

The answer is simple: attraction. In the beginning of a relationship, men and women are so inexplicably drawn to one another that they overlook potentially divisive differences. Men and women do not come together in relationships because of what they have in common, but *despite what they lack* in common. They are mysteriously and irresistibly drawn to each other. There is a gravitational pull between them that does not lend itself to rational explanation, becoming stronger the less it can be expressed in words.

That's what we mean by the expression "*falling* in love." The words aren't "tiptoeing" into love or "ambling" into a relationship. The expression is "falling" because you are overtaken by a force over which you have no control. Sadly, however, attraction is now waning between the sexes.

A simple case in point is the world's beaches. We all think of beaches as erotic places where scantily clad women parade their shapely breasts and well-toned thighs, and where men, like peacocks strutting their feathers, proudly sport their six-packs. But if the world's beaches are truly such exciting meeting places, why are half the people at the beach fast asleep—literally! Why are the other half reading books or magazines? Surely, with so much exposed flesh, you would think that their adrenaline would be rushing so much that they could scarcely read, let alone fall into a deep slumber.

But the answer is that men and women are not as excited about each other's bodies as much as they once were, and are generally not as strongly attracted as in days gone by. We'll examine why later. For now we note that in the absence of attraction as the principal engine in romantic relationships, men and women have been forced to fall back on "compatibility" and "friendship" as the forces holding their union together. Having things in common simply isn't strong enough to keep a man and woman together for the duration of their lives. Whereas attraction is a nuclear force, compatibility is much weaker by comparison. And, with such a tenuous bond cementing them together, it is not long before "irreconcilable differences" seep into the cracks and begin to tear them asunder. When couples speak of "irreconcilable differences," they are really saying that whereas once upon a time their attraction to each other was much greater than their differences, something has changed to make their differences much more powerful than their attraction.

The number-one cause of divorce today is loss of attraction—or what we may call *erotic boredom*. Some people refer to it as "the seven-year itch." It's the brick wall that virtually every marriage hits and more than half of them will never surmount. Sometimes it leads to adultery. No matter what it's called or how it surfaces, the symptoms and consequences are the same: Couples don't desire being around each other as much as they once did; they go out to movies instead of talking over drinks, and sex often becomes a predictable routine rather than a glorious night of lovemaking.

Experiencing this syndrome doesn't mean that you are no longer in love. On the contrary, falling in love can often exacerbate the problem. When you get married, nobody bothers to tell you about the great paradox of love: The more deeply you fall in love with each other, the less passionate you become. Passion and excitement are at odds with feeling close to another person. Being lovers and companions are inversely proportional, so that the more of the former, the less of the latter, and vice versa. Since passion is predicated on novelty and newness, we're never excited about things we see every day. It's looking forward to the unexpected that creates excitement. How many of us are excited about reading yesterday's newspaper? Do we vacation in the cities where we work and live—or do we search out new exotic destinations?

On the other hand, we grow close in marriage only through sharing time and life experiences together. Not only do we want passionate nights, we also want warm days and a tender companion to hold us when life is unfair. We want the security of having the same person to come home to at the same address. Routine is essential to the security and companionship that marriage offers. But routine is also the water that extinguishes the fire of passion.

This inverse relationship between passion and familiarity is so pervasive that, historically, few have tried to prevail over it. From the beginning of recorded time we witness that men of means—and especially princes and rulers—always seem to have two women in their lives: One exists for companionship and the other for passion; one for kids and one for desire; one for pedigree and respectability and the other for fun and excitement.

The Passion and Mystery of an Affair

A number of years ago, I received an e-mail from a thirty-five-year-old woman named Melissa who discovered that her husband was having an affair with his secretary. As she describes:

. . . First I cried for a week, but then I decided that rather than sit and sulk, I was going to win my husband back. I was going to become the most desirable woman in the world for him. So I planned this really special night. I went for a complete makeover and had my hair permed. I bought this incredibly sexy outfit from Victoria's Secret and I studied The Joy of Sex and planned a whole bunch of new sex positions. . . . I then had the kids sent to his parents and when he came home, there were rose petals all along the entrance to our home. He opened the door and I was standing there in this really sexy outfit, holding two glasses of champagne. He just looked at me with a blank expression on his face and said, 'What do you think you're doing?' He then walked right by me and asked if there was anything for dinner. I started to cry and he said, 'I can't help it if I'm not attracted to you.' And he went upstairs to our bedroom. I was destroyed by what he did. I have never felt so rejected, so humiliated. I cried the entire night. The next morning I demanded that he move out of the house, but he is still refusing. I am not an unattractive woman. I have tried everything to get him to notice me. I can't understand what she has that I don't have?

Melissa's mistake is that she blames herself for this situation. Melissa could be the world's most ravishing supermodel, but that still would not guarantee that her husband won't fall for another woman.

What does the other woman have that you don't, Melissa? *She is not his wife.* That's it. He has never grown familiar with her, he has never settled into a routine with her, she has never become committed to him, and he has therefore never become bored with her. In a word, *to him* you are old and she is new.

The following letter, sent to me from a Presbyterian minister, gets to the heart of the matter of how passion has been stripped out of marriages.

Dear Shmuley,

I'm writing to you because you seem to be one of the only spiritual figures willing to openly address some of the sexual and emotional issues that arise among religious couples. I have a problem that I've been grappling with for some time, and I don't know where else to turn. I'll try to be as brief as possible.

I'm an ordained Christian, Presbyterian minister, raised in a traditional yet modern home. Being a "normal" American male, I discovered girls and sex in my early teens, but understood (not so much from parents and teachers but from my own research) that my religion forbade any sex before marriage, and even masturbation was to be avoided. As I think is the case with most boys, I didn't adhere to that particular guideline very carefully.

During my teen and college years, with the advent of the Internet, I found myself e-mailing and chatting with girls all over the world, and I enjoyed the witty repartee and flirtation I could engage in without the pressure of an "in person" date. I dated for marriage purposes, but socialized online purely for cheap thrills.

I got married five years ago, and for various medical reasons over the first two years of our marriage, my wife and I could not engage in regular sex for months at a stretch. I turned to pornography, masturbation, and online flirting as an outlet. We've since regulated the problems and even had a child, but I still find myself searching the Internet for engaging exchanges with other women. My wife does not know about this pastime of mine, and I don't let it interfere with my home life. But I've gone so far as to post ads on singles sites telling the world that I'm looking for cheeky fun via e-mail.

This week, a single girl answered one of my ads. I led her to believe that I was also single, and we e-mailed intensely for a matter of days. I don't know whether it's a testament to my writing skills or a sad commentary on the state of affairs among singles today or both, but I had this girl hooked within a day. In all fairness, she was equally charming and clever, and I'm sure that we'd be dating were I single. She was ready to exchange photos with me and meet me and she couldn't understand why I was reticent. I grappled with the issue for a few hours, and I decided to come clean and tell her the truth before things went any further. I admitted my sin last night. She said she was hurt and upset, I apologized, and we went our separate ways. I also deleted my personal ad.

I know I did the right thing. I also know that I deceived and hurt someone who I don't even know. I also know that I'm perfectly capable of doing it again.

So what I need, Shmuley, is practical advice. How can I come to a point, emotionally, where I don't crave this added stimulation? My wife is loving and wonderful and supportive and a great mother, and I would rate our sex life as fair. None of this is her fault. It's possible that God is punishing me for my preoccupation with sex by frustrating me sexually, but the vicious cycle continues. If I'm frustrated, I seek other outlets. If I seek other outlets, I engage in deception and behave reprehensibly. I don't feel as though I have any friends or fellow Christians with whom to share this story, because they'd be shocked at my behavior. I'm shocked.

I know that you're busy but if you have a moment, please respond. Thank you.

Dominic

What this minister and his wife need—like every other couple experiencing sexual doldrums—is something that will undo the familiarity that has destroyed their interest. This husband makes the mistake of feeling guilty for his legitimate need for forbidden sexual erotic thrills. He errs in believing that his sin lies in the fact that he wants to sin. But stifling his urge to feel the stirring ecstasy of forbidden pleasure is not the way to go. Rather, he should be sinning with his wife. He could easily have had the same exhilarating encounter by having a secret e-mail affair with his wife, as I will teach you to do later.

This is where adultery comes in. Studies have shown that men and women who are involved in an extramarital affair never seem to lose erotic or sexual excitement. To be sure, they suffer from other relationship problems, like constant anxiety, fear of getting caught, and jealousy of the spouse that their lover goes home to every night. But they almost never suffer from diminished passion.

Lillian Ross, the famous journalist, created a scandal a few years ago by writing of her forty-year affair with William Shawn of *The New Yorker*, after he died. She maintained that: "After forty years, our lovemaking had the same passion, the same energy . . . as it had in the beginning."

Sounds impossible right? But read almost any revealing chronicle of an adulterous affair and the two participants will claim the same thing. For the duration of their affair, they had really great sex. Their erotic desire for each other did not lessen with the passage of time. If they broke up it was for other reasons: The mistress became too possessive and demanded that her lover leave his wife; one of the two lovers was found out by his or her spouse who gave an ultimatum; the affair simply became too complicated; and so on. But lovers in an illicit affair almost never break up because the relationship simply becomes dull or boring. Now, let's be honest here. How many married couples can claim to have the same intensity of sex forty years after marriage?

The same fate awaits adulterous couples that move in with each other. Suddenly, without warning, their passion quickly fades.

One of the most satisfying letters I have ever received came from my friend Rabbi Harold Kushner, author of *When Bad Things Happen to Good People* and several other bestselling books. He wrote: "You deserve to know how you helped me save a marriage and help two basically good people."

He then proceeded to tell me of how a wife came to him for counseling. The husband had started an affair with another woman, moved out of the house, and wanted a divorce from his wife of many years. The wife asked Rabbi Kushner what she should do. As Rabbi Kushner wrote in his letter to me: "I remembered something I had once heard you say, that once the mistress is readily available, without the thrill of a clandestine affair, she becomes less desirable. I told [the woman] to do nothing, not to throw him out, not to call him names or tell people what he had done. Don't put him in the position of choosing between a wife who curses him and a girlfriend who caresses him. Sure enough, just as you had predicted, a few months later, he left the girlfriend and moved back with his wife as if nothing had happened. She still bears the scars of the event, but she's better off now than if she had thrown him out in righteous indignation. And you deserve the credit."

Now, Rabbi Kushner is giving me way too much praise. This was not my insight, but one that has been documented in countless studies about relationships. About 90 percent of men who leave their wives and move in with their mistresses end up leaving their mistresses within the first year of living together. Clearly, something about the passion and mystery is lost when the vagaries of everyday life set in.

Experimenting with the Adultery Mystic

Putting aside whether we accept this custom of retaining separate partners to meet separate needs, we cannot deny that the dichotomy continues to exist today as much as it always has. In counseling couples I constantly encounter husbands and wives who claim that their sex lives are in the morgue. Here is one e-mail I received from a woman in Wisconsin:

> Dear Rabbi Shmuley,
> My husband Stan and I have been married for eight years. We have three kids and we don't fight much. My husband's not perfect, but he is an affectionate father and a responsible husband. . . . But with every passing month, I grow more and more unhappy. . . . I don't think my husband is that attracted to me anymore. He doesn't look at me, certainly not the way he looks at other women. When we make love, it's like he's on another planet. And I'm in my mid-thirties, for goodness sake, and still in shape. . . . I've tried to buy new lingerie and to do some of that kinky stuff. Initially it worked. But now we're back to square one. The most infuriating thing of all is that he won't talk about it.

He's too busy watching television. Now, I'm beginning to feel like a nag, and he resents it. I do nag him, but when he's not focused on me, I begin to feel lonely. Can you give me some advice as to what I can do?

Sincerely,
Georgina

Steve, a chiropractor from Atlanta, wrote the following letter to me after we spoke on the phone:

Dear Rabbi Shmuley,

. . . The problem, as I explained, is something like a loss of interest, rather than a loss of love. You asked me if I love my wife and the answer is yes, I do love her. But I love her like a sister. I'm protective of her. You asked me if I consider myself a good husband, and I do. But by that I mean I do the right thing by my wife and the kids. I work hard to support them and they lack for nothing. But my wife just doesn't get my juices going anymore. She always complains that when she undresses, I'm never looking. And I'm not. I'm going crazy with distractions. There was this woman at the office whom I started fantasizing a lot about. Something could have happened between us, but I decided that I didn't want an affair, particularly with someone in my hometown, and especially with someone in the office. But that hasn't stopped me from having sex outside my marriage, usually when I'm on business trips and conventions. These women are a lot different than my wife. They're not as classy. But at least they like sex. My wife *doesn't* seem to like sex. She seems to go through with it as a way of keeping me content. But I find that patronizing and demeaning. Maybe my wife and I just aren't sexually compatible . . . .

Mark

Well, Georgina and Mark, your dilemmas are exactly why I'm writing this book. The biggest marital problem of all is the loss of passion in long-term relationships and the resulting alienation of husbands and wives.

This is where the subject of adultery comes in; locked within its mysteries, we can unravel the secret to restoring passion in marriage. Adultery is perhaps the only thing that can restore excitement and wonder to a marriage. Having counseled hundreds of couples, I have reached the conclusion that couples are not meant to be married to one another. Rather, men and women are specifically designed to *have affairs* with each other. My journey to arrive at this conclusion began when a strange story came to my attention:

Jack, a forty-two-year-old partner in an accounting firm, was married to Linda, his thirty-eight-year-old wife, for sixteen years. By both of their accounts, their marriage was strong. Jack could always make Linda laugh, and Linda could always comfort Jack as he faced work challenges as a corporate executive. They trusted each other with every secret and were there for each other in their sadder moments. Only one major component was missing from their life together: *passion.*

Jack accepted that this was primarily his fault. He loved his wife, but he no longer found her exciting. Although he readily agreed that she was very attractive, the novelty had worn off. It had been years since they had had a truly exciting sexual encounter. Jack's lack of sexual interest was, unavoidably, detected by his wife. This led to some difficulties in their marriage, but none that either of them thought they couldn't surmount. Still, the more she saw him looking at younger women, the more she began to crave attention from other men. When he flirted openly with women at parties, she was hurt and enraged. The situation escalated to the point that they were incapable of discussing the matter. They reconciled themselves to the idea that their marriage provided stability, albeit at the expense of passion.

This deterioration led Jack to begin contemplating having an affair. He thought that he might regain the lost excitement of early love with a girlfriend and found himself eyeing many of his female coworkers, as if he were picking out a potential candidate. There were times when he was startled to discover how many willing partners he could find. Thoughts that hadn't been more than a passing fancy in his mind were now being entertained in great detail in his head. And there was an even more troubling development: Whenever he was in bed with his wife, he thought about other women. He would mentally undress coworkers or make love to phantom women he saw walking down the street. He felt the need to contemplate other women in order to find his sexual experiences with his wife exciting and satisfying.

But there was something else going on in Jack's erotic mind as well. He noticed that whenever his *wife* stared at another man or other men stared at her, he suddenly felt passionate about her again. For instance, once when his wife remarked that she found the parking attendant cute, Jack suddenly felt an erotic electric current passing between him and his wife. What were these deep, dark emotions rising up within him? Sure, jealousy, but it seemed like there was something else setting him alight. He knew that a sociologist would dismiss these feelings as mere territorialism, but Jack felt that this was more than just trying to reclaim what was rightfully his. Rather, he felt that he was once again viewing his wife as a *woman,* as a sexual creature, rather than just as the woman who provided a comfortable home for him and his children.

What was he to do about developing this passion? How could he fan these embers into a more powerful flame? Should he encourage his wife to have an affair and then tell him about it? He was wary of this option. He knew that the kind of jealousy and hurt that would arise from such an experience would destroy him. He resolved to close his mind to that possibility, and yet he couldn't help feeling that the excitement of seeing his wife with another man might be the saving grace of his marriage. For months Jack wracked his brain about what do to.

Proceeding with caution, he finally decided to take action. While he and his wife were making love, rather than automatically closing his eyes and thinking about other women he found exciting, he started mentioning other men whom he thought his wife was attracted to. At first she was silent and didn't take the bait. She even protested that he was being a fool if he thought that that sort of thing excited her. She asked that he stop. But he wouldn't be denied his fun. Now, almost every time they were together in bed, he said to her, "I know that you're attracted to Matt. I know that Jerry has a crush on you." Gradually, he wore her resistance down and his wife admitted her excitement. It wasn't long before he had her saying other men's names when they made love.

Jack felt he was making progress. Hearing his wife call out the other men's names—and fantasizing about her with those other men—finally liberated him from the ghosts of all the women who were floating around his mind. He didn't feel haunted by these strangers any more, and he felt his wife becoming sexier to him every day.

He also noticed his wife changing. She started dressing up more, even around the house. He started watching her innocuous interactions with delivery men and the gardener, but they didn't appear to be that innocent anymore. Now his wife was aware of the fact that they were all potentially interested in her—and not just for her business. Jack was watching his wife come alive as a woman fully aware of her magnetism.

He now found himself thinking far more about keeping his wife faithful than being unfaithful himself. The dynamics of their relationship were beginning to change: His wife was now becoming the more powerful one; she was now the object of his desire; and he was doing all the pursuing. It struck him that this is the way it was all those years ago when they were courting. There were a lot of guys who showed interest in his wife when she was single, and he had to outdo all of them in love and devotion.

Still, Jack had a long way to go before he could feel that his wife was the center of his erotic attention. One day he became more adventurous and devised an elaborate plan to go on vacation together to the U.S. Virgin Islands. They spent the first two nights of their trip in luxurious hotel room content— but essentially dissatisfied. There was the simmering of sparks, but no inferno of passion.

The next night, while walking with Linda on the beach, Jack dropped a bombshell. He declared that they must take radical steps in order to resurrect their marriage. If not, he feared that he might have an affair. He presented his wife with a choice: Either she would agree to have a woman prostitute join them in their hotel room for a ménage a trois, or else they would invite a man into their hotel room for Linda to enjoy. He knew his wife would object to both of these options, so he told her that all he wanted was for her to be massaged by a man in his presence. He also made it clear that while the masseur would not actually have sex with her, he might go a long way down that path. After much haggling and cajoling on his part, Linda reluctantly agreed. "What choice did I have?" she later told me. "I love my husband and he suddenly confronts me with the possibility of his having an affair because he thinks our sex life isn't satisfying. I agreed because I would do anything to prevent that."

Jack pulled out a phone book and made a few calls in his wife's presence until he found Ricardo, a male masseur (who supposedly had other specialties as well). Jack arranged for Ricardo to come to their hotel room that night and give his wife a massage for $300. Linda vociferously protested that she didn't think she could go through with it, but Jack would not relent. "The only thing I'll give in on is that you don't have to be naked," he said.

Later that afternoon, Jack was surprised to find that his wife was actually showering, applying her makeup with care, and putting on her best lingerie in preparation. Sure, she was anxious and continually voiced concerns, but on the other hand, she could barely mask her own erotic excitement. "I hope we're not making a mistake and this isn't just going to hurt us," Linda told him, as she blow-dried her hair in the vanity mirror.

Just before Ricardo's scheduled arrival, Jack came up with a strange stipulation. He told Linda that she would have to wear a blindfold. "I don't mind you being with this man," he said. "In fact, I know that you are doing it for me, and I do appreciate it. But I don't want you to see his face. If you saw him, the experience would be too intimate. I want him always to be a stranger to whom you have no attachment. I don't want you to be able to fantasize about him later." His wife agreed that this was a good idea, saying that she would be far too shy if she had to look back at him anyway.

But here's the twist. *There was no Ricardo. Jack* was Ricardo. He had carefully orchestrated the entire evening so that his wife would think that a strange man was coming to their hotel room, when, in fact, no one was coming at all. Jack had paid a hotel bellboy to pretend to be Ricardo on the phone and, later, knock on the door, announce himself as the masseur, and tell Jack that the massage would take about ninety minutes. Earlier, Jack had bought new cologne that his wife would not recognize and an expensive wig that gave him longer, curlier hair. He had also devised a completely new sex routine. He even went so far as to get the bellboy to record one or two lines on tape, which Jack replayed during the massage to have her believe that Ricardo was in the room. Finally, he had given his wife a drink before the massage, ostensibly to calm her nerves, but, in reality, to impede her faculties of discernment.

In the guise of Ricardo and with his wife blindfolded, Jack began to massage her back—slowly, patiently, and better than he had ever done before. He was careful not to say a word for fear that his voice would give him away. He moved leisurely over every part of his wife's body, paying more attention to detail than at any previous time in their married life. He caressed and kissed her so that she felt he appreciated each and every part of her. Slowly, she turned on like a light, all the while thinking he was Ricardo.

After a full hour of touching and stimulating Linda, Jack became more ambitious. He knew his wife to be naturally shy and was sure that she would resist his undressing her. But she did not. He removed every stitch of her clothing, and she did nothing to protest. As this happened, all kinds of things went through Jack's head. Was this really his wife? This woman who was so opposed to getting naked for another man? Suddenly, her husband's approval didn't matter at all to her. Jack felt traces of anger and jealousy developing within him. Why didn't she stop him? They had agreed only to a massage. But these feelings were easily drowned out by the explosive eroticism that Jack was feeling, and he plunged ahead further.

He went even further than Ricardo's mandate, and still

she did not stop him. He held her hand softly and she clasped his back. He kissed her passionately, first on the cheek, then on the lips. At first, she moved her head away so that he could not find her mouth. But slowly, as he kissed her neck, her resistance was gone and he found his wife giving into him completely, kissing him back passionately with the long strands of his fake hair dangling across her face.

The couple shared four action-filled hours of both tender and raucous lovemaking. Jack was simultaneously in shock and enraptured. This was by far the best sex he'd ever had in his life—and with his wife no less. But *was* she his wife? It felt to him like he was making love to a stranger. His wife came alive like never before, and he began to wonder whether she would be as passionate if she knew it was her husband with whom she was having sex.

When it was all over, "Ricardo" wordlessly kissed Linda gently on the cheek and departed. Her husband opened the door to allow him to leave, and then returned to his wife and removed the blindfold. Linda was tired, but she looked radiant. She thanked her husband for having organized the night and told him how much she had enjoyed it. She also insisted on knowing whether or not he was upset, since things had far surpassed the original intention. He insisted that he was not, but deep down he felt a curious but immensely potent blend of passion and excitement mixed with shock and immeasurable hurt.

His wife had, in theory, allowed herself to have sex with another man. Even though it had not really occurred, it had in her mind. Jack could never look at her in the same way again. The loving, caring, loyal and devoted wife whom he thought he knew had turned out to be none of those things. He now saw his wife in a totally new light. He had no idea he was married to such a passionate woman, such a sexual creature, a woman who would *risk anything in the pursuit of physical pleasure.*

For the next two days, Jack drove himself crazy about what he really wanted—a consistent, loyal wife on whom he could depend, or an exciting, adulterous wife, who would always keep him guessing? The passion he now felt for her, knowing what she had done, exceeded anything he had ever experienced before. But the pain was unrelenting. How could she do this to him? How could she cheat?

He tried to talk himself into the fact that his wife knew all along. But in questioning her about the evening—and seeing the occasional remorse she exhibited—it was clear to him that she did not know. And in truth, he was glad that she didn't. He had to admit that her willingness to be with other men, and having witnessed it with his own eyes, transformed their marriage immeasurably.

For weeks after their vacation, they made passionate love that lasted for hours. Jack could not wait to get home from work. Linda thought that her husband's newfound passion and desire for her resulted from her having slept with another man in his presence. Little did she know that the real reason was that he felt that he had discovered a totally new woman. "I honestly felt," Jack later told me, "like I was having an affair. Only, I was having an affair with my own wife. It was all so weird, but infinitely worthwhile. I felt more alive than at any point in my life. I used to get the greatest buzz from doing deals, but my work now suffered in favor of my marriage. I kept on thinking of other ways that I could fool my wife into thinking that guys were interested in her and seeing how I could gauge her response."

Jack now found his wife Linda to be the most attractive woman in the entire world. His attraction was so great that he didn't even look at the bikini-clad women who infested the beach near their home. Instead, he gazed lovingly upon his wife the entire time.

The Lesson Learned

What had happened here? How could Jack and Linda have been so transformed by these experiences?

Jack's dilemma is not new. Almost every man who is lucky enough to be married to a sexy woman—and at some level all men are—experience the same elation and agony, the same pleasure and pain, the same irreconcilable tension of excitement and torment when they realize that ultimately a woman cannot be possessed.

In fact, it is the tension itself that generates the excitement. Tension is not the enemy of marriage, *complacency* is. Lack of predictability in a marriage is a blessing, so long as it doesn't totally destroy the foundation of the marriage. Breaking routines is one of the most necessary elements in any fiery relationship because the element of surprise is the soul of passion. What the story of Jack and Linda demonstrates is that while adultery is one of the most destructive and harmful sins that erodes the foundation of a marriage, the *possibility of adultery*—a.k.a. *kosher adultery*—is necessary to sustaining passion and novelty within a marriage.

Kosher adultery is the perfect antidote to the greatest problem facing marriage—namely, that husbands gradually become complacent about their wives, leading their wives to be less loving and supportive and, in turn, leading the husbands to justify further estrangement. Just suppose . . .

- Husbands could never afford to become complacent because they were married to voracious sexual seductresses that constantly need to be re-seduced.
- Wives became the living embodiment of a man's sexual fantasies—a woman with an insatiable appetite who would do anything for sex.

If this were to occur, would men still need to turn to manufactured porn entertainment when the real thing is in their bedrooms? Would it not lead us to be constantly attracted to our partners?

Today, it seems, we learn about sexual attraction from Sarah Jessica Parker and Kim Cattrall on *Sex and the City*. At its best, our sexuality today is copied and contrived, artificial and invented. I believe that we can all reach deeper and find something a lot better. But how do we unlock that latent sexual potential? Try the following exercise.

Exercise
THE EROTIC INTERROGATION

FOR HUSBANDS:

Let's take a page from Jack's brave marital experiment. The key to Jack's renewed desire for his wife Linda was being reminded that she was, at her core, a woman. Remind yourself that your wife is a sexual being. Take her out to dinner and tell her that you want to take your marriage to the next level; you want greater passion and intimacy.

Without rushing the conversation, ask your wife the following questions, making it clear to her that she will be given the same opportunity when you're finished with your erotic interrogation.

1. Do you find yourself attracted to other men whom you meet in casual interactions?

2. If so, who are they?

3. What is it about them that attracts you to them?

4. Do you think that they're attracted to you as well?

5. What makes you think that they are interested? Is it a woman's sixth sense, or do you have more tangible proof? Do they, for example, stare at your chest instead of making eye contact?

6. Did the men in question ever do anything out of the ordinary that would confirm their interest?

7. Did you ever do anything, however innocent, that would confirm your interest in them?

8. Do you ever find yourself thinking about them?

9. Have you ever sexually fantasized about them? Have you ever done so when we are in bed together?

10. Tell me more about your sexual fantasies. (Press her to hear at least three.)

THREETHREETHREETHREETHREET
HREETHREETHREETHREETHREETH
REETHREETHREETHREETHREETHR
EETHREETHR three ETHREETHRE
ETHREETHREETHREETHREETHREE
THREETHREETHREETHREETHREET
HREETHREETHREETHREETHREETH

Curiosity—
THE
SINGLE
MOST
IMPORTANT
INGREDIENT

A woman, I always say, should be like a good suspense movie: The more left to the imagination, the more excitement there is. This should be her aim—to create suspense, to let a man discover things about her without her having to tell him.

—ALFRED HITCHCOCK

If men knew all that women think, they'd be twenty times more daring.

—ALPHONSE KARR

The most exciting attractions are between two opposites that never meet.

—ANDY WARHOL

43

The story of Jack and Linda in the last chapter teaches us a very valuable lesson: The most important ingredient needed to sustain a relationship is curiosity. Insatiable inquisitiveness is the soul of marriage. Wanting to always know your partner in the most intimate way is the key to sexual excitement. A man who wants to discover what a woman sounds and feels like—how she moans, how she writhes and wriggles—when he takes her to the heights of sexual ecstasy will always want to make love to her. A man who thinks he knows already might be more interested in watching the Lakers game.

We must be constantly inquisitive, because a predictable routine will be the death of a marriage. What causes husbands and wives to lose interest in one another is their belief that they already know everything about each other. It's at this point that we begin to see husbands and wives who sit at dinner tables together barely exchanging a word. Why should they talk? They already know everything the other one is going to say. They can finish each other's sentences. They can read each other's minds. Why bother articulating it?

Likewise, adultery arises only where there is boredom, complacency, and neglect. A husband will go about having an affair when he feels that he has a wife, rather than a sexy woman who is hot for sex. He treats his wife as his partner. But who wants to make love to a partner? What a cold and distant term that is. A partner is for business, or in this case, having children and paying the mortgage. Partners are made for sharing resources, not for making love.

A husband who views his wife as his partner feels that he knows her so well that there is nothing left to know and thus sees her as inherently boring.

At the same time, a wife looks for someone new when she feels she is neglected because her husband spends all of his time at the office. In her book *The Erotic Silence of the American Wife,* Dalma Heyn refers to a study in which husbands who were having affairs were asked the following question: "Since you're cheating on your wife, what do you think the likelihood is that she is cheating on you?" Ninety-three percent of husbands gave the same response: "My wife is not the type." And that's just the point. It was because they thought that their wives were not the type to have an affair that they were out on the prowl in the first place. In their minds their wives had ceased being women. They were house-keepers, mothers, chauffeurs, and organizers. But they were not women. They had lost their attractiveness.

One unfaithful husband answered the question in his own words, "My wife has, I believe, never been 'unfaithful' to me. Knowing her lack of interest in sex, I would be aston-ished to find out she had ever indulged herself elsewhere." Likewise, 83 percent of wives having affairs were asked the same question about their husbands and responded in kind. One woman said, "My husband? Forget it. He's just not the type. He's not interested in sex enough to do something like that." This mindset explains why these women are running around with strangers rather than being at home with their husbands.

Faulty "Equipment"

A famous relationship writer and I recently compared notes about infidelity. I spoke to her about my firm belief that pas-sion can be restored in monogamous relationships, and that the erotic attraction of sex was not in the body but in the mind, meaning it could be renewed at any time even without new bodies. She told me I was wrong. Suddenly, she came out with a confession: "I had an affair . . . I was married for four years. I loved my husband, but the sex was terrible. I worked at a restaurant at the time, a man came in one day and we just hit it off. The two years of my affair with him were the most exciting of my life but they ended up destroying my marriage. It was not that my husband ever found out—he didn't. The problem was that after the excitement I experienced in those two years, and the sensuousness of my lover, my husband simply couldn't compare. . . ."

I asked her how her husband couldn't compare. "He lacked the equipment," she told me without so much as a blush. "With all the goodwill in the world, and whatever effort he made in bed, his plumbing simply didn't measure up. My lover was much better endowed and I discovered that bigger is better."

I asked her if it was possible that her husband had also had an affair. "No," she answered. "He'd never do that. He probably didn't notice anything anyway because he's preoccupied with so many things other than our sex life. Classic workaholic."

Well, just two weeks later—and I'm not making this up—I befriended the woman's husband, and we had a heart-to-heart. He also had a confession: "I've been having an affair. It's tearing me up. I love my wife, but this other woman is so sexy, and she makes me feel like an Adonis. I've tried to break it off but the other woman won't let me. She's crazy about me and it's the best sex I've ever had. Not to mention the fact that she's ravishingly beautiful."

In the end, the husband stopped his affair and gave up his mistress. The couple remain together today, albeit with outstanding problems that still lack resolution. Still, their story proves three important points: So much for his lacking the right equipment. So much for being a bore. And so much for not being the kind of man that would ever be interested in an affair. Perhaps if this wife had recognized her husband's sexual potential prior to her own affair, she might have salvaged the core of her marriage. As it happened, she wrote him off too quickly and found passion elsewhere, and in the process lost her husband, for a time, to another woman.

I've heard a thousand stories like this. A husband will complain to me that, "my wife's not interested in sex," and use that as a justification for fooling around. Inevitably, I will hear from his wife that, "I am a very sexual woman but I have a husband who has no thought or interest in satisfying me." Here is a letter that I received from a seventy-four-year-old woman who read one of my books:

Dear Rabbi Shmuley,

I read your book *Kosher Sex* with great interest. What particularly intrigued me was your assertion that women are more sexual than men. This is certainly true in my case, although my husband never knew this nor did anything about it. He had a string of affairs all throughout our forty-year marriage. Everyone seemed more exciting to him than me. I don't know why I tolerated it. Maybe it was because he had so diminished my self-esteem that I lost the will to fight back. But I was erotically charged throughout the marriage and in great pain at not finding an outlet for it. I contemplated having an affair a few times, and there was even a neighbor of ours whom I think would have welcomed it. In the end, though, I didn't do anything about it because marriage meant something to me. My husband is dead now, and I have forgiven him in my heart for all the pain he caused me. But I forgive him mostly because I pity him. All those years he had a woman in his life that would have taken him to the heavens with great sex. All he needed to do was show me some interest. He was the one who missed out and, through his failure, I ended up missing out as well.

Sincerely,

Elaine from Montana

The first step in restoring passion in every marriage is to know that: (a) Sexuality is a state of mind more than body and it can, therefore, always be stimulated and coaxed out of hiding; and (b) the potential for each and every married spouse to commit adultery—which we all undoubtedly possess—is indicative of the fact that we are all sexual beings who are both passionate and exciting.

The Sexual State of Mind

Sexual attraction is all in the mind. If romance or passion is missing in your marriage, what you really need is a new attitude, not a new partner. Once you are aware that your spouse is capable of having an affair, you will see him or her in a completely new light. Where there is no possibility of faithlessness in a marriage, there is also no possibility for passion in that marriage. The husband who thinks that his wife holds no attraction in the eyes of other men will find her unattractive himself. Similarly, a wife who feels that her husband is boring to other women will also find him boring.

At this point, the story of my marriage bears relevance. As a child of divorce, I was lonely and yearned to marry. When I had attained the mature age of twenty-one (in Yeshiva we grow up pretty quickly), a wonderful young woman came along from Sydney, Australia, and I jumped at the chance to get to know her better. After a few weeks we became engaged, and a few months later, we married.

I was elated. I was going to build a home myself—one that had been robbed from me by my parent's divorce. The morning after the wedding, I went to a shopping mall in search of a camera to take pictures of my new beautiful wife and me. As I departed the camera store, a terrible thing happened: I noticed an attractive woman walking by. I was devastated with guilt. I went back to the apartment to confess to my wife. Of course, my "confession" that I still noticed that other women could be attractive just made her laugh and think she had married a complete loon. For me, however, the situation was much more serious. I had always thought that true love was complete and total. I believed that it was meant to completely consume you like a raging fire. If true love was an overwhelming experience, how then could I still be attracted to other women?

After giving the situation a bit of thought, it began to make sense to me. A husband and wife actually have to choose each other anew every day. When a husband walks home from work and notices (not ogles) the many pretty women walking down the sidewalk yet still comes home happily to his wife, it's as if she has won a beauty pageant. He's saying to her, "Today I saw a beautiful woman, but I still chose to come home to you, not out of obligation or responsibility, but because you're the most beautiful of all." The alternative would be that he marries her under the wedding canopy and then never needs to marry her again. His commitment is never challenged and his devotion is never renewed.

Seeing your wife through another man's eyes is sometimes the perfect remedy for boredom. So many husbands have gorgeous wives at home, yet they embarrass themselves by eyeballing women at the office or brushing against women on the subway. The funny thing about this is that while they're leering at random women all around them, there are guys leering at their wives. Isn't that a bit ridiculous?

One of the solutions is for the husband to take his wife to cocktail parties or double-date with friends and watch how the other guys stare at her with apparent desire. What a husband is missing is not a beautiful wife, but the novelty of a new and unknown woman. If you're bored with your wife's body, it's not beauty she's missing, but novelty. With time, our commitment to our own attractive wives can become weary through familiarity; but, if we looked at our wives the way other men do, it will remind us just how alluring our wives really are.

Husbands need to go out and notice everyday occurrences in which other men are attracted to their wives. I can guarantee that the man who converses with her—even if he is just a friend—sees her as a woman, particularly when something about her suddenly becomes revealing, like a bra strap or her panty hose. Watch his eyes as your wife bends over; his eyes will gravitate in that direction. Study another man's eyes as your wife moves to get up from a chair and she pulls up her skirt tightly, exposing her figure. His eyes will follow her movements. You don't have to force this situation because it is happening all the time and is all around you. Everyone is aware of it, except you.

Once, when I was the rabbi at Oxford, a man I knew told me that his marriage was finished: His wife was just not attractive to him. "She's put on weight since having our kids and she's just let herself go. Our sex life is in the dumps. The greatest thrill I get these days is from the adult programming on cable TV that I watch when my wife's not home." I asked him if they had tried to spice up their sex life. "Are you kidding?

We've tried everything. Counseling, lingerie, sex toys, the works. We've even watched crazy erotic movies together. But it's all just a waste of time. I've completely lost interest in her body. I know it's awful, but I'm just not attracted to her."

I knew this man's wife and, by all accounts, she was a beautiful woman. I gave him this advice: "Tonight, I want both of you to go to a nightclub, but not one that's near your home. Go and drive somewhere that's at least an hour away where nobody knows you. I want your wife to put on her sexiest dress. She should go into the club before you and sit at the bar. Nothing more. Just sit at the bar. You come in about a half hour later and sit behind her, inconspicuously. There should be no communication between the two of you; no one should know that you're together. You just sit there looking at her back." "And then what?" he asked me, "I'm just supposed to sit there?" "Precisely," I replied.

His wife was a modest and dignified woman who objected to my plan, but I called her up and reassured her. "I respect your desire to preserve modesty and mystery. It's what makes you such a special woman. But sometimes you have to jumpstart a moribund marriage with a booster cable from another car. Trust me on this one," I said. "I would never tell you to degrade yourself. When this slightly dangerous exercise is over, your husband's going to be ripping your clothes off." So she relented.

The next day the husband called me. "You were right, I got the point. We had the most amazing night imaginable. . . . My wife went into the club before me. By the time I got in, there were all these guys swarming around my wife like bees to honey. One guy's trying to ask her to dance and another's buying her a drink. Another guy is jealous of the guy who got to her before him. It made me hot. After a while I got so jealous that I couldn't sit in the back any more. I got up, took her hand, and led her out of the club and away from some good-looking guy who was talking to her. Not knowing I was her husband, he almost punched me out. Could you believe it? Another guy was gonna fight me over my wife because he was dying to take her to bed. I couldn't even wait until we got home to be with her. I made love to her in the car for about three hours. This morning she could barely move. It was the best night of sex we've shared in years."

Now, to be sure, I wouldn't prescribe this very extreme advice in all cases—just as a doctor wouldn't give every one of his patients an electric shock from a defibrillator. Later I will even discuss how situations like this in which women wear skimpy clothing can significantly decrease erotic attraction. But the purpose of this exercise was to open the eyes of a bored husband so that he could see what everyone else saw. Every night, in his very own bed, he could make love to a woman that other men would go to battle over, like Helen of Troy. There are many things a husband and a wife may do in order to be reminded of each other's attractiveness, thereby rekindling their passion.

This is not intended as a primitive form of open marriage or ménage a trois, which it most certainly is not. It is merely a healthy way husbands and wives can play with, and thereby learn to appreciate, each other's sexuality. But remember to retain modesty at all times. Don't do anything stupid that will make your spouse hate you or accuse you of having degraded yourself. On a daily basis this comes down to simply allowing your sexuality to speak for itself by feeling sexy and therefore carrying yourself sexily. Going to a club in order to attract men is a very extreme maneuver. But for wives to simply dress in a dignified but attractive way at all times is an essential ingredient in a steamy marriage. I believe that all married women should wear lacy bras and silky underwear, not just for their husbands but for themselves. Feeling attractive means projecting attractiveness. Men will see your confidence and they will stare at you. And your husband will notice them staring at you and will never forget how gorgeous you are.

The Ultimate Curiosity Stimulator

Answer this: When a husband discovers his wife has been unfaithful, what does he do? Does he shout and yell? Break the door down? Raise his hand in violence? Go out and cheat himself in order to punish his wife?

None of the above. Rather, one of the most common response of a cuckolded husband is that he pulls his wife into bed with him and makes passionate love to her. The reason for this response is not, as some misguided feminist authors have suggested, that he is trying to reclaim what's his or make a declaration of his territorial rights to her body. If that were the case, he could just as easily lock her in the closet.

Since the number-one cause of female infidelity in a marriage is neglect by the husband, his attitude changes completely the moment he discovers that she is someone else's mistress. Suddenly, the woman who once bored him has surprised and excited him as a seductress who will risk everything for great sex.

In her book *Tempted Women: The Passions, Perils and Agonies of Female Infidelity,* psychologist Carol Botwin documents that as soon as a husband discovers his wife's infidelity he ". . . may want to have sex with you right after learning about your affair. It is a strange enough phenomenon, but it happens frequently enough. Some men may get excited thinking about you as a sex object again. Others get a perverse thrill from imagining you with another man." Unfortunately, by this time she has often already become emotionally attached to the other man and it is too late to salvage the marriage. Nevertheless, the principle of her husband's renewed interest still applies.

The same is true about open marriages. Among the downright strange arrangements that have been practiced in marriage, this one is one of the strangest. To be sure, an open marriage is a betrayal of the nourishing intimacy that makes a husband and wife into one flesh and in the long term, as nearly every study has shown, proves very destructive and infinitely painful, tearing couples apart with insidious jealousy. So why have so many ordinary people practiced it?

The most interesting feature of open marriages is who initiates them—it's almost always the husbands. Statistics show that at first it is the husbands who desire to have the best of all possible worlds: new sexual partners, but with the consent—even participation—of their wives. Husbands were finding their wives dull, and sought sexual encounters with their friends' wives as a way of finding new excitement. But the massive experiment of open marriage prevalent in the 1960s proved a colossal failure, and now accounts for less than 2 percent of marriages, where it once accounted for as much as 14 percent, according to the *Janus Report on Sexual Behavior* (1993).

Why did open marriage fail? Was it the wives who stopped it? Most definitely not. It was the same people who pushed for it in the first place: the husbands. Statistics show overwhelmingly that it is the husbands who at first are most willing to initiate an open marriage, yet are also the ones who insist on ending this bizarre marriage arrangement. And it is the wives who are at first hesitant but later enthusiastic about the arrangement. But the two are not contradictory. The husbands initiated open marriage because they were bored with their wives and wanted the license to have many sexual partners with the vague consent of their wives. Later, however, when they saw that their wives were beginning to enjoy it—and that they had many suitors interested in them—husbands suddenly wanted their wives back because they unexpectedly became sexual and seductive all over again. In most cases, however, they came to their realization too late. The recipe really is simple: No man who thinks that other men are not attracted to his wife will be attracted to her either. And no man who notices how other men lust after his wife can resist being strongly attracted to her himself.

Affairs don't last, either. Studies show that 91 percent of men who leave their wives for their mistresses end up leaving their mistresses within the first year of the new marriage. *Ay caramba,* you say! Your surprise is well justified. After all, isn't this the same man who just a year ago was prepared to throw away everything for this woman? Isn't this the guy who just twelve months back was prepared to sacrifice everything he had worked for—his wife, his kids, his home, a lot of money in divorce settlements—all for this one woman because he couldn't live without her? Yet, as soon as she moves in, he gets rid of her!

The explanation for this is simple. When she was the mistress who had to be wooed, she was exciting. But the moment she became the wife at home, balancing the checkbook and scheduling garbage pickups, she became boring. Once he fully possessed his mistress, the eroticism was lost. Hence the famous saying of Oscar Wilde: "A man who marries his mistress leaves a vacancy in that position."

Marriage thrives and prospers when a couple is reminded of their attraction to one another, and not just their mutual interests. Jealousy can destroy marriage utterly—or it can enhance it. In every interaction between the sexes there is some level of attraction between a man and a woman. This is what Ronald Reagan's celebrated speechwriter Peggy Noonan meant when she wrote, "People ask me, 'Do you ever get crushes on the men you work with?' And the truth, which I usually find ways not to say, is 'yes, often, don't you?'" (*What I Saw at the Revolution*)

Attraction between the sexes is innate and unstoppable (although it is being severely diminished through many modern factors such as sexual overexposure). The trick is to enhance that quality of attraction where the sexual component is crucial, as it is in marriage. I am firmly committed to the belief that every couple is fully capable of leading the most passionate sexual existence, so long as they set their minds to it. It is not about how your partner looks, but rather about what you think of your partner.

The greatest proof of this is what I call "The Billy Joel Syndrome." The pianist/composer was married to Christie Brinkley, one of the world's top supermodels, yet he allegedly had numerous affairs with other women who, objectively speaking, simply could not have compared with his wife's looks. So what did these women have over Brinkley that caused Joel to allegedly forsake his wife, the mother of his child, and the woman who had sacrificed her career for him? The answer: They were new, she was old. He was excited about the novelty they presented, and dulled by the monotony of his relationship with his wife. Of course, he sought to justify his actions by telling her, as reported in the press, that she was no longer a "spring chicken," "Have you looked in the mirror lately?" and so on. But all of this is balderdash. His alleged unfaithfulness to her had nothing to do with the real facts about his wife, but rather his mental outlook toward her. The same could of course be said of other celebrities, like Mick Jagger, who apparently cheated on his supermodel wife, Jerry Hall, numerous times.

The principal solution to the loss of passion in marriage is to have an affair with your spouse—to bring adultery into your marriage by cheating with each other. The goal is to see your wife not as a complacent and content woman, but as a sexual adventuress, a seductress, and a potential mistress. Conversely, the aim for a wife is to see her husband as a sexual tiger and her would-be ardent lover. Every wife has the potential ability to dig and unearth the Don Juan that lurks within every husband. The problem is how do we achieve this sexual awareness and always keep its lesson before our eyes?

The Tools of Passion

Back in England, I once counseled Hector and Hillary, a couple who had been married for four years. They had a number of problems, but perhaps the most daunting was that, in the words of Hector (and confirmed by Hillary): "We can count on two hands the number of times we've had sex since the beginning of our marriage." Oh my.

The following dialogue ensued among the three of us ("RSB" stands for me):

> HECTOR: My wife is frigid. It's like she's not even sexual. We have this huge king-size bed. She always stays on her side. She would never dream of coming over to my side, and I'm sick of making advances and having her rebuff me. Her grandmother told us when we got married to have a smaller bed so that we'd be forced to be close to each other. What a wise old woman she was.

> HILLARY: The problem is not that I don't like sex. I love sex. Before I married I had very satisfying sexual relationships. But...

HECTOR (interrupting): Oh, come on, even on our honey-moon you would barely let me touch you! Shmuley, I took her to Pukeit in Thailand, the most sexualized country on earth where everybody was bonking like bunny rabbits. Everyone except us, that is. And we hadn't even had sex before we married because you were into this whole "born-again-Christian-virgin" thing.

HILLARY (gritting her teeth from having been interrupted): As I was saying, Shmuley . . . I love sex, love it. I just don't love it with my husband. Before we were married we may not have gone all the way, but that doesn't mean we didn't have great sex. Because he couldn't actually have intercourse with me, he was forced to engage in foreplay. We would kiss and hug and do other things for hours, and he was never in a rush. But on our honeymoon, foreplay? Ha! And I began to notice his selfishness. In all areas of our marriage, it was only what was important to him that took precedence, never what was important to me. We did everything he liked; we took up all of his hobbies. He liked scuba diving, so I had to wear this enormous tank on my back and look at sharks that wanted to eat me alive. And I also saw clearly how selfish he was in bed. Sex would last five minutes and then he'd turn the TV on—on our honeymoon! So I closed up to him. And yeah, he's right, I'm not coming over to his side of the bed. What am I, a prostitute? He snaps his fingers and I spread? Forget it. I want a lover, not a lazy lay.

RSB: I understand your frustration, Hillary. But your big mistake is having given up on your husband so quickly and now rebuffing him every time he gets near you. If you're complaining about how your husband is distant, how can withholding sex, intimacy, be the answer? By your own admission he can be very passionate. Isn't that what you said he was like before you married? So why haven't you taught him to be that man again? Why haven't you expressed to him that the foreplay he used to engage in was necessary to your sexual engagement? You've taken the worst possible route. You've decided to use sex, or rather the withholding of sex, as a power tool to assert your independence. It would be a lot more productive if you used sex to teach your husband to be the kind of lover you desire.

HILLARY: But I didn't marry a boy. I married a man. And I don't want to have to teach him how to be a man.

RSB: You have to stop wanting a finished product. Marriage is about teaching one another and, in the process, bringing out each other's sexual fire. You've got to rub sticks together in order to get a spark. The spark isn't just there. You have to create it.

Unfortunately, far too many wives like Hillary lack the sexual tools and the mental desire to make their husbands into passionate and patient lovers. All too many wives argue that they can't reach the part of their husband that's alive deep within the mummified remains. Later, we are going to learn these methods so that every wife is well-armed with the tools she needs to make her marriage into an ardent affair.

Let's summarize what we've learned thus far:

1. The number-one cause of modern divorce is boredom, which starts the slippery slope downward to drifting apart and, subsequently, falling out of love.
2. Boredom is caused by loss of curiosity and onset of routine.
3. Illicit affairs are one of the most destructive sins in a marriage.
4. While point number three is true, the possibility of adultery—the belief that your spouse is sexually voracious and desirable, attractive to strangers, and can betray you at any time—is essential to a marriage.
5. Husbands and wives who cheat on each other are almost always convinced of the fidelity of their spouses.
6. Husbands who are anxious about their wives' fidelity rarely ever cheat themselves because their mental and sexual energies are too absorbed in guaranteeing the faithfulness of their own spouses.

7. Husbands, and wives especially, who reveal to one another their harmless and natural attractions to other people have a greater potential for passion.

8. Just because your husband or your wife seems to lack sexual passion doesn't make it so. Every human being is sexual. It is then our challenge (as a husband or wife) to find the tools to help ignite a sexual fire.

9. If a wife seems bored to death of sex it could very well be that her husband has killed her libido.

10. If a husband seems too goal-oriented in sex, and neglects the practice of foreplay, his wife is likely to turn off to sex (with him, at least). This doesn't mean that a wife cannot teach her husband to learn to enjoy the sensual thrill of patience and the erotic barriers that heighten the excitement.

The Progress of Knowledge

The reason we search for higher meaning in our relationships is that humans are endowed with perception and insight. We are constantly peering under the hood to see how things work. We crave intimacy because we seek to know people intimately and to understand how they work. This thirst for knowledge is the single most important ingredient in any healthy male/female relationship. As long as a man and a woman still want to know each other, their relationship is healthy and strong. They are still leaning inward toward one another, desirous of peeling off layer after layer—both in terms of clothing and psyche. But the moment they think that they completely "know" each other, the relationship has functionally terminated.

Imagine if you will, a man sees a woman from across a restaurant. She catches his eye. Sure, he's attracted to her. But he doesn't know her name, her interests, or her background. So what causes him to slowly angle his way over and talk to her? It is his desire to know all those things. They start talking and he invites her out on a date, which she accepts. They start going out. At first they share expository conversation, about their hobbies, their parents, and the weather. Later, however, as time progresses, they begin to speak more intimately. They share secrets. As they continually delve deeper and deeper into each other, their relationship continues to flourish.

There are basically four levels of progressive knowledge within every relationship:

1. Exterior—What is your name, "rank," age, ethnicity, profession, etc.?
2. Interior—What was your upbringing like; what are your values, your dreams, your hopes, your aspirations?
3. Emotional—What are your fears, your anxieties, your secrets; what is the crisis point of your existence?
4. Physical—What are you like when all the layers have been peeled away?

The relationship is dead the moment a couple hits a brick wall or when he thinks he's got her all figured out. His questions about her day at the office will stop. His desire to know how she can be sexually pleased will cease. Her hopes to be at his side through his long trek through life will diminish. Why accompany him when he has forfeited his own male magic and exchanged it for *Seinfeld* and *Simpsons* reruns? Why be his partner when he has become a potato? This is the kind of marriage wherein the only thing he offers his wife from the depths of his being is a belch, and the only thing she offers her husband from the wells of her feminine springs are tears of sorrow over what might have been. The relationship has gone from being an exciting journey to a boring destination.

Hence, in an age where the human personality remains largely uncultivated, and superficial pursuits like shopping and TV are prevalent, the life expectancy of relationships and marriage has gone from decades to years. For many it can even be measured in months or even weeks. We all tire of each other much too quickly. Notice how this is especially true in celebrity marriages, which are often measured in days. (Remember Tom Green and Drew Barrymore? Or Dennis Rodman and Carmen Electra's two-week fling?) Since celebrities are addicted to life's highs—from film premieres and holidays at Cannes to the kind of highs that come from white Bolivian marching powder—they lack an appreciation for life's more subtle moments. They tire of the adventure that daily life and shared experience is designed to offer. Attraction between the sexes has the capacity to make ordinary moments into extraordinary encounters, natural events into miraculous memories. But only if you can take the everyday and make it unique.

The truth, however, is that lurking beneath the seemingly boring monotony that so many men and women find in each other—especially if they have been living together for a few years—is infinite human depth. The challenge is simply to unearth it.

In the Biblical book of Ruth, the Jewish nobleman Boaz shows unusual kindness to the Moabite woman Ruth by granting her special agricultural privileges. Ruth turns to Boaz and says, "Why have you made an effort to recognize me, when I am a stranger?" (Ruth 2:10) But the words literally translate as, "Why do you claim to know me when I am unknowable?" Ruth was saying to him, "I am a woman, and a woman is a riddle, wrapped within an enigma, wrapped within a puzzle. How can you claim to know me?"

Indeed, the greatest insult you can give another person is to claim to know him or her. After all, don't you hate it when people do that to you? You're having an argument with someone, and that person looks you right in the eye and says, "Don't tell me what you're going to do or what you think, because I know you." To claim to know someone is to claim to have someone all figured out. It's as if you're someone's master and lord. The reason it's so insulting is that it implies that the person has no profundity to him- or herself—all surface and no depth. All humanity and women, who are especially mysterious, are essentially unknowable.

To sustain novelty in a relationship, we must therefore introduce new parts of our persona and reveal them to our spouse on a regular basis. Some of the ways to accomplish this are straightforward. They can be as simple as coming home and telling your spouse what you did at work that day. Or they can be much deeper. You may be one of those people who have meaningful insights into life. You might be a modern Mark Twain, for whom everyday experience was enough to write novels about. But even if you're not, you are capable of offering your husband or your wife new insights into yourself (for which there must first be self-reflection). Or you might read books regularly and share with your spouse the knowledge you've gleaned. You may even finally decide to reveal to your husband or wife your deepest sexual fantasies and use your marriage as the arena in which to act them out.

Sexual Knowledge

Just as the human personality cannot stagnate, the same is especially true of our sexual natures. The Bible establishes sex as the quintessential form of knowledge with its use of the word "knowledge" to describe the act. This also makes sense, since sex is indeed the deepest form of knowing. Sex involves real nakedness. It involves exposing your vulnerability, your defenselessness, and allowing someone to enter your innermost heart. You lift the veil that separates you from the rest of the world. Every other endeavor in life involves doing, but sex is the only time we submit entirely to instinct; it's all about *being*. It's only when our defenses come down that truthfulness comes out. It's no wonder that drunkenness often leads to sex (usually really bad sex, or sex with the wrong people), as both involve taking down our defenses and a desire to draw close.

Moreover, whereas talking with someone is intellectual, making love to someone is *experiential*. You are actually holding that person in your arms. Words can only reveal one facet of a person and only in one syllable at a time. But touching, sharing, and making love reveals our essence—all at the same time. The relationship has been transmuted from understanding and exchanging to embracing and sharing.

Since sex is the deepest form of knowledge and serves as the foundation of the entire relationship, it follows that we must never allow our sexual nature to stagnate. If a man or a woman thinks that they already know each other sexually, the relationship is dead and has lost all passion. This is where men start fantasizing about other women, contemplating, "I wonder what she's like in bed" or "I wonder what she's like naked."

Hence, our sexual nature must be utterly unpredictable. There are two ways of making it so. One is the functional mixing up of sexual venues and techniques. If your sex life starts getting boring, you may try a new position or kinky lingerie. But this just begs the problem rather than truly addressing it. Simply put, if you're not interested in your spouse, what's going to motivate you to try all these different positions in the first place?

Rather, instead of relying on technical variation in the bedroom to sustain or resuscitate a marriage, it is far more necessary for a husband to feel that his wife is an utterly unpredictable sexual creature. That she is a radiant and magnificent sexual temptress who is deeply desirable to other men and who is deeply desirous of other men as well. Her sexual nature is utterly unknowable. Like a tempest, its direction is changing constantly and can never be controlled. Sexually, she is an unsolvable riddle. Indeed, every time he asks her about her fantasies, he is dumbstruck by what he discovers. The guy married to this mysterious sexual woman needs no one else because he gets all the variety he needs right here with his wife.

Exercises
ENCOURAGING
SEXUAL CURIOSITY

1. Call your spouse at work or at home and say you have something special waiting for him or her. It doesn't matter what it is, the important thing is that your spouse lives in constant anticipation. Mix and match. Buy a small gift one day, an erotic plaything the next. Keep your spouse guessing.

2. Think of something new about yourself to tell your spouse at least three times a week—something insightful and not obvious. It could be a childhood story that you never mentioned before.

3. Think of something sexual and erotic to say to your spouse three nights a week. Saying it softly at the beginning of sex is usually the best course.

4. FOR WIVES: Always keep your husbands guessing. If he is on a business trip and calls home at night to say goodnight, every few nights, have a baby-sitter or the housekeeper answer and tell your husband that you're out and she doesn't know where you are. When your husband later catches up with you and asks where you were, just say, "Out." You don't have to lie. It could mean you walked out to the garden. After the kids are asleep, if you have a baby-sitter, then go out to visit friends or just to do shopping. But make him wonder what you're getting up to when he's away.

5. FOR HUSBANDS: Always keep your wives on edge about when you're going to have sex with them. Again, mix and match. Some days, get dressed in your suit and tie only to rip it off just a few moments later just when she thinks you went out to the car.

6. HUSBANDS: Be voyeurs when it comes to your wife. Some nights, when it's really dark, stand outside your bedroom window and watch her get dressed and undressed when she thinks that nobody is looking. Again, mix and match. While she's in her undergarments, throw a stone at the window and startle her to look out to see who the Peeping Tom is, staring at her while she changes. Hide behind a tree when she looks.

7. WIVES: Make it a common practice to buy a new sexy bra or underwear at least once a week. But make sure it looks great. And I mean it. Once a week. Then, in the morning as you get dressed, or at night as you go to sleep, model it for your husband. It need not be any great striptease. A simple and nonchalant, "Oh, I got this yesterday, how does it look?" will do.

8. Practice having sex together in the tantric tradition, stopping short of full intercourse, for an entire week. Re-experience not just the pleasures of foreplay and long, sensual massages, but also the erotic thrill of delayed gratification.

9. FOR WIVES: Never undress fully in front of your husbands. Always undress in the bathroom or only partially in front of him, or in the dark. Make him lust to see you. Make him earn your body. Only when he is begging to see your body should he be granted a private audience.

10. WIVES: During sex, when you really start getting into lovemaking, tell your husband that there is a man whom you think notices you. Ask him, "Do you want me to tell you his name?" or "Do you want me to tell you who it is?" If he takes the bait and you see him getting excited, don't just say the name, relate the whole experience. For instance, "I went to fill up the car with gas and there was this guy across the station who kept staring at me and then asked me where I lived. . . ." By all means, get carried away. Whatever you say in the throes of passion is beyond your control; it just comes out. If, however, he seems resistant or suddenly unromantic, pull back gently; for some husbands, the thought of your being interested in another man can be an instant passion killer, at least in its initial stages. You can wait a few weeks and try again to see if his reaction changes.

FOURFOURFOURFOURFOURFOURFO
URFOURFOURFOURFOURFOURFOU
RFOURFOURFOURFOURFOURFOURF
OURFOURFOU four FOURFOURFO
URFOURFOURFOURFOURFOURFOU
RFOURFOURFOURFOURFOURFOURF
OURFOURFOURFOURFOURFOURFO

THE Insatiable WOMAN AND THE MALE Animal

I married beneath me. All women do.
—LADY NANCY ASTOR

I myself have never been able to find out precisely what feminism is; I only know that people call me a feminist whenever I express sentiments that differentiate me from a doormat.
—REBECCA WEST, *THE CLARION*, 1913

Some of us are becoming the men we wanted to marry.
—GLORIA STEINEM

Are women insatiable in their sexual appetites? Are men truly animals in their pursuits of sexual conquests? This chapter explores the very nature of female and male sexuality and demonstrates the erotic mindset and dynamic that must occur between men and women to have passionate marital relationships.

First, let's examine a few female stereotypes . . .

The Female as Sex Symbol

In December of 2001, I debated twenty-year-old Lindsey Vuolo, *Playboy* magazine's first acknowledged Jewish playmate, on the effects of pornography on human dignity and relationships. At first I thought the debate would be an imbalanced contest, *not* because I have had more experience as a debater than Lindsey, but rather because the audience would be sympathetic to my cause. I could only imagine that men and women alike would agree with my opposition to a woman taking her clothes off for money to please and pleasure men. Talk about being out of touch.

To begin, the men in the audience—who outnumbered the women two to one—arrived with their *Playboy* pictures of Lindsey, eager for autographs. I don't know if anyone reading this has ever had the experience of facing off against the pinup idol of 200 salivating and lecherous men; let me tell you, it can be unpleasant. But the big surprise was the women. From the very moment I stepped up to my podium, the females in the audience were hostile toward me. How dare I object to this young woman's "bravery," as one female audience member put it, evidenced by her confidence in showing her body to the entire world? "Women have to be liberated from caring what men think of them!" she declared.

"Liberated for what?" I asked. "Liberated to indulge men's lust and need to objectify women? Whatever happened to the idea of men having to be gentlemen in order to get a woman?"

I then turned to Lindsey. "And doesn't *Playboy*—the overwhelming majority of whose readers are married men—just encourage husbands to fantasize about other women while making love to their wives?"

"So what?" Lindsey exclaimed. "What's wrong with that?" She turned to the audience and flashed a smile, eliciting support from her admirers in the audience. "Yeah, what's wrong with thinking about someone else while you make love to your spouse?" the masses thundered, almost in unison.

Anything You Can Do, I Can Do Better?

Of the many tragedies of the modern relationship, perhaps the greatest tragedy of *all,* is the equalizing of the sexes. For women, being treated as equals was a drastic demotion. Throughout history all the great romantic writers exalted women as the spiritual and emotional superiors of men. This is especially evident in the stories of the Bible, and reached its zenith with the troubadours who invented courtly love in the court of Eleanor of Aquitaine in Provence. A woman stood upon an elevated pedestal that a man had to climb, if he was ever to prove himself worthy to even stand in her presence. He had to be a gallant knight, battling dragons and winning honor and virtue if he was to be worthy of the lady of his affections. He was taught to speak to a woman gently and reverentially, as if addressing the divine presence, and he had to focus on a woman's pleasure in bed before his own.

That's what courting was all about. Prior to the First World War, couples would not date, they would "court." The onus was on the man to win over a woman. He would go to her home and produce his card. The young woman would then decide if she would indeed receive the man or not. If she chose the latter, then he was sent away. If he remained interested— and usually this rejection made him all the more interested— he would do everything possible to win her over.

Today, it is quite a different story. Now, women usually yearn to be deemed worthy of the man—to be deemed pretty enough, thin enough, smart enough, funny enough—and thus to win the "honor" of a first date. Even after that elusive first date, it is the woman who has to wait by the phone for the man to call again. Hence, women today are riddled with insecurity. Many starve themselves, quite literally, in an effort to look attractive for men.

The sexual revolution of the 1960s was not a masculine revolution. In fact, it had very little to do with men. Men have always craved casual, commitment-free sex. They just had no one to do it with. But in the 1960s women said, "Hey, we're grown up about this whole sex thing now. What do you think, we're weak? You think we need a guy to marry us just to have sex? We're just like you guys. We love having sex even if it's not part of a relationship."

Suddenly, the male-female covenant was broken. Men could behave like pigs and still get a woman. They could be lecherous and two-timing, they could date a woman for four years and not ask for her hand in marriage, they could get women pregnant and leave them to fend for themselves—and women would put up with it—initially. (Even as I write these lines, the newspapers tell of how Liz Hurley just had a baby, alone, since the man whom she claims impregnated her—former boyfriend Stephen Bing—says that the two "were not in an exclusive relationship" when Hurley became pregnant.) But then one day the women woke up with two realizations:

1. Women aren't wired like men. They don't enjoy casual commitment-free relationships. For men, sex is an out-of-body experience. It is doing something to someone else, making it very easy to compartmentalize between the heart and the body. For women, however, sex is an internal experience; it is an invasion of one's body and one's heart—particularly from a stranger.
2. Men don't value them any longer. Men became coarser and more selfish, and were taking the women in their lives for granted.

But instead of going back to the original ideal of courtly love, where women had to be earned, women chose an extreme alternative: They largely gave up on men and no longer look to them for happiness; they look to their careers instead. It would seem that we now face an entire generation of women who see themselves as potentially marriage-proof.

The masculinization of love and the disempowerment of women in relationships has been a tragedy. Men are in the driver's seat in most relationships today, to the detriment of all. Things were a lot more romantic when women were in charge— and a whole lot more passionate. In instances where it is not the men who are running the show, it's the women who behave as men, having taken their love cue from men. These are the women who are just as commitment-phobic as men and suffer from other male mistakes, such as subordinating love to their careers, overcompetitiveness, and an inability to spark romance.

Remember the famous date scene in the movie *As Good as It Gets?* Jack Nicholson plays a sociopath who insults every person he meets. But he has developed a crush on a waitress at his neighborhood restaurant, played by the charming Helen Hunt, and finally ends up alone on a date with her. Soon into the dinner, she wants to leave. She complains that he has done nothing but insult her the entire evening. "Give me a compliment, or I'm going home," she tells him. So he tells her that her dress is beautiful. But it's a simple dress, undeserving of flattery, so she gets up to leave. He then tells her, "Wait, I took my pills this morning." She's confused. How can this possibly be a compliment? Finally, he offers the immortal line, "You make me want to be a better man." It was his knowing that he was going to see her that motivated him to take the medication that controlled his obsessive-compulsive disorder. Without anyone to love or live for, he didn't see any reason to take his medication.

There is a wealth of empirical evidence that supports the theory of female superiority as well. Women are responsible for only 3 percent of all violent crime in the United States and account for more than 70 percent of regular church and synagogue attendance. They are five times less likely to abandon their children than are men. Not only are they naturally more spiritual than men, they are also apparently better investors as well. A 1998 University of California-Davis study reports that while men act more confident in investing, women achieve 1.4

percentage points better on their returns.

The Talmud says that women are "wiser than men," and have an innate sense of compassion and justice that men lack. In the Jewish religion, the masculine days of the week are far less holy than the feminine day of the Sabbath, which Jews have always called their "bride" and their "queen." Similarly, the all-encompassing presence of God is known as the "shechina," the feminine divine presence.

The greatest Jewish mystic of all time, Rabbi Isaac Luria, founder of all modern Kabbalah and known as the Ari, the Lion, stated more than half a millennium ago that the Messiah would not come until men started listening to their wives. What he meant by that was that the world would not be perfect until the feminine principle became predominant. Men had to start developing their feminine side, and letting their wives exercise influence over them. Paradise on earth will arrive when men and women are more compassionate, less envious, more understanding, less judgmental, more feeling, and less self-seeking. And paradise will come into marriages when men finally become more passionate about foreplay and less impatient for climax; when men become more appreciative of commitment and less loving of variety; and when men learn to make love with their minds much more than with their anatomy.

Women on Top

The area that most clearly demonstrates female superiority is sexual relations. First of all, notice how in the quintessential male/female interaction, when the man and woman are finally united in sexual embrace, it is the woman who envelops the man. It is her anatomy that encircles the male's. In my book *Why Can't I Fall in Love*, I called it "the envelopment of the line by the circle." Simply put, a man's sexuality is a pittance compared to a woman's—which is more passionate, lasts longer, and is more deeply rooted.

But today it is the *men* who are perceived to be the ones

interested in sex, while the women are more interested in the emotional commitment of a relationship. You know all the famous sayings: "Marriage is the price that men pay for sex. And sex is the price that women pay for marriage." Or "Women need a reason to have sex, men just need a place." When a wife isn't interested in sex, she says to her husband, "Not tonight, honey, I have a headache." And yet a man can have an axe lodged in his head and still he's ready for sexual action.

But in ancient times, it was the women who were seen as sexually voracious and men were the ones who lacked the stamina to keep up. Men were seen as not being able to satisfy a woman sexually, and thus husbands always had to be on their guard to protect themselves against being cuckolded by their wives. Now it's the guys who are perceived as being sexual tigers and the women as sex kittens.

Even the most cursory examination of the sexual differences between men and women proves the opposite. Men experience single orgasms, while women are multiorgasmic. When a man makes love to a woman, one minute he's screaming her name, professing his love, swinging from the chandeliers, promising he's going to do this all night. Yet the very next second, right after he reaches what D. H. Lawrence calls his "crisis," he is out for the count. He's slipped into a virtual deep coma. He's gone from needing handcuffs to needing a mortician.

When it comes to sex, men are like microwaves while women are like conventional ovens. Men pride themselves on their ability to heat up really quickly. They can get into the sexual mood much more rapidly than women. They think that all they need to do is zap the woman, and she'll be all hot. Little do they realize that their own heat is external. Having been generated so quickly, it dissipates just as quickly.

What Killed the Female Libido?

If women are so much more sexual than men, why don't we see it more? The secret is that, while women are much more sexual than men, they require their sexuality to be brought out and made manifest. Like the power of the atom that needs a catalyst to be ignited, men have the great pleasure of detonating the female libido. They get to ride the roller coaster of the unlimited female sexual response. And what a ride it is. One of the greatest sexual thrills for a man is to witness a woman surrendering herself to the total loss of all sexual control. As Bob Guccione once remarked, "If I were asked for a one-line answer to the question 'What makes a woman good in bed?' I would say, 'A man who is good in bed.'"

Unlike the male sexual organs, the vagina is naturally hidden, and female sexuality is about subtlety and hiddenness. It's like the fire within a coal that must be fanned into a flame. When he spends the day making her feel desirable and giving her lots of affection, and then engages in hours of foreplay (yeah, right!), he ignites her fuse and their mutual pleasure is immeasurable.

Sadly, however, the same way that men can ignite the spark, they can snuff it out. Years spent neglecting her deep sexual needs can make the fire go incredibly cold and become more and more hidden. All too many men kill off their wives' libidos. Instead of giving her love, he gives her credit cards to shop and get out of his hair. Whereas once she loved sensual massage, now she loves going to the mall. A wife's sexuality is lost due to an inattentive husband.

Death of the Female Sexual Experience

The Monica Lewinsky story briefly resurrected the ancient image of the female sexual predator. According to Lewinsky's own testimony, she pursued President Clinton voraciously, and cast her body at him in a bid for instant intimacy. Betty Curry later admitted that for weeks on end Monica would pester her, just to be admitted to the oval office so that she could engage in such intellectual discourse as reporting to the President (Nov. 12, 1997) how pleasurable oral sex is with Altoids mints. "Ms. Lewinsky was chewing Altoids at the time, but the President replied that he did not have enough time for oral sex.

They kissed, and the President rushed off for a State Dinner with President Zedillo [of Mexico]" (the Starr Report).

But for the most part, Monica was a twentieth-century anomaly. Today it is usually men who are perceived as the great sexual hunters. But in Biblical times it was radically different. Scores of ancient writings portray women as the ones you had to watch out for. Proverbs 2:16 warns the innocent youth: "Be saved from the loose woman, from the adulteress with her smooth words. . . ." And again in Proverbs 7:10–12: "Then a woman comes toward him, decked out like a prostitute, wily of heart. She is loud and wayward; her feet do not stay at home; now in the street, now in the squares, and at every corner she lies in wait."

Why has this changed? I mentioned earlier that sexual boredom is the number-one cause of divorce today, with more husbands than ever before complaining that their wives are frigid in bed, constantly complain of headaches, and seem to prefer shopping to making love. Studies today report that the overwhelming majority of women enjoying cuddling and romantic walks far more than sex. Ancient women may have enjoyed an occasional cuddle now and again, but surely it was not the need for romantic strolls that earned those warnings in Proverbs!

Here is the primary explanation. Women have a far more mature approach to sex than men. Many men who cheat on their wives deflect their guilt by telling themselves that, "It wasn't love, it was only sex." I know that this is the ultimate cliché, but women, on the other hand, have always found it difficult to separate their bodies from their hearts. Unlike men, women have always treated sex as an act of love, a consummation of the road of intimacy. This is also why their sex drive is so much stronger than a man's, because the well from which it courses runs so deep.

Another Blow to the Female Libido

The monumental 1995 study, *Sex in America: A Definitive Study,* by Robert T. Michael, et al., showed that young people no longer believe sex to be a central component of a relationship—which demonstrates just how shallow our views of sex have become. Rather, communication, shared values, and common interests are the strongest criteria for long-term relationships. Hence, 94 percent of American College graduates will marry only someone of similar education, while 96 percent of American women will date or marry only someone who earns as much or more money than they do.

This study proves what I have long suspected to be true. The more casual and commitment-free sex people have, the less it matters to them. But these singles have it all wrong. No amount of rousing political conversation or matched funds in a joint bank account have the power to bring forth our most intense emotions, making us feel intensely good about ourselves and our partners, the way that sex does (or *should*). When things don't work well in the bedroom, they're not going to work in the living room either. Hence, it is imperative that we respect our sexuality and recognize its ability to maximize the intimacy and closeness that we feel within a relationship.

Sadly, however, with the rise of casual sex, men have lost the incentive to take the time necessary to light a woman's fire. So the embers of the woman's libido eventually extinguish as a result of negligence and lack of attention on their partner's side. Psychologist Debbie Then, quoting a study by Ellis and Symons, finds that while a man's favorite activity in bed, other than sleep, is sex; a woman's favorite activity in bed, other than sleep, is reading. But who is responsible for the death of the female libido? Is it the women, who have always dreamed of a Prince Charming who would sweep them off their feet—or is it the men who became Prince Selfish and Rush-to-the-Finish Line in bed, thereby turning women off sex and on to books?

The Desire to Acquire

Studies show that when two men are left alone together in a room, their conversation inevitably gravitates toward five very linear subjects. In order of frequency:

1. Money and finance (which for men is a line, or a graph—up, down, etc.)
2. Sports (which is all about lines—think baseball bat, hockey stick, gridiron)
3. Women (which men reduce to lines and measurements—think 36-24-36)
4. Politics (the scepter of rule, the linear measurement of power)
5. Cars (another line, zero to sixty in 3.2 seconds)

And what do two women usually talk about when left alone in a room? Two cyclical subjects. In order of frequency:

1. Relationships (circles of intimacy, closeness, and exclusivity)
2. Shopping (bringing objects into their circle of possession)

The interesting thing about the female subjects is that the less love a woman has in her life, the more important shopping and acquisition become to her. The more the healthy circle closes, the more the unhealthy one opens. And boy, can it become insatiable, as I have discovered from the countless husbands who complain to me about how their wives are reckless with spending. If she cannot fill her life with the healthy circle of love and intimacy, she settles for the unhealthy circle of acquisition and property. That's why I always tell these husbands who accuse their wives of being inveterate shoppers that if they wear their wives out in bed the night before, they won't have the strength to go to the shopping malls the morning after. And in a way this is true. A woman who receives the emotional and erotic fulfillment from her husband does not feel the emptiness that leads to material acquisition.

Women make these tradeoffs all the time. Think of the stereotypical gold-digging woman who will marry some old business tycoon so that she can shop until she drops for the rest of her life. But this is happening increasingly among women who have much more wholesome values. Many women who cannot satisfy their erotic needs within their marriages sublimate "the desire for sex" into "the desire to acquire." Having given up on being really satisfied with a man who is passionate about them, they become passionate about shopping, career, and making money. When a man destroys his wife's self-confidence and her libido by transferring his own libidinous energies onto another woman, a wife has usually three choices:

1. She can sulk and be miserable and wallow in self-pity.
2. She can run out and have an affair of her own to take revenge and to bolster her macerated ego.
3. She can vent her pent-up anger and suppressed eroticism in shopping.

In the end, both husband and wife suffer. He snuffs out her fire and pushes her to shallow pursuits like shopping because buying colorful clothing or feminine shoes is the only way she can feel feminine. And he has to go and find some sexual excitement with strangers because, to him, his wife has ceased to be a woman. As one wife—whose husband has an extensive collection of pornography at home and invites her to look at the magazines with him so as to assuage his guilt—told me, "When I look at these magazines with my husband, he thinks *I* get turned on by watching *him* get turned on. But really I just feel like a man."

Feminine vs. Masculine Marriages

Unfortunately, we have evolved (rather *de*volved) to a time when men take the initiative in relationships and women follow their example. As I have suggested, this was not always the case. Until the past century, it was women who took the initiative. They understood that the soul of a relationship was to always make sure that their partner had something to look forward to. They would surprise them with the unexpected, delight them with their innocence and naiveté, and most important of all, maintain a sense of fun and discovery. After all, what is sex other than two adults at pleasurable play?

When marriages stopped following the feminine sexual

lead and became masculine in nature, they lost their erotic and edgy quality. Husbands and wives went from being lovers and mistresses to each other to being just that—husbands and wives. They went from having an affair with each other, to having a marriage.

Below is a quick summary of the differences between a feminine marriage and a masculine marriage.

The Feminine Marriage

1. Making love comes before making money.
2. Functional elements of a relationship are subordinated to the romantic side of the relationship. Thus, paying the mortgage or taking out the garbage is trumped by activities such as sitting together in front of a fireplace, having candlelit dinners, and going together for a drink to talk about nonfunctional issues.
3. Marriage is based on surprises. A husband calls up his wife in the middle of the day to go meet at a midtown hotel, just as if they were secret lovers.
4. Husbands and wives are open and emotional with each other. They pour out the contents of their hearts, revealing their sexual fantasies, their frustrations and fears about career and life. They are complete soul mates.
5. Husbands turn off the TV in the bedroom to watch their wives undress at night.
6. Husbands recognize their wives as sexual goddesses who cannot suppress their passion. The husband, therefore, is totally focused on making sure she is sexually satisfied and thereby ensuring that she doesn't stray.

The Masculine Marriage

1. Making money comes before everything else. According to the study *Sex in America,* the national average of couple lovemaking is about fifteen minutes at a time, twice a

week, because husband and wife are completely tired at the end of the evening. According to American Demographics, February 1998, however, Americans are having sex an average of only once a week. Hard to believe, but true!

2. The relationship is mostly functional. Husbands and wives are like project managers, always discussing the running of the "corporation" (the family). Endless discussion is directed toward where to take family vacations, kids' after-school activities, new cars to buy, and the latest tax benefits.

3. The marriage is based on routine. The husband calls up in the middle of the day to remind his wife to pick up his dry cleaning.

4. Husbands and wives are guarded with each other. He tells his shrink his secrets, she confesses to her mother.

5. Husbands change the channel whenever their wives enter the bedroom, so as not to be caught watching the Playboy channel.

6. The only one who would cheat in this marriage is the husband. The wife's sexual fire was extinguished long ago in favor of becoming a breadwinner and/or someone who raises the kids. It's the husband's libido that is out of control—his tongue hanging out at every waitress or female colleague or feminine neighbor, alienating his wife, and further distracting him from his marriage.

More than anything else, the feminine marriage possesses a single, worthy quality that is lacking in the masculine marriage: the very *possibility* of adultery. The woman's sexuality is always evident—enticing all who see or come near her—and the husband's own passion is deeply fired by being married to this woman who can be controlled only if he satisfies her insatiable feminine needs.

The Male Animal: Fact or Fiction

One of the most frequently asked questions about relationships is, why do men seem to be driven, nearly beyond their control, to seek out variety in women? Some relationship authors maintain that men are all animals, or predators, by nature. Therefore, to keep a man interested a woman has to play hard to get, thus keeping a man constantly on the prowl.

Other people, evolutionary biologists in particular, hold that men aren't actually predators, but they are following the rules dictated by the "survival of the fittest" theory. They assert that humans are biologically programmed for the widest possible distribution of their gene pool. Evolution has embedded within them an unconscious desire to inseminate as many women as possible. Thus, men are basically walking sperm banks, willing and able to offer a free loan to any applicant. In his bestselling book *The Moral Animal*, Robert Wright even goes so far as to suggest that, based on this evolutionary evidence, we should no longer label adultery a sin since its practice may be for the good of the species. Interestingly, throughout history, many writers have suggested the very same thing and, later, I will deal with why they are all thoroughly misguided.

For now, let me say that this shallow and superficial understanding of men is flawed. Are we really bringing greater understanding to the field of human relationships by assuming that all men are animals? With the man/animal explanation, aren't we denying those unique qualities inherent in the man/woman *human* relationships? Reading about these superficial ideas in other relationship books, I sometimes feel like standing up and proudly proclaiming the words of the Elephant Man, "I am *not* an animal!"

Demonstrating the vast differences between humans and animals would fill an encyclopedia and is well beyond the scope of this book. But let us consider briefly some of the undeniable differences that separate human and animal sexuality.

1. Human beings are the only mammals (with Bonobo chimpanzees being the only exception) who make love face to face. All other animals copulate back to front. There is a reason for this. Animal sex is all about procreation. Therefore, the identity of the female makes no difference to the male, who never even looks at the female's face.

Sex is not a distinguishing or individual act; its only purpose in the animal kingdom is the perpetuation of the species. The purpose of human sex, however, is closeness and intimacy.

2. The ability to have face-to-face sexual relations is facilitated by the disproportionately large male sexual appendage. Yes, in some respects, size does matter. Okay, I know that in *Kosher Sex* I quoted the insightful aphorism that it's not the "size of the stick but the magic in the wand" that counts—and that's still true. But size does matter insofar as it allows a man and a woman to make love in a uniquely human way. The male gorilla is approximately three times the size in mass of the average human male, about 600 pounds to 200 pounds. Yet, the gorilla's sexual appendage is approximately half the size of a human's. Evolutionary biologists have long been puzzled at the large size of the human penis. Why so large, you wonder? Well, now you know the answer—it allows men and women to make love front-to-front, face-to-face. (And there you have it, an answer that gives you your money's worth for this book already!)

3. To demonstrate #2 further, we note that the human female is the only one on the planet who has attractive features on her front rather than her back. In the animal kingdom, it is the rump that is the most attractive feature of the female. The male is therefore attracted to the female in a way that allows for procreation but not for intimacy or "knowledge," to use the Biblical word for sex. The human female, by contrast, has breasts on her front, thereby attracting a man to her distinctive features—her face—rather than the part of her that has no personal, distinguishing characteristics—her back. Female animals only develop breasts when pregnant or nursing their young. Thus, the human female is constructed in a way that invites a man to "know her" rather than merely fornicate with her.

4. The human female is further distinguished in being the only one who enjoys having sex even while pregnant. This is an impossibility for a female animal, who will never accept a male once she has been impregnated. There are no

exceptions. In addition, human females enjoy sex even when they are postmenopausal, thereby demonstrating conclusively the separation of human sex between pleasurable intimacy and its procreative function.

5. In the animal world, the female goes into heat, usually once or twice a year, and this is the only time that she will accept a male for copulation. At all other times she is simply not sexual. The same is not true of human females. Sure, they get their headaches, and it is also true that women do feel particularly sexual at certain times of the month, like around the time of their ovulation; but, generally speaking, human females are sexual almost any time that a man makes them feel desirable. They're raring to go if they find a man who is worthy of being invited into their inner sanctum.

6. Animals have no concept of sexual excitement, flirtation, erotic games, or fantasy. Nor is there any significant idea of foreplay or teasing each other. The procedure is simply about going into heat, followed by attracting the male, penetration, and insemination. There is nothing a female can do to add or subtract her attraction to the male. It's not about her. It's about him. His hormones draw him to her rather than anything intrinsic about her. But this means that sexuality for an animal can never be a form of personal expression and attraction as it is with humans.

To sum up our points about humans vs. animals, for an animal there is nothing higher than the mere sexual release or sexual dispensation. Even after animals have had sex, they do not feel any closer to one another, nor do they engage in sex out of a genuine desire for intimacy. On the contrary, animals engage in sex for no other reason than genetic imperative and instinct. To be sure, for humans the same path is possible and, for many, perhaps even the norm.

The ultimate difference between humans and animals is, of course, that two humans have the capacity, if they decide to exercise it, of becoming fully fused as a result of their intimate behavior. They are capable of creating an unbreakable nuclear unit that we call the family. Therefore, to compare men and women to animals, and to guide them in their relationships based on this shallow understanding is not just degrading, but ultimately, it does not accord with the facts. Only humans have the unique capacity of achieving what the Bible says is the purpose of sex, namely, to become "one flesh" as a result of engaging in intimate human behavior. As it says in Genesis (2:24), "Therefore shall a man leave his father and leave his mother, he shall cleave unto his wife, and they shall become one flesh."

Exercises
FEMALE AND MALE
SEXUALITY

For wives, here's how to be even sexier than usual:

1. Always acknowledge to yourself that men find you attractive. But don't purposely court it. The whole point of the attraction is that you're mysterious and above it all. Simply be aware that you are the focus of male attention. While sprinkling cinnamon on your Starbucks White Chocolate Mocha (after having mortgaged the house to pay for it), or while picking out asparagus in the supermarket, you'll see men giving you a glance. Notice this.

2. Allow #1 to feed your own sense of sexual confidence and desirability. Absorb that attention and bring the sexual energy back home, so that by the time you walk through the front door you are very positively sexually charged. This will instantly draw your husband to you.

3. Casually mention to your husband how the guy at the checkout counter noticed you; how your male secretary at work stayed late to do a project for you but refuses to do so for any of your other colleagues; how the cop who stopped you for speeding suddenly became very friendly and let you off with only a warning; or how the supposedly married hairdresser who spent twice the time finishing your do than he did with any of the other women he worked on. Try to be casual when you mention these occurrences. The idea is that he will notice them, but to you they are simply fodder for conversation.

4. Indulge your natural mystery at home. You cannot be fully possessed, even by your own husband. Never allow your husband into the bathroom, whenever you're there, even if you're just brushing your teeth. When you change in and out of your clothes, dim the lights so that it's hard for him to see. As we said earlier, wear sexy undergarments always—no exception—just as a mistress would.

5. Don't take a cell phone with you everywhere you travel. I told you before, but I bet you didn't take me seriously: Your husband should not be allowed to reach you at every moment. If he calls you on your cell phone and you're at the shoe store, your response is going to be, "I'll be right home. I'm just at the shopping mall." But if he can't reach you and has to wait till you get home for an accounting, your response can *then* be, "Oh, I just went out to buy some shoes. But it got really weird when the salesman kept on insisting on helping me try on my boots, even when I told him I was fine on my own. Then he gave me his card and told me to call him any time I need anything from the store." Your husband not being able to reach you at all moments also leads to greater anticipation and anxiety on his part. Let him lust for you.

6. Read an erotic novel before bed instead of watching *Conan*. Show your husband that you have sex on your mind. Have an intimate conversation over your morning coffee. Tell your husband you had the sexiest dream about the FedEx man. If he starts getting jealous or angry, tell him that in the dream the FedEx guy suddenly morphed into him. Show him that you are always thinking about sex.

Special exercises for the "male animal" (the husbands):

1. When asking your wife to reveal the attractions she has to other men, or for her list of men who she thinks are attracted to her, make sure you never say, "Oh him, of course he'd be attracted to you. He's Hugh Hefner's twin brother. He's the most lecherous man in the world. He'd be attracted to anyone." Make sure your wife understands that *you* understand that it's her attractiveness, rather than his lechery, that draws him to her.

2. Be inquisitive about your wife. Always seek to find out more and more about her. Don't just ask her about her day—get details. "Okay, so you went to get the dry cleaning. Did you meet anyone there?"

3. When making love to your wife, if it feels like it lacks erotic energy at times, imagine your wife with a man who you think is attracted to her. Keep the fantasy on your own wife and *her* paramours, rather than allowing yourself to think about other women.

4. If you still feel distant from your wife erotically, as you try to make love, ask her during lovemaking if she has recently met anyone whom she finds attractive. No need to press for details about the man (or men) in question. Simply say, "Did that make you lusty? Did it make you think about sex?"

5. If your marriage is strong emotionally and you have a strong ego, go ahead and ask her to identify the men in question. (Wives, if you're naughtily reading this section, always make sure that these guys are distant and men you don't bump into a lot. This is a fantasy, not reality. So, if you're attracted to your husband's brother, better get over it and choose the guy at the car wash instead.) Go further and ask her to say their names or to recount to you episodes where casual strangers showed an interest in her. This is an infinitely healthier alternative to husbands thinking about themselves with other women, which immediately sucks the erotic energy out of the lovemaking session.

6. Get your wife to surrender to you. At least once a week, give her a long sensual massage. Do this especially when she is tired and says she has to get to sleep. The greater the resistance, the greater the passion. It's getting her into the mood that is the erotic part, especially when she swears she's not in the mood. Use deliciously scented massage oil. This will put even the most reserved wife in the mood for love.

For husbands *and* wives, here are ways to love like a woman:

1. In your next conversation with your spouse, discuss your fears, your anxieties, your vulnerabilities, and your dashed hopes. Don't worry about appearing less than macho or of opening yourself up to be hurt later. Learn to trust and don't be afraid to be hurt. Invite your partner into your deepest spaces.

2. Cordon off a "function-free zone" of time every night. Stop being project managers and start being lovers. Every night, for thirty minutes, do not mention perfunctory issues, and do not allow your spouse to do so either. Nothing pertaining to the children, to repairs at home, or financial plans for the future.

3. Practice being romantic. Do things for each other that have no purpose other than to make each other feel desirable. When going to the grocery store together, stop and give each other a kiss when no one is looking.

4. Hold hands under the table when you have guests at the home. Also, always sit next to each other at the dinner table when you have guests. Don't go for any of the aristocratic "hosts sitting at the opposite ends of the table" nonsense. You are lovers, not hosts.

5. HUSBANDS: Stop being sexual and learn to be sensual. When making love, stop rushing to the finish line. Stare at the clock if you have to and make sure you are touching and pleasuring your wife for at least thirty minutes before coitus. Otherwise, it's just breaking and entering. Learn to indulge all your senses in lovemaking. Stop having sex for a week, and work on developing your "foreplay vocabulary." It will be much easier to focus on the journey now that the destination is closed for a while.

6. HUSBANDS: Start staring at your wife as she undresses every night. Go to department stores and buy her sexy underwear and lingerie. Do not give her the undergarments you've bought. Leave them on the bed for her, with a rose, nothing more. Silence is golden. While pornography shouts, eroticism whispers.

7. By now attraction should be significantly heightened. Start giving each other long sensual massages that don't lead to sex or sensual release. Focus on every erogenous zone.

8. Take pleasure in seeing each other light up. Husbands, learn to take pleasure from making your wives feel like women. Engage in erotic transference, whereby giving pleasure is much more delectable than receiving it.

9. Reduce the amount of male "visual" attraction and focus more on female "sensual" attraction. Make love with the lights off. Focus on the sounds, scents, feel, and tastes of lovemaking.

10. HUSBANDS: Record the sounds of your wife when you make love, and take it with you to work. Tell your wife that you are listening to her ecstatic calls during your lunch break. (Make sure you use headphones in the office rather than speakers!) If you're really busy at work, burn her love-tones onto a CD and listen to it in the car on the way home. You, too, will be burning by the time you get home.

11. WIVES: Kiss and hug your husbands at every available opportunity. Soften them up, get them used to showing affection, and make them talk about their emotions. Show them that real strength and courage is losing their fear of being soft.

The
Pain and **Power**
of Infidelity

FIVEFIVEFIVEFIVEFIVEFIVEFIVEFIV
EFIVEFIVEFIVEFIVEFIVEFIVEFIVEFI
VEFIVEFIVEFIVEFIVEFIVEFIVEFIVEF
IVEFIVEFIVEFI five EFIVEFIVEFIVE
FIVEFIVEFIVEFIVEFIVEFIVEFIVEFIV
EFIVEFIVEFIVEFIVEFIVEFIVEFIVEFI
VEFIVEFIVEFIVEFIVEFIVEFIVEFIVEF

ADULTERY 101: WHAT MAKES ADULTERY Hot?

Can a man take fire in his bosom, and his clothes not be burned? Can one go upon hot coals, and his feet not be burned? So he that goeth in to his neighbor's wife; whosoever toucheth her shall not be innocent.

—PROVERBS 6:27–9

When Moses came down from the mountain with his tablets in hand, according to one apocryphal source, he told the assembled elders and scribes: "I've got good news and bad news. The good news is, I got him down to ten. The bad news is, adultery is still on it."

—ANONYMOUS

Adultery is as American as apple pie.

—ROBERT SCHEER, *LOS ANGELES TIMES*

The adulterer goes into the booth and admits his sin but refuses to name whom he had committed adultery with. The priest asks him, "Was it Mrs. Richards?" "No, father," he replies, "and I cannot tell you who it was." "Was it Mrs. Brown?" "No, father."

The priest then tells the man that he has one more chance to confess properly and, if he does not, he will be excommunicated for two weeks. "Was it Mrs. MacLanahan?" asks the priest. "No, father." "That's it," says the priest, "You're excommunicated for two weeks."

The man leaves the cubicle with a big smile on his face. "How did it go?" asked the other man. "Great," he said. "I got two weeks off and three good leads!"

The Deadly Sin We Can Make Jokes About

Adultery jokes go on and on, but they almost always have one thing in common—the joke involves the concept of sin. Indeed, when many of us even broach the idea of sin, the first digression that comes to mind is adultery. It is the most mysterious, the most erotic, and, for most nonpathological individuals, the most enticing of them all. The fascination with adultery is such that experts maintain that it is the most common theme found in world literature.

But before we just look at adultery as something evil, ponder this for a moment. In a world that today divides itself neatly into religious and secular, the only thing that actually bridges the two worlds is adultery. It is the only act that does not involve an infringement of civil rights or a deadly assault weapon but that most people still agree is wrong. Remarkably, it is also something both religious and secular people label a sin. In an age when almost every sexual taboo has fallen by the wayside, when people don't think twice before having premarital sex or spending the entire night downloading images of bestiality off the Internet, nearly everyone still considers adultery to be a gross transgression.

The Nuclear-Powered Libido

A 2001 Gallup poll showed that 89 percent of Americans felt that adultery was always "morally wrong." Clearly, the vast majority of Americans still believes in the sanctity of marriage and feels that any violation of that tradition is morally reprehensible.

There is also the issue of pain. When women, who had experienced both serious illness and a husband's infidelity at some point in their lives, were asked which experience was more painful, 67 percent said it was discovering that their husbands had been unfaithful. This study includes women who had been (may God spare us) cancer patients and the survivors of such invasive treatments as mastectomies and radiation. This gives you a sense of the incredible degree of hurt that adultery can cause, pain that is about as severe as anyone may experience in life.

In fact, a recent study shows that women who had just discovered a husband's infidelity were *six* times more likely to be diagnosed with a major depressive episode than other women. Being cheated on clearly causes intense psychological pain. Indeed, while the attitude toward so many other forms of human behavior is hotly debated between religionists and secularists, they are (nearly) all in agreement on the subject of adultery.

But there is something in these statistics and studies that can't simply be overlooked. Aren't we saying that adultery possesses some sort of mighty charge—like that emitted in a nuclear reaction—that is as powerful as any explosion one can experience in life? If this is so, is there not some way that its energy can be harnessed for something good? An atomic explosion occurs when we somehow split the atom and release the energy that kept that particle together. So, using this nuclear explosion as a metaphor, adultery is the explosion that comes about when the force that held a husband and wife together is destroyed. It's the pain, the anguish—even the passion and the pleasure—that explode when the sexual interactions that husband and wife are meant to reserve solely for each other, are channeled, are *dispersed,* to another party.

But in a strange sort of way, isn't the fact that such a force exists a good thing? The fact that such a pulverizing power exists in a marriage is near miraculous. Isn't the greatest problem associated with marriage the fact that it wilts after a while? The longer you stay married the more you lose interest in sex, not just with your wife, but in general. Scientists show that the level of male testosterone decreases not only with age, but also with every additional year that a man is married. Couples who once had an intense physical life settle into the glorious routine of "transcending" the need for sex, watching late night TV together every night before they fall asleep, holding each other, perhaps even "spooning," but doing so as best friends would. The intense becomes casual, the casual develops into complacency, and the complacency withers into custom.

Yet, when an affair occurs, all of a sudden this steady decline is disrupted. While traveling down this inclined plane toward the gradual deadening of erotic senses, there is an explosion—kaboom! One of the partners in the marriage, refusing to go silently into that dark night, has an affair. Suddenly, a wife who thought that she had altogether lost her erotic feelings for her husband is out on the warpath because he violated their marital bed. Or, a husband who thought he was bored to death with his wife, suddenly wants revenge—or to be dead himself—because of the phenomenal pain his wife's infidelity has caused him.

Objectively, does this not show phenomenal promise? It turns out that this couple is not dead after all! Lurking beneath the calcifying skin is a nuclear libido that wants to love and live again.

The Scary Facts of Adultery

All of the available statistics show that there is a dramatic increase in extramarital affairs in the world today. A 2001 study conducted at Stanford University reported that an estimated 50 percent of husbands and 40 percent of wives commit adultery. To put this shocking prevalence into perspective, a 1998 *Time*/CNN poll found that two out of every three people know someone who has committed adultery. And the amazing thing about this is that adultery is usually something practiced in secret.

The United States is not alone in its rising adultery statistics. In the United Kingdom, a 2002 study by the *Guardian* newspaper found similar numbers to the aforementioned Stanford University report: 42 percent of spouses admitted to committing adultery. In Canada, marriage is apparently still held more sacred, although once again men seem to stray more: According to a 1998 *McLean's*/CBC poll, 16 percent of married men and only half as many married women have committed adultery.

Adultery is a universal problem, however, and does not only manifest itself after years of marriage. A study of college students in northern California found that 60 percent of them had experienced sexual betrayal at some point.

Why Bother Walking Down the Aisle?

With adultery so prevalent, why do we marry? If it's an inherently flawed institution, why not bid it good riddance? Marriage exists because it actually presents the possibility for *synthesizing* the twin aspects of familiarity and passion, thereby affording men and women the opportunity of reaching the summits of sexual excitement and emotional intimacy.

Chasing as many sexual partners as possible or having someone new in your bed every night may provide passion, but it deprives us of intimacy. You get excitement with formality and passion with awkwardness. When a couple barely know each other and they have sex, they are as focused on impressing each other as they are on having a good time. This is the reason that more than 74 percent of American women admit to faking orgasms. (When I mentioned this statistic to Helen Gurley

Brown in a television debate, she said she thought the figure was much higher.) It also accounts for why Viagra is advertising to younger men in their thirties and forties who experience impotence as part of "performance anxiety." They are as hell-bent on demonstrating their sexual prowess as they are in enjoying the experience. The result is an occasion that lacks spontaneity and cannot be fully enjoyed.

Is that what we want? Thrilling sex with both participants hoping that it will soon be over so that they can exhale? Sex where the man and woman may be physically naked but are all dressed up with inhibitions? Sex that is bereft of *emotional* nakedness?

And so while the experience of commitment-free sex may seem very passionate, it is not nearly as exciting as sharing the same experience with someone you love, someone whom you know is not judging you, someone with whom you can be natural and uninhibited. This is when you can have the kind of sex that is totally spontaneous, uncontrived, instinctive, and electric. It leaves you feeling as close to your partner when the experience is over as you felt when it first began. It's the kind of sex that can be found only through familiarity, closeness, long-term commitment, and marriage.

The Soul of Adultery Can Invigorate the Body of Marriage

The only way to overcome the monotony that almost inevitably develops in a relationship is by ensuring that your marriage is as sexually exciting as it can possibly be. Don't worry for a moment about all the other problems that may exist in marriage—arguments, lack of common interests, incessant needling of each other. Studies show that when a couple's sex life becomes inviting, exciting, and pleasurable, most of marriage's peripheral problems subside.

The indifference that destroys so many relationships cannot fester when a husband and wife can't bear to take their eyes off each other. Why else do trivial matters become so blown out of proportion in marriage if not because the pleasurable closeness that once existed and consigned the less important matters to their rightful place as trivial, is no longer present?

Rutgers University's 2000 report on *The State of Our Unions* estimates that more than half of recent divorces occur not because of high conflict, but because of "softer forms of psychological distress and unhappiness." One of the leading divorce lawyers in Britain once told me that more than half the divorces she handles are between men and women who complain that their partners are too untidy to live with. Can you imagine husbands and wives leaving each other because one leaves toothpaste smeared on the bathroom basin? Would a wife leave a husband who looked like George Clooney and made love like Valentino just because he had soup stains on his tie? Obviously, she leaves him because *all he has left* are soup stains on his tie. He has long since stopped dressing up for his wife, and makes love with the football game blaring in the background.

When single folks are invited home by a member of the opposite sex for a nightcap, they don't first look around to check whether or not the room is tidy. Sure, they may notice it. But that's not what's important to them. They are interested in one thing and one thing only: great sex. And that one thing is so thrilling that everything else is so much less important by comparison. A one-night stand is, of course, radically different from a marriage, and I am not implying that by having a passionate love life all the other problems in your marriage will disappear. What I am saying, however, is that strong and passionate attraction is the very soul of a marriage, breathing life into every other aspect. A great sex life takes the edge off so many of life's problems and is strong enough to compensate for a lot of lesser things.

Living together in marriage is not radically different from how the two of you met in the first place. You were drawn to each other not because of what you had in common—after all, you were strangers at first—but because a force that was greater than you, namely attraction, compelled you toward one another. It is that nuclear force of attraction that must keep the two atoms of husbands and wives together within the framework that we call marriage. Whereas marriages that are sustained through commonalities can always unravel—people change and may become incompatible—marriages that are held together by the mystery of attraction will survive all of life's vicissitudes. Because attraction is utterly mysterious and has no intelligible underpinning, it can therefore never be refuted. It is not subject to the law of point and counterpoint. That's why parents always love their children. They have no reason to love them other than the transcendent mystery of the parent/child bond.

What Happens in Sexless Marriages

Once I was counseling a young married couple in Australia who fought constantly. Adrienne, the wife, told me that her husband showed her no respect and even undermined her authority with the children. "Last week, I told our son to take a shower before he went to sleep. He came back and told me that daddy said that what mommy says isn't important. Could you believe he would do that?" I spoke to Bob, the husband, separately. He was a gentle and decent man, so it seemed inconsistent that he would drag his kids into the parental battleground. But I soon discovered that Bob and Adrienne had a disastrous love life. Adrienne felt belittled by Bob, so she retaliated by withholding sex. The couple had not made love in eight months. And Bob in turn retaliated by provoking his wife at every turn.

Judaism has always been at the vanguard of understanding the centrality of sex to a marriage. In Jewish law, the denial of sex in marriage is a functional termination of that marriage. In the Tenth Commandment God forbade the lusting after a neighbor's wife, which clearly implies that a man should be lusting after his own wife, and his own wife alone. There is not enough lust in matrimony as it is now, so we should not diminish it further by misguided views as to the shallowness of the flesh.

It may sound naive to imply that a great sex life can cure all of a marriage's ills. Nevertheless, I believe that one of the most prevalent modern-day fallacies is that a successful marriage is more about compatibility of interests or great communication than about great passion. If compatibility is more important than attraction in a romantic relationship, then homosexuality makes much more sense than heterosexuality and should therefore be more common. Men should marry other men instead of women. After all, the average man or woman has more in common with members of the same sex than with the opposite. The fact that when we marry we look forward to sharing a life with the *opposite* sex teaches us that marriage is primarily about *attraction,* rather than compatibility. And it is uniquely the power of a satisfying sex life that can transform the tedium of waking up to the same face and going to bed with the same body into a welcome experience.

The Myth of Compatibility

This is a lesson that has sadly been lost on today's singles. In nearly every survey, modern men and women say that of the twin pillars of a relationship, attraction and compatibility, the latter is more important than the former. Being best friends is more important than being lovers. The insistence on common interests, as opposed to the strong gravitational pull between men and women that we call attraction, has actually had a negative impact on relationships. In the pursuit of common interests, men and women are becoming increasingly alike. This tendency toward a unisex culture is diminishing the magnetism between the sexes.

Moreover, as men and women focus more on common education, hobbies, background, and profession, they have transformed the pursuit of love from an exercise primarily of the emotions to one of the mind. What used to be a spontaneous, natural, and hot-blooded process has become detached, calculating, and cerebral. The result is that men and women treat each other today as partners rather than soul mates. They examine each other with the cold indifference of a balance sheet. The downright silly marriage-as-a-professional-contract approach to marriage of yesterday's royals and aristocrats has now been adopted by everyman. But the mind—built as it is on objective truths—cannot produce the subjective attraction that glues a man and a woman together as one flesh. Only the heart has that power.

The Downward Spiral of Marriage

When I had just turned twenty-one, I returned to the United States from Australia where I had been a student for two years. I was sitting with a close married friend talking over old times in a hotel lounge in Manhattan, when a young couple entered the lounge and immediately grabbed everyone's attention because of the distracting volume of their conversation. The man was handsome, with a dark complexion and impeccably styled hair and an expensive suit. He appeared to be suave and charismatic—the quintessential Manhattan "ladies' man." His wife (or so we guessed her to be) while certainly attractive was disheveled and distraught.

They sat down at a table not far from us and, even if I had had no desire at all to eavesdrop on their conversation (though I admit I was tempted), I could not have avoided it because of the way she shouted, "You promised me never to speak to her again. How could you? After everything we've been through because of her, how could you smile at her and be so nice to her?" She was pounding on his chest from the stool she sat perched on next to his at the bar. "How could you? You promised. I thought she was out of our life forever! And here you go and pull her right back in. How could you?"

Her husband, or so he seemed to be, clasping both her hands in his, tried unsuccessfully to calm her. But it wasn't going to work. She was clearly hurt and upset. He spoke to her gently, caressing her cheek, seemingly oblivious to the fact that others were listening. He was concerned only with consoling her. "Honey, you know I love you. You know that she meant nothing to me. I promise. She's history." He petted her softly as he spoke, kissed her on the lips, and it appeared as though she would forgive him. She allowed herself to drop softly into his arms, but then immediately she recoiled—and with a vengeance. She stood up, pounded her fists against his chest, and shouted even louder: "No! I won't let you do this to me again. No, I won't forgive you. You *don't* love me. If you loved me you wouldn't do this to me." They argued a bit more in this way, with her shrieking and crying amidst his futile attempts to console her with his promises of future fidelity.

I still remember the raw pain on the woman's face; the frazzled hair, the long black mascara streaks down her cheeks. She was apparently hurt so badly that she was completely oblivious to the spectacle she was making of herself. She did not care about her appearance or about others' impressions of her.

The cycle of adultery, even when it is the wife who is being unfaithful, usually *begins* with the husband. Men innately desire (some would say require) many sexual partners and associate passion with newness. They may love their wives, but they still seek out new bodies. They become restless with the limitations of monogamy, as their wives become too familiar to them to instigate their excitement. As that happens, husbands begin paying less attention to their wives. The monotony they feel causes them to ignore the woman with whom they share their everyday existence. The husband who in the early years of the marriage would take his wife cycling every Sunday, now watches football for hours on a sunny day. The man who once called his wife at her office every day, now calls to remind her to have the car washed on her way home.

Women have a giving and generous nature. They will devote their lives to the man they love. But when a woman feels she has given her man everything, but senses that she is now losing his attention, she becomes bitter and she begins to retaliate—subtly at first, and then more and more as time passes. This is especially increased if a husband shows his wife attention only when it's time for sex.

A married woman named Sophie demonstrates the problem:

For many years, my husband has not made any overt demonstration of affection towards me. Held my hand or

*patted me on the shoulder or any of those things, and it is
one of the things I have great problems in coping with. I
mean it is one of the reasons why I went into an extramarital affair, and yet [my husband] wanted sex very regularly,
and I eventually got to the stage where I got out of bed in
the middle of the night . . . and said, "I cannot allow you
to have sex with me if you are not prepared to show that
you care about me because my body is the one thing that I
own and I will not use it for any purpose that I don't want
to use it for and I don't want to have sex unless it is part of
a wider relationship."* (Adultery by Annette Lawson)

The husband begins to detect his wife's resentment, but usually he doesn't really get it. He says to himself, "I work so hard,
I do everything for my wife and kids. I kill myself to support
them. And then I come home to a cold, unappreciative spouse."
He retreats into himself and becomes even less communicative.
This in turn alienates his wife even further. In her mind she does
everything *for him* and yet when he comes home he doesn't
even have the decency to take a little bit of time to talk to her.
Instead, he just plunks himself down in front of the TV.

What often happens next is that the husband, feeling lonely
and unappreciated, begins to get close to a woman in his office,
or at his gym, or one of the mothers of his children's playmates.
He can't figure it out. This new woman thinks he's amazing. She
laughs at his jokes and compliments him on his achievements.
He feels like a person around her. "Why doesn't *my wife* ever
make me feel like that?" he asks himself, all the while rejecting
his own responsibility for her estrangement. "How unfair it is
that I must seek out a stranger to get some tenderness!"

Yet all the while, he is the one who snuffed out his wife's
suppleness. He is the one who took a once-fawning wife and
made her bitter through his inability to focus on her, his
inability to treat her like a person who needs to talk, laugh,
and complain. By now, the wife has noticed that her husband
is even more distracted, and she begins complaining to her
husband about every little grievance, in an attempt to get him
to notice and listen to anything. While she once took pleasure

in presenting him with a well-ordered home, she now excoriates him for leaving his socks around the house.

Now the husband says to himself, "My wife isn't merely unappreciative, she's downright mean." He begins to feel sorry for himself. In his perception, everyone he knows has a soft and loving wife, except him. His self-pity assuages his feelings of guilt about his budding affair.

Her husband's mental and emotional preoccupation rapidly depletes the marriage of its necessary "nutrients," leaving the wife feeling lonely and unloved. She knows full well that her husband's mind is not on her. As a writer who counsels husbands and wives on their marriages, I cannot begin to tell you how emotionally drained one can become in listening to the agony of so many modern wives, who feel they have sacrificed so much for men whose attentions are so often diverted onto complete strangers. They feel they are living in a barren wilderness, devoid of any real emotional appreciation or intellectual validation.

So one day, while watching the kids in the park, a stranger who is there with his kids strikes up a conversation with her. He compliments her on how patient she is with her children and admires what an outstanding mother she is. It's not necessarily a romantic compliment. But she's certainly never heard it from her own husband. In fact, she doesn't hear anything from her husband lately. She feels comfortable with this new man. A week later, he's at the park again. They talk some more. This time he tells her she looks sad. He asks if she wants to talk about it. She declines. But the next week he calls her up and they agree to have coffee. Now she's embarking on an affair of her own. Often, she feels no guilt at all for what she's doing because she sees it as a matter of survival. As one unfaithful wife told me, "The compliments my boyfriend gives me are like oxygen to a suffocating victim. They're enough to keep me breathing for an entire week."

Tragically, this downward spiral into mutual infidelity could easily have been avoided if the husband had worked on countering what I call "MADSS: Male Attention Deficiency to Spouse Syndrome." The name is appropriate because the average husband who neglects his wife *is* MAD. Only an act of unwitting insanity would have a man alienate his most important emotional support in the entire world. Most of the blame lies with the husband, which is why I'm so tough on men when couples come for counseling. Indeed, Shere Hite showed in her famous study on female sexuality that, whereas husbands may engage in adultery even if they have a loving and attentive spouse, 94 percent of married women will never cheat if they are satisfied with their marriages. But the wife is also somewhat to blame in the scenario of the inattentive husband because she could have made more of an effort to coax her husband into conversation instead of allowing him to retreat into his cave.

Women are naturally more vulnerable and more emotionally open than men. A wife yearns for the love and affection that existed at the outset of her marriage. If she is lucky, and both she and her husband work hard enough, their affection can be rekindled. But if she gives up hope—especially if she knows her husband's attentions to be with other women—she will either close up and grow unhappy and embittered, or she will look outside the marriage herself.

In my counseling sessions, I have noted of late a dramatic increase in husbands who have simply removed the erotic attention from their wives. They have lost attraction to their wives, which is not all that surprising in an age that glorifies youth and a culture that streams images of so many beautiful women into every home. This has a far greater impact on men who are more visually attracted to the opposite sex, than on women, who are more holistically attracted. When a husband loses his attraction to his wife, it creates the common situation of the emotionally abusive husband. Since he does not feel physically drawn to his spouse, she becomes like a dead weight to him, a burden that he wishes to cast off. The characteristics of the emotionally abusive husband which are becoming so prevalent in our society are:

1. The husband who rarely ever talks to his wife about anything other than the most mundane aspects of their lives.
2. The husband who is emotionally undemonstrative. He never shows his wife any kind of affection. When she hugs or kisses him, he instinctively pulls back as if he were being licked by a shaggy dog that slurps on him.

3. The husband who is hypercritical of his wife. Wherever he looks he finds fault. In his eyes she can do nothing right. He treats her as if he is her high school gym teacher, reproaching her at every turn.

4. The husband who blames his wife for anything bad that happens in their life together, from a rusting car to the children's illness. Had she been more careful, these bad things would not have happened. Had she been a better mother, the kids' report cards wouldn't be so bad. His complicity is overlooked or denied.

5. The husband who makes constant comments denigrating his wife's looks. Her appearance is something that irritates him. When she dresses up for him, she is wearing too much makeup. When she puts on lingerie for him, she wears it awkwardly, making her instantly unsexy. When she loses a few pounds, she is still way too fat.

6. The husband who accuses his wife of being insatiable. In his eyes, she is way too demanding, and he tells her as much. She spends too much money and he accuses her of being lazy and selfish. In his mind, he is always giving to her, but it is never enough. Whatever little morsels of affection she asks for is an indication, to him, that nothing he does will ever make her happy.

7. The husband who accuses his wife of being just like her mother. Whatever faults the wife has are a genetic inheritance from his impossible mother-in-law. He is constantly saying "like mother, like daughter." The same contempt he shows toward his mother-in-law he displays toward his wife.

8. The husband who is constantly accusing his wife that unless she changes—becomes more responsible, less demanding, more in control—he will leave her or will find a girlfriend. This is the husband who is a control freak. Everything has to be on his terms. If his wife shows any sign of rebellion, if she in any way asserts her independence, he threatens to be out the door. By doing so and holding over her head the constant threat of divorce, he bullies her into submission.

9. The husband who accuses his wife of being emotionally unbalanced or mentally insane. She is delusional, filled with anxiety

and worry. He blames her for trying to make him crazy as well, with her insane demands and insatiable need for affection. He accuses her of being terrified of everything, plagued with psychotic fear. Why can't she be tough like him?

10. The husband who disempowers his wife in front of her own children. This is the husband who says to his wife things like, "If only mommy would love you as much as she loves her grandma and grandpa," or "I want to take you to the park. But mommy says you have to do your homework." This husband makes it a point to embarrass the mother in front of her kids and undermine her authority in order to feel more secure about the children being closer to him than they are to her.

To be sure, we can give advice to counter each of these individual points and teach husbands how to be loving spouses. But the shortcut to all of this is to deal with the root cause. Husbands who lose attraction to their wives treat them really poorly. They search for things to complain about and, in the gritty details of everyday life, they find a treasure-trove. The solution is not to get wives to strive to be more attractive to their husbands—although this is important as well—but rather, to create erotic desire in the minds of the husbands. Can you imagine any man, a control freak included, denigrating a woman to whom he is strongly attracted and wants to get into bed?

Amidst the many useful ways of enriching marriage and preventing adultery to be found in this book, none is as important as the techniques by which a couple can achieve passion and newness in marriage and the methods by which we create mental desire. A husband who can be taught always to see his wife in a passionate light will be able to cater to his natural disposition without repressing his essential sexual nature. The result will be that his wife will feel like the most desirable woman in the world. Both will abstain from adultery, not for religious or social reasons alone, but because they feel immensely happy and sexually satisfied.

Exercises
CREATING A SPARK

1. HUSBANDS: Tell your wife how great she looks; how in awe you are of her ability to balance successfully the many aspects of her life; how much you enjoy discussing movies or books or politics with her at the end of a day; and how much you appreciate everything she does for you. "You must be superwoman. To look beautiful, excel at your profession, give me and the kids so much love, and be so patient while doing it."

2. WIVES: Give your husband what I call "manly applause." This is the kind of praise that men especially appreciate, because they have inevitably grown up with the expectation that they must be a good provider. Tell your husband, "I was at Cheryl's house today. You know her husband is that fancy, corporate lawyer. And yet he doesn't provide his wife and kids with half the things you give us, and he never spends time with the family. You're so good to us. You're always thinking of me and the kids before yourself. I'm so lucky to be married to you." Even if this is not exactly accurate, find something you can say to him that will make him feel he has done something good. Words create their own reality. The more you compliment your spouse, the more you give him something positive to live up to.

3. Give each other a neck massage when you get home from work, even if it's only for five minutes. If your hands naturally gravitate to areas of your spouse below the neck, so much the better.

4. Ask yourselves if there is anything you may be overlooking, missteps that are casualties of a busy life and harried existence. Do you show appreciation for everything your spouse does for you—or do you take it for granted? Do you occasionally call your spouse from the office for no other reason other than to thank her for a favor she performed for you? If your wife buys you your favorite beer, have you told her how much you appreciate the effort? If your husband takes the kids out on a

Sunday afternoon so that you can have time to yourself, do you tell him how much it means to you?

5. Take one night off a week and make it your time together. Don't let anything prevent you from doing so. Make it your weekly date. Go to the theater, have coffee at Starbucks (even though you might have to sell one of the kids in order to pay for it), or just take a stroll in the town center.

6. Have a weekly sporting event that you do together. Play racquetball, basketball, or go jogging or Rollerblading together. If you're not the sporty type, do something less exerting. Go bowling, or simply take a walk around the neighborhood.

7. Make each other laugh. Tell each other jokes. Do imitations of family, friends, or the kids. Share jokes that are told around the workplace or funny stories that occur during your time apart during the day. But always keep each other laughing. Laughter, like sex, is a great stress reliever.

8. Read erotic literature to each other. Try to make it tasteful classics, like D. H. Lawrence's *Lady Chatterley's Lover* or John Cleland's *Fanny Hill*. Avoid the trashy stuff with titles like *Harriet's Horny Henhouse* that leaves little to the imagination. Reading erotic literature, especially great love stories, certainly awakens erotic desire.

9. Once a week, take a long hot bath together. It doesn't have to be sexual, but it might be. Focus more on the soothing aspect than the erotic. Add bubbles and bath salts. You might even light candles. Learn to comfort and rid each other of anxiety as a prelude to sex.

SIXSIXSIXSIXSIXSIXSIXSIXSIXSIXSI
XSIXSIXSIXSIXSIXSIXSIXSIXSIXSIX
SIXSIXSIXSIXSIXSIXSIXSIXSIXSIXSI
XSIXSIXSIXSIX six XSIXSIXSIXSIX
SIXSIXSIXSIXSIXSIXSIXSIXSIXSIXSI
XSIXSIXSIXSIXSIXSIXSIXSIXSIXSIX
SIXSIXSIXSIXSIXSIXSIXSIXSIXSIXSI

MONOGAMY AND THE Sin OF ADULTERY

Do you give up the great marriage for one incident that was yes, painful, yes, terrible, and yes, horrifying? When someone you love disappoints you on a deep level it's devastating, but you have to weigh the love with the hurt, the good with the hurt, the great memories with the hurt. If the scales are tipped [toward love], that puts it in perspective. Would I ever want to go through it again? Never. And I will not go through it again. Frank knows that I won't.

—KATHY LEE GIFFORD COMMENTING
ON HER HUSBAND'S ADULTERY

One cardinal rule of marriage should never be forgotten: "Give little, give seldom, and above all, give grudgingly." Otherwise, what could have been a proper marriage could become an orgy of sexual lust.

—RUTH SMYTHERS, *MARRIAGE ADVICE FOR WOMEN*, 1894

My wife has cut our lovemaking down to once a month ... but I know two guys she's cut out entirely.

—RODNEY DANGERFIELD

107

Is monogamy viable? Was it viable in the first place?

Recently, I watched several wives of an outcast Mormon polygamist speak on television. They made a case for polygamy arguing that, "Well, Jacob had several wives! Solomon had *more* than just several wives!"

So, does our nature accord with monogamy or is it merely a modern artificial imposition? In the face of such widespread marital infidelity and divorce, perhaps it is time to really question whether monogamy is not just some wishful fantasy born of religious mores. The soaring rates of infidelity and divorce mentioned in earlier chapters surely point to the failure of long-term monogamy as a way of life. Certainly, it's not very encouraging to young people contemplating marriage.

There are many people who argue that extramarital affairs are a good thing, healthy for marriage, and should no longer be condemned. Helen Gurley Brown, international editor for *Cosmopolitan,* once urged women "to borrow other women's husbands for sex." Many famous people have embraced the idea, including Colette and Jean-Paul Sartre, Pablo Picasso, William Faulkner, H. G. Wells, Errol Flynn, and, of course, Bertrand Russell, who became a leading advocate of open marriage. Innumerable psychologists, researchers, and authors maintain that at times having a lover on the side can help to keep husbands and wives together. Currently, there are even social groups such as "Beyond Monogamy," founded by Carl Turney in Australia, that exist solely to support like believers.

When it comes to plural marriages, people seem to focus on places like the state of Utah—with its scores of defrocked Mormon polygamists living in the hills (although the Mormon Church officially abandoned polygamy and excommunicates those who practice it). But even in places like the San Francisco Bay Area, with its traditionally open-minded environment, there are high concentrations of so-called "swingers." Many licensed sex clubs around the world, particularly in Europe, offer couples a safe haven where either partner can quickly pick up and have sex with a new partner, or where both can openly engage in group sex.

In *The Hite Report: A Nationwide Study of Female Sexuality* (1976), many married men and women assert that, while they desire to remain married, the only thing that enables them to do so is the fact that they are having extra-marital affairs. One wife, "Judith," who is forty-eight and has been living in such a relationship for twelve years, claims that she "personally couldn't get into a relationship which required [her] to be monogamous. A closed system runs out of energy. An open system keeps a relationship alive and fresh and current and honest." She continued on to explain that the sexual variation "keeps you from getting into the old, boring drudgery that people get into after making love to the same person for fifteen years."

I have counseled several couples who have told me the same. Timothy, married for twenty-one years, told me that had he not cheated repeatedly on the side he would have left his wife long ago. "I found marriage to be completely stifling. I needed some excitement or I would have left my wife. And what would you prefer, Rabbi," he asked me, "that I break up our family and leave my kids without a full-time father at home, or that I engage in a bit of harmless sex with strangers from time to time?"

Dorothy, married for thirty-four years, told me the same thing. "I loved my husband but he had never been the warmest of men. He was too self-absorbed, too focused on his work, to fulfill my emotional needs. But I never thought of leaving him. I loved him in my own way, and I suppose he loved me about as much as he could love anyone. In our fifteenth year of marriage I found a lover. We would meet about once every two weeks and make love. It lasted for eight years. He told me I was beautiful, something that my husband never did. And with my husband the sex was mediocre. But with Harry it was great. If I hadn't had Harry on the side I would probably have just died on the inside. My affair never adversely affected my marriage, my husband never knew, and I don't think I did anything wrong."

The Missing Piece

In many instances, a good marriage will be missing one component—sexual passion, for example—which can sometimes be provided only by someone outside the marriage (at least that's what those having the affair will maintain). In other cases, what leads a partner into adultery is the desire for an adrenaline rush and excitement; they stray outside the marriage to escape what they perceive as the inevitable drudgery of marital routine. If this adulterous affair satisfies their curiosity, and thus leads to the long-term viability of the marriage, then what makes it so wrong?

Although, as I have mentioned, there are those who would argue that adultery may have positive consequences, such opinions are not generally aired within mainstream society and they specifically call attention to themselves because of their rarity. Amidst a general loosening of moral strictures in nearly every other area of society, adultery is inviting greater condemnation than it would have just a few decades ago.

The classic modern case in point is of course Bill Clinton's affair with Monica Lewinsky. JFK had a string of affairs just thirty years earlier and yet reporters not only did not report it (there was a general reluctance to invade a politician's private life back then), they didn't judge him for it either. But President Clinton was ultimately impeached because he lied about his affair.

Many other modern politicians could commiserate with President Clinton. He is not alone. Governor Nelson Rockefeller was the clear frontrunner for the 1964 Republican presidential nomination, until the scandal over his extramarital affair was revealed and resulted in a dramatic drop in popularity. Remember Gary Hart? He was forced to withdraw from the 1988 presidential nomination race after his candidacy imploded from media exposure of an extramarital affair. In 1995 Senator Bob Packwood of Oregon was forced to resign over his sexual advances to women in the office, while in 1998 Army Major General David Hale—once a top NATO commander in Southern Europe—was forced into early retirement for committing adultery with the wives of his subordinates. Then, of course, in that same year, former Speaker of the House Bob Livingston stepped down from office after his affair became public, and claimed he was setting an "example" for President Clinton. The list goes on and on.

When I was the rabbi at Oxford, there were back-to-back scandals of two British government ministers who were caught having affairs. Both had to resign their positions. Commenting on the scandals, the *Independent*, a daily British newspaper, commented: "Whatever the failings of their political leaders, the British people are overwhelmingly in favor of monogamy. Nearly 80 percent consider extramarital sex to be always or mostly wrong, thus echoing Dr. George Carey, the Archbishop of Canterbury, who denounced adultery as a sin yesterday. . . ."

Since then, the sentiment has grown only stronger. A 1998 study reported that 90 percent of Great Britain felt extramarital sex was "always" or "almost always" wrong.

Other Taboos

Then there is the phenomenon of group sex—or "three-" and "foursomes." While it may not be as widespread as premarital sex, the *Janus Report* claims that 17 percent of men found group sex "very normal" or "all right." A far greater number actually admitted to having been involved in group sex. In Finland, while foursomes are rare (only 1.4 percent of men and 0.8 percent of women); threesomes are not so uncommon, with almost one out of ten men having participated in a threesome, but only 2 percent of the women.

In the United States, an unscientific but revealing survey of students at California State University-Long Beach showed that of almost 100 students ages eighteen to twenty-nine, 29 percent of the men and 14 percent of the women had already engaged in group sex; almost half of the men who hadn't done it yet claimed they were willing to try. This is born out nationally, as roughly 2 percent of couples—or approximately 3,000,000 people—are engaged in a "swinging" lifestyle, of which group sex is an integral component. Dr. Robert McGinley, founder in 1975 of Lifestyles, a swinging organization, contests this statistic, and claims that as many as 15 percent of American couples have engaged in swinging at some juncture in their marriages.

Apparently, this is not solely a male fantasy. *The National Health and Social Life Survey,* published in 1992 by the National Opinion Research Center at the University of Chicago, discovered that 10 percent of women aged eighteen to forty-four "found the thought of sex with a stranger appealing" and 9 percent of women aged eighteen to forty-four "found the thought of group sex appealing."

Those Who Tolerate Infidelity

According to Dr. David Buss's *The Dangerous Passion: Why Jealousy Is As Necessary As Love and Sex,* almost half of divorcees cite a spouse's extramarital affair as one of the main reasons for the breakup. However, it is possible for extramarital sexual activity to occur within an otherwise stable marriage and transpire without causing a breakdown. The *Janus Report* found that 28 percent of married men and women had had more than one extramarital sexual contact without their marriages dissolving. More recently, it's been found that over two thirds of marriages survive the betrayal of a spouse.

Among the many married couples I have counseled over the years, there are understandably numerous examples of marriages dissolving—often violently—after one single case of infidelity. But I have also been involved in many cases where the wife or husband is forgiving of the other's infidelity, and believes that their love for each other is far more important than a momentary breach of their marital bond.

One woman tolerated her husband having a mistress in another city where he frequently went for business. "When we first got married I had an affair. It was really stupid and it pushed my husband away from me. But we worked it out. Now he's having an affair and I guess it's only right that since I did, he should be allowed to as well. I have no right to stop him." I was incredulous. "No right to stop him? He's your husband. No matter what you did in the past, he has to be faithful to you. By all means go to him and say how sorry you are for what you did. Tell him you recognize the pain and anger you caused, that you will do any kind of penitence to put it right. But you simply cannot allow him to make the same mistake. It's bad for both of you and it's bad for your children. Tell him you're in a relationship without integrity or dignity when a husband has a mistress." I pleaded with her, but she wouldn't listen. "I'm afraid that if I do what you say, Rabbi, I'll lose him."

More often than not, tolerating a spouse's affair happens in cases where the unfaithful spouse is honest enough to inform his or her partner of the new arrangement. But make no mistake about it. The very first casualty of adultery in any marriage is the trust upon which the marriage is built, and this is only partially reinstated by a spouse's confession. (To be sure, I started this book by saying that too much trust in a marriage snuffs out the passion because it allows you to take your spouse for granted. I will deal with this later, where I discuss what *real trust* in a marriage consists of.) But if the marriage is healthy enough to sustain the impact of an affair on either side, why did this not prevent it from happening in the first place?

I believe wholeheartedly that adulterous acts are not irreversible problems within a marriage. In fact, adultery is far more a statement about human nature than it is about the state of matrimony. I say this with one important proviso, however; it applies only to acts of adultery committed by the husband. While acts of adultery on the part of either spouse are equally sinful and equally serious, and I am not advocating an unjust double standard, nevertheless all studies bear out that it is the wife's straying that is indicative of a much more serious problem within the marriage. Firstly, when a husband is unfaithful, often the cause is not his marriage at all, but a natural sexual predisposition towards variety. Secondly, husbands are far less prone to become emotionally involved with their mistresses than wives are with their lovers. By and large, the adultery on the part of a husband seems to be motivated by a desire for novelty, while the unfaithfulness of a wife seems to be driven by a desire for attention and affection.

In fact, *The Hite Report on Male Sexuality* (1981) reported that 87 percent of husbands who were being unfaithful to their wives claimed to love their wives. A study by Shirley Glass, published in *Psychology Today* in 1998, found that over half of the men sampled who had an extramarital affair said, "their marriages were happy." They were cheating because of the thrill of the chase with a new woman and the thrill of a new body.

This is also the reason why more than 90 percent of husbands who promise their mistresses that they will leave their wives and marry them instead are lying. Even if the marriage breaks up as a result of the infidelity, 90 percent of these men never end up with their sexual partner. In *Women Who Stay with Men Who Stray*, Debbie Then quotes an only slightly lower statistic: "Eighty-five percent of philandering men don't leave their wives."

These men still feel connected to their wives. The reasons they cheat are varied. For some it's an escape from the routine of marriage, for others it is out of a desire to augment their sexual confidence by affirming that they are attractive to another woman, thus corroborating their manliness. For others it might be the latest hostility directed against their wives. As Dr. Joyce Hamilton Berry, a clinical psychologist in Washington, D.C., notes, "When I counsel clients, I compare male infidelity to a man walking into the kitchen and seeing a chocolate cake sitting on the counter. It looks good; it smells good. He is not hungry, but he will eat the cake anyway. In other words, men sometimes cheat when they see a woman who is attractive and appears to be interested, and even though there is nothing lacking in their marital relationships, they initiate affairs anyway." But they still love and stay with their wives, and the wives accept them. Eighty-eight percent of women say they would stay with their spouse even if he had strayed.

This is further borne out by research done by Dr. David Buss at the University of Texas. Dr. Buss and his fellow researchers tested how willing men would be to have sex with a woman who was a complete stranger. The researchers had men go up to women on the street and say to them, "Hi, I've been noticing you around town lately, and I find you attractive. Would you go to bed with me?" Not a single woman who was asked this question accepted the proposition. But when a woman posed the same question to men, 75 percent immediately agreed to have sex with her—and even told the woman that they were flattered by her proposition.

However, a wife's cheating leads to divorce in approximately 25 percent of marriages. Indeed, Annette Lawson, in her landmark study *Adultery: An Analysis of Love and Betrayal,* and Dr. Lana Staheli, in her book *Triangles: Understanding, Preventing, and Surviving an Affair,* both show that a wife's infidelity is cited as the leading cause of husbands divorcing their wives. When a wife commits adultery it is not because of her nature but rather because of her *marriage.* This does not mean that women are less interested in sex than men. Indeed, I maintain that the female libido is much stronger than a man's and wives are capable of far greater sexual ecstasy than their husbands, as anyone who has compared the intensity of the male orgasm to the female orgasm can attest.

Husbands frequently state that even if they stray they still love their wives and they are doing nothing to hurt the marriage. Many of them actually believe, however mistakenly, that their acts of infidelity do not seriously affect their married lives. (Later in this book, I will demonstrate the fallacy of their thinking.)

There is a well-documented difference between men's reasons and women's reasons for committing adultery. *In the minds of many adulterous men, love is something they get from their wives; excitement is something they get from their mistresses.* They often talk themselves into the belief that they are unhappily married and their wives don't understand them, when really all they are feeling is boredom brought about by a natural inclination away from monogamy and a shallow male need for superficial novelty. Emotional fulfillment has little or nothing to do with it.

Many commentators maintain that a husband or wife's adultery is an indication that something is seriously, even irrevocably, *wrong* with their marriage. In most cases I do not believe that a marriage should break up as a result of a sexual indiscretion. Moreover, throughout this book I shall argue that it is specifically the *possibility* of adultery that can resolve the greatest of all challenges to marriage: the loss of sexual passion in long-term relationships.

Adultery Is a Sin of Omission

What is the true sin of adultery? Have you done something wrong, or have you failed to do something right? I maintain that the truly damaging part of adultery is the latter. Adultery is a sin of omission. People seem to think adultery is a sin of *commission:* You do wrong therefore it is a transgression. But that is not the most harmful part of adultery. Rather, it is the void the couple creates that hollows the marriage out and renders it susceptible to collapse. Cheating is wrong not just because you have done something wrong, but primarily because *you haven't done something right.* All of the affection, emotion, and attention you lavish on the person you seek to seduce should be shown to your spouse. Instead of putting it into your marriage, you're focusing outside your marriage. You are taking the life-giving waters of love that stem from the fountain of the heart and diverting its flow away from your marriage and into another pool of water. The resulting diversion will make your marriage into arid earth, bereft of nourishing affection. A marriage is like a stomach: When it's not fed it begins to ache. It's a hungry animal, an electric, alive institution that needs constant nourishment. It needs to be fed with attention, devotion, and love if it is to last.

In almost every case of adultery I have dealt with, if a

marriage died after the adultery it was because of the depletion of affection and attention rather than due to the act itself.
If a man and a woman love each other, they will almost
always stay together after an act of infidelity and try to better
their relationship. But if a man spends half a year chasing
after another woman—making her feel sexy rather than his
wife—his marriage dies the painful death brought on by neglect. The same is of course true of a wife's infidelity.

In my first year at Oxford, a twenty-five-year-old woman
wanted to be divorced after only two years of marriage. She
caught her husband red-handed in their very matrimonial bed
with another woman. She was hysterical. "Out!" she cried to
the woman who was scrambling to find her clothes. After she
had left, she shouted and cried to her husband at the top of her
lungs, "You're an animal. You brought that whore into my
house and into our bed. How could you?" And she cried for
three weeks. Finally, inconsolable, she packed her bags and
moved in with her best friend.

This couple were friends of mine and I struggled to keep
their marriage together. The husband was most repentant. He
begged her to take him back but she slammed down the phone.
Knowing her commitment to Judaism, I called her up and said,
"Look, our faith is a forgiving religion and people deserve a
second chance, so if he wants to repent and swears never to do
it again, why won't you consider forgiving him?"

"Shmuley," she said to me, "This isn't about his hideous act.
That was just the straw that broke the camel's back. Had he
been a husband the rest of the time, had he been loving and
considerate, I could overlook it. But this is a cold and unfeeling
man who never once complimented me for going to a gym and
keeping up my figure and looks, for his sake. When I was sick
he never made me a cup of tea. He comes home late at night
and reads by himself. He's a stranger, and there's no reason to
forgive a stranger for hurting you."

She had a point. A woman is prepared to forgive the man
she loves. But not the man she doesn't love. In life, if a brother
or sister or child hurts us, we can forgive that person because
he or she is our flesh and blood. But if a stranger steals from

us, we tell that person never to come to our home again. And when a spouse becomes a stranger through continued neglect, it becomes almost impossible to forgive that person for the pain he or she causes through an additional act of infidelity.

But the same would also be true of far lesser offenses. When a husband and wife become strangers to each other, even minute things like annoying habits can serve to sever them. Renowned marriage expert John Gottman says in his book *Why Marriages Succeed or Fail: And How You Can Make Yours Last* that in order for a marriage to succeed, it must have five times as many positive moments as negative ones.

I would do almost anything to drill this point into a husband's head. I see husbands all the time who subordinate their home lives to the pursuit of riches. The only thing important to them in the first stage of their lives is getting ahead. They put their marriages on the backburner and grow old before their time. Suddenly, in their early forties when they finally have financial security, they come to life. *Now* they're ready to be married. They want to recapture their youth. They want to live again. And they get angry and disappointed when their wives aren't ready to play ball.

Larry was a classic example. He left high school when he was sixteen to start his own business. At twenty-one, he married Kim, his high school sweetheart. He planned a dream life for them and worked his guts out in order to attain it. By thirty-five he was a rich man, but in their fourteen years of marriage he had taken his wife away on vacations only twice, and had come home late almost every night. As a result of his work addiction, he was way too tired on weekends to give his wife the affection she was dying for. When they did talk, they talked only about his business. Inevitably, his wife drifted away from him. It wasn't that Larry didn't notice. It's just that he thought he could later make the effort to win her back.

Larry recently brought in a high-paid manager to look after the business while he jet-setted around the world in an attempt to recapture lost time. But he was puzzled and angry that his wife didn't want to join him. "I can't leave the kids this week," she told him. He brought in nannies and expensive tutors. Still, his wife wouldn't leave the kids. "My wife's an ice queen," he told me. "Don't blame me if I have an affair. Every man deserves some happiness. It's like I'm not married."

I said to Larry, "But she wasn't an ice queen when she went against her parents' advice and married a nobody with no money and with no high school degree. Do you still remember that woman? If she loved you enough back then to follow you to the ends of the earth when you didn't have a dime in your pocket, ask yourself why she won't follow you now to Aruba when you have bags of money falling out of your suit. Maybe, just maybe, you alienated her. Maybe you became a stranger to her. And the only woman who will go on a vacation with a stranger because he's rich is a whore. Your wife is no whore."

The even worse scenario, which is becoming increasingly common, is for many of these same men to simply dump their wives, who have stood by them all those years, just as soon as they make a couple of bucks. In Hollywood, this attitude is par for the course. Successful actors regularly trade down for younger actresses, forgetting about all the years their wives stood by them while they were building their careers—and then leaving them to age alone.

The True Crime of Adultery

Larry's story brings us to an important point. Adultery is not about hurting your wife. Rather, it is about taking the affection and desire that are hers by marital right and giving them away to a stranger. *By committing adultery you do not become an adulterer. Rather, you cease being a spouse.* The story also shows that infidelity need not be sexual, and it need not even be with another person. Any time a person, place, or thing becomes more important to you than your spouse and your marriage, the effect is the same as if you had committed adultery—even if you haven't. You are depleting your marriage of the love it needs to flourish.

From time immemorial it has been debated whether or not

a man or a woman can love two people at once. Can a husband love his wife and his mistress equally? Can a woman remain focused on her husband and her paramour simultaneously? The question is immaterial. Even if a man *could* love his wife and his mistress simultaneously, he still could not show them both enough attention and affection to sustain a relationship properly with either of them. The same applies even more so to women, who seem to get more emotionally involved in their extramarital affairs.

Thus, adultery serves as a double wrong: first, because it betrays a marriage and causes terrible pain to one's spouse; and second, because it robs a marriage of the input it needs to survive and prosper. On a more individual level, adultery erodes, if not utterly destroys, the faith and trust that one partner has in the other. Worse, it causes an almost incurable feeling of inadequacy that the partner who has been cheated on cannot shake. "What do I lack that he has found in someone else?' the wife asks herself. "Have I not been loving or caring enough?" the husband asks himself. What is particularly unjust about this introspection is that it is the *victim* who feels responsible.

This feeling of inadequacy is particularly acute when the betrayed spouse feels that the areas in which he or she is seen to be deficient just cannot be changed. It is one thing for a husband or wife to feel that his or her spouse's infidelity perhaps resulted because he or she was too career minded and showed too little affection. At the very least, this can be redressed. But what if the wife discovers that her husband's mistress is stunningly beautiful and sexy; or the husband finds out that his wife's lover is far more successful than he is, better looking, and of more athletic build? How can either of them avoid the feeling of being an inferior lover, unable to compete?

This was one of the points behind the 1993 movie *Indecent Proposal*. Woody Harrelson's character is torn apart by his wife's having spent a night with another man for a million dollars. After all, he agreed to the deal because they both felt they needed the money. But near the end of the movie he tells his wife that the real reason he agreed was that he thought that she *wanted* to be with the other man (Robert Redford), and worse, he feared that she was justified in wanting to be with Redford's character because he was the "better man." But what he finally came to understand was that Redford was not the better man; he just had more money. Of course, not all husbands come to that mature conclusion.

Prostitutes Are Not the Paradigm of Sexiness

Notice that in reading even countless "Lonely Hearts" postings you will never find a man who advertises "Successful man looking for hooker for long-term relationship and marriage." Now, this is curious because one would think that a prostitute would make the ultimate wife. Think about it: she's usually highly attractive (or else she'd be broke!); she is experienced in the art of pleasuring men (or she'd have no clients); and she is likely to be streetwise to boot! Are these not the ingredients of the perfect woman?

But the reason some men have sex with prostitutes but cannot foresee anything romantic with them is that a prostitute can't make a man feel sexy. He can never feel exclusively special to her. There are too many prints already present, making it impossible for his own fingers to leave any indelible mark.

A man wants to be with a woman who on the outside appears somewhat naïve about sex, because then he gets the erotic thrill of bringing out her sexual fire. He gets to change her from being an asexual *person* into a *woman*. He gets the pleasure of fanning her nascent sexual fire into a burning inferno. His manliness is corroborated by her losing all control and submitting to his seduction. That's why men find innocent women incredibly sexy. It is when a woman wishes to resist a man's advances but simply cannot resist his charm that eroticism is brought to its apogee. Her sexual guard falls as she slowly succumbs to his irresistible appeal. But if she has no sexual guard up in the first place, there can be no erotic attraction. Notice all the raunchy jokes about nuns, virgins, and nurses. Virginity and nurturing types who wear white are obviously extremely enticing to men.

I once heard a sex therapist speaking on CNN. Interestingly, she was a former prostitute herself. She said that whenever she counsels couples about marriage, she walks over to the husband and asks him to point to his principal sexual organ. Inevitably, the man blushes, and instinctively looks sheepishly down to his crotch. She then points to his head and says, "Silly! *This* is your most powerful sexual organ." This is absolutely true. Sexual excitement and elation lie in the mind, not in the genitals.

It is for this reason that marriage—and marriage only—possesses the greatest erotic potential. Since marriage involves the greatest degree of commitment, it is also the greatest statement of interest. Two people are saying that they are so interested in each other that they are even prepared to close off all other sexual possibilities and partners. To make the marital bond effective, it is necessary to see it primarily as a sexual commitment. Instead of seeing a marriage proposal only as a statement of "He loves me and therefore he wants to spend the rest of his life with me," we must equally view it in these terms: "He sees me as so sexually desirable that he wishes to spend all his days talking with me, *and also his nights with me in my bed.*"

The Marriage Commitment: Monogamy

Marriage does not come easy to everyone who undertakes its commitments. In fact, there are very few couples who adjust to it instantly. Nor should it be that simple! I have always believed that the greatest statement of love from one human being to another is when a constant, ongoing effort is made to remain loyal, faithful, loving, and caring amidst the natural inclination to selfishness, apathy, and sexual variety. Any husband and wife for whom marriage comes easy are deprived of making that most sublime statement to each other—that is, I love you so much that I seek to transcend my nature by remaining totally focused on you at all times.

Anything in life that does not require great effort to attain is simply not worth having. Marriage is the greatest demonstration of this. There is nothing more special, more loving, more worthwhile, more sublime, and better able to cure humankind's hurts and woes than marriage—when it is done right. But, equally, there is nothing so miserable, hurtful, devastating, or tormenting to the soul as a marriage gone wrong. We must therefore make an effort—our *greatest* effort—to be loving at all times, and caring, faithful partners, even while we feel a natural attraction to men and women outside our marriage. Monogamy is not a concession that religion asks humans to make in the name of holiness and decency. On the contrary, it is the very vehicle through which the ultimate sexual passion can be experienced and sustained to make our marriages pleasurable, glorious, and, above all, holy.

Having said that, is monogamy *natural?* The answer is an emphatic NO! Monogamy is as unnatural as the desire to remain constantly hungry. This knowledge is the single most important realization in any successful marriage, and the more quickly we confront this fact, the better, because we will then be on alert to actively make our marriages work.

Judaism maintains that the fundamental challenge of human living is for humankind to rise above its nature. We dare not allow our natures to rule over us. Rather, we must focus and align our inclinations. Only then can we guarantee fulfilling lives that are not the product of mere impulse.

I read a story once about a white Bengal tiger in the Miami Zoo who ate a zookeeper. The zoo decided not to destroy the animal, as is normally done in such cases. Part of the reason was that the white Bengal tiger is virtually extinct already. But the more important consideration was that the zookeeper himself had made the fatal mistake of leaving the cage open as he fed the animal. It was felt that the animal should not be punished merely because its predatory nature surfaced in the face of human error.

But such clemency would never be granted a human. If a man gets into a bar brawl and knifes his adversary, he would be prosecuted. The excuse "I lost my temper" would not be acceptable before a judge. Because we are human we are expected to control our emotions and rise above our instincts; we are held accountable for any failure to do so.

The same standard applies to humankind's natural gravitation to having numerous sexual partners. The fact that your natural instinct leads you to stray will not serve as an adequate excuse for hurting your spouse and destroying your marriage. Therefore, when we speak of "holy matrimony," and when we speak of marriage as a Godly institution, we should attune our ears to the serious implications of these words, namely, that *marriage is not a natural institution, but a supernatural one.* Marriage is a Godly pursuit and we do not slide comfortably into marriage and monogamy. They have to be worked at. We must never take these commitments for granted.

Those of you who aren't taken with that must now ask yourselves: *Why then are you prepared to marry?* Have you taken leave of your senses? Exiting from this commitment comes with a substantial price tag. In fact, there is no circumstance in life *besides marriage* where an individual is prepared to commit himself to a lifelong prospect. Even your children will *eventually* move out (or so we hope!). But not so with marriage.

So how do you know that things won't go wrong? If you're so infatuated with someone that you wish to be with that person always, sure, go ahead and live with that person; hold that person in your arms and make that person yours for a time. But for goodness sake, don't be silly enough to say things like "Till death do us part" or "through sickness and in health" when you have no guarantee that person's foot odor won't turn you off just a month later! We are all only too aware of the unpredictability of emotions. The partner you can't *live without* today somehow becomes the person you can't *live with* tomorrow. Better to take things gradually, see how it goes. It's the reasonable, logical thing to do. You wouldn't commit yourself this way to anything else. Why, then, to a marriage?

The only answer is that what we humans wish for in life is not to be free, but to be special. And becoming the permanent center of someone else's life is the highest corroboration of our own uniqueness. That someone else is prepared to become an earth orbiting around our sun substantiates the fact that we have much light to give.

But that doesn't mean that it is natural or easy. The same aversion humans have to monogamy seems rampant throughout all other species as well. Indeed, the rate of infidelity in nature is truly shocking. Ninety percent of all species and 97 percent of all mammalian species are promiscuous.

No, marriage and monogamy are not natural or logical, and the belief that they are has led to terrible misconceptions and inestimable damage in relationships. Happiness in marriage, unlike the passion of adultery, requires effort. And because it is divine rather than of human construct it requires the blessing of Heaven and a healthy spiritual component in order to endure.

You're Not the One I Fell in Love With

A common complaint among married couples is that the relationship changes once they actually get married. They often feel that the person whom they married is different, sometimes radically, from the person they were dating. When a man is courting a woman, he's on his best behavior. He showers before the date, dresses up, and he discloses to her the inner contents of his heart in long, intimate conversations. But the moment they marry, he has odors coming from every orifice of his body and he doesn't cut his toenails for months. What happened to this woman's real husband? Was he snatched by aliens and replaced with a lesser clone?

Every potential mate seems so much more sensitive, caring, and responsive to each other before they've closed the deal. In the words of a female friend, "The probability that my husband would open the car door for me now, as he did when we were dating, is the same probability that I would bring him breakfast in bed, as I did every Sunday in our first few months of marriage."

How can this be? Does marriage have a magical, yet sinister capacity for transforming a woman from Snow White into Lady Macbeth or a man from Casanova into Howard Stern? Why is it that so often marriage is not nearly as pleasant or fulfilling as dating is? It is this reality that has given rise to the oft-repeated aphorism, "How do you kill a great relationship? Get married."

The real explanation lies in a couple's mistaken belief that they will instinctively know how to be married. Whereas when they date they exert every effort to impress their intended partner, when they finally marry they suddenly exert no effort at all, thinking that bliss will just flow automatically from their union. In other words, their mistake is in thinking that two people can simply *get* married, and that the rest will automatically fall into place. They believe that they can cross some symbolic threshold and enter a new realm of existence. But that never really happens. Since marriage is unnatural, we never just *get* married. Rather, we must always engage in the art of *becoming* married. As Gabriel García Márquez put it, "The problem with marriage is that it ends every night after making love, and it must be rebuilt every morning before breakfast."

The men and women who are surprised to see their spouses change do not see marriage as a constant endeavor, an endless challenge, in which a person must be on alert at all times. Rather, once you get married, they believe, you need hardly do anything at all. You simply stay married.

Everyone knows that in order to build up and sustain attraction with a member of the opposite sex, one must work very hard. To be sure, there is occasionally "love at first sight" or immediate attraction. You meet in a restaurant, and you just know that you would love to go out with the girl sitting at the table near the picture window. But even this sort of attraction will dissipate almost immediately if nothing is done about it. If you do not ask her out, you will forget about her quite rapidly. If you do ask her out, you must do your utmost to impress her. Why else should she be interested?

We all recognize the need to show our most caring side in winning a member of the opposite sex over to marriage. We know logically that it just doesn't happen *naturally,* or even particularly easily. People don't fall for each other if they don't *do* anything to earn it. People will not commit themselves to a lifelong adventure impetuously. Rather, after a laborious and time-consuming courtship, a man gets on his knee and pops the big question—and it's worked. She blushes and with elation says yes. The big day comes, and now they are married. So what then? He is no longer on his best behavior, and loses his temper frequently and with little cause. Nor is he as generous, complaining that they must save all their money to pay the mortgage. Nor is she as loving to him as she once was. The little things about him that were once so charming, like how he always got lost while driving her on a date, now become endlessly irritating. So what went wrong?

The answer is staring them in the face. They have made the mistake of assuming that once a couple gets married, the process of impressing each other is over. But marriage is not just a single act; it is a constant process, and we must always engage ourselves not just in *being* married, but rather, in *becoming* married and in *staying* married. Marriage is not a natural state, and our natural resistance to its monogamous demands and huge commitment necessitates a constant and conscious effort to make it successful.

Marriage Needs Constant Nourishment

But rather than looking at this effort as a curse, we can turn it to our advantage. The knowledge that we never *become* married, but rather must always *engage in the process of becoming married,* can have enormous implications for passion in marriage. The words *lover* or *mistress* carry with them an erotic mystique. Even the words *manly* and *womanly* have sexual undertones. But the words *husband* and *wife* do not. They ring solely of form and function. To think of your wife not as a *woman* but as a *wife* is to consign her to the realm of familiarity and boredom. The knowledge that none of us ever becomes a wife or a husband, but always remains just a man or a woman trying to remain faithful despite a powerful inclination to do otherwise, serves as a constant reminder that we are married to sexual creatures who are not naturally monogamous and who are always attractive to others.

The great medieval thinker Maimonides, who ranks as one of the foremost Jewish thinkers of all times, noted that in the Bible there is no word for wife. The word is *isha,* meaning woman. Thus, Sarah was "the woman of Abraham," rather than his wife. Unlike the English language that has two separate words for "woman" and "wife," Hebrew has only one. The lesson: No woman ever exclusively becomes a *wife.* Even after she marries, she is still a woman. She has all the passion of a woman, she remains attractive to other men as she would as a single woman, and she has the propensity to attach herself to other men like a single woman would. She can't ever be taken for granted. When you neglect her, she fantasizes about other men. When other men see her looking lonely, they engage in the hunt. They compliment her and she feels drawn to them. She makes love to you, her husband, but it's them she's thinking about.

This point bears repeating. The secret to retaining passion in marriage is *knowing that we never get married.* Humans will always lean away from commitment. Thus, a wife may take your last name but her heart never becomes yours exclusively.

So a wife is never only your wife; she is also your personal mistress. The metaphor may sound unappealing, but bear with me long enough to examine the idea; a single woman agrees to become the mistress of a married man when he lavishes her with so much attention that she can't stay away. She takes off her clothes for him when he takes her to the heights of sexual pleasure. She reorients her work schedule to meet him for secret rendezvous in hotel rooms because he makes her blood simmer and her libido sizzle. She lies down with him because he makes her skin tingle. And when he does none of these things, she breaks off the affair. After all, why should she still meet him? The unbalanced risk-to-reward ratio makes it a really bad venture. And the same is true of your wife. If you don't take her to the moon and back, if you allow your sex life to become stale and boring, she effectively leaves the relationship. Her body may still be there, but her spirit has taken flight.

We must therefore work to preserve our spouse's loyalty always by showing them love, attention, and romance. Never take your spouse's fidelity for granted. The only success we will ever have in marriage is if we always focus on what we can put into marriage, not just on what we can take out of it. As a rabbi, I hear all too often young couples complaining that they do not "get anything" from a relationship. Before marriage a man and woman are separate and distinct beings. If they are to join successfully together as one, they must both reach inward towards each other. They have to always put in rather than take out. But if they focus on what they receive rather than what they can give, effectively leaning *away* from each other, they are sure to grow apart. This is especially so with regard to human sexuality. If indeed monogamy is unnatural, then we must do all we can to make our intimate lives passionate and exciting enough to satisfy our spouses.

Don't get me wrong; I am not arguing that we do not deserve any benefits from marriage. Nor am I suggesting that there are no legitimate needs on the part of each spouse in a marriage. But if both a husband and a wife focus on what they can *contribute* to a marriage, both will be receiving and enjoying the benefits of companionship and marriage not as strangers, but as loving halves of an indivisible whole.

Exercises
STARTING A SECRET AFFAIR

Start a secret e-mail affair with your spouse. Before I tell you how, here's a story for inspiration from Karen, a thirty-six-year-old woman married for eleven years with two kids:

For the last four months I've been carrying on a secret e-mail affair. It's the greatest thing that ever happened to me. I've never seen my lover, but he sends the most erotic messages to me. When I get one of his messages, I drop everything to run and read it. I bought myself a little laptop so that I can always access his messages wherever I am. I don't walk these days. I glide. My husband doesn't know, but he has noticed how much more alive I've been. And it's done wonders for our sex life. My husband's not an erotic man, but I am bursting with all this sexual energy and we've been having the greatest sex. I fantasize about what my lover must be like when I'm making love to my husband. It's amazing. I don't feel guilty about it. It hasn't disrupted my life, and I deserve some excitement after all the sacrifices I've made.

But there's one thing that Karen doesn't know. Yup, you guessed it. Her secret lover is her very own husband. And I own up: It was all my idea. When her husband Kenny came to me complaining that the couple's sex life was in the morgue, I suggested he pretend to be someone else and see how much his desire for his "unfaithful" wife would increase. I also told him that he would have to give up the charade after six months, at which time, his wife would begin to see him for what he really is, an incredibly erotic man who simply lost his edge through too much familiarity with his wife.

1. Go to a Web site like *www.secretadmirer.com, www.ecrush.com*, or *www.wholikesme.com* where you can write secretly to someone without that person knowing who is actually writing.

2. Write your spouse a message. Take great care to change your writing style, so as to eliminate any suspicion that it could be you writing. Make the message sound like it comes from someone whom you think your spouse admires or is attracted to anyway. Make it broad enough that he or she really has to keep on guessing who it is.

3. When your spouse receives it and accuses you of writing it (and inevitably, he or she will) you should simply profess shock, anger, and outrage that your spouse received a message from a secret admirer. Tell your spouse there is no possible way that it was you who sent it. Tell your spouse that your e-mail was down at work or home, and that you could not have had access that day. Delete the "cookies" from your computer that Web sites place on your computer for easy access to repeated information (such as Web site preferences) but can also show where you surfed the Web. (Most programs, such as Microsoft Internet Explorer and Netscape Navigator, have the option to delete these cookies as well as the "history folder" that records which Web sites you visit. See the "Help" file in the program.) Profess ignorance of the Web site.

4. Make your spouse swear to you that he or she will delete the message and not respond. Have him or her delete it in front of you. Say how hurt you are that your spouse has been communicating with a secret admirer; even if he or she has not responded, tell your spouse that in your opinion some signal must have been sent to this person suggesting that your spouse was open to such a possibility.

5. That night, in bed, still show interest and even disturbance about the e-mail. Speaking out loud, speculate about who might have sent it. Get your spouse involved in the conversation and ask who he or she thinks the sender could possibly have been.

6. Even if your spouse swears that he or she has no idea, go through all your spouse's daily contacts with him or her, trying to figure out who it could be that admires or is attracted to your spouse. Wait two or three days and then send another message. Pretend to be the same person who sent the first message. Express your disappointment that you haven't received a reply.

7. If you get a response, great. You're on the road. The journey has begun. If you don't get a response, wait two days, then go to your spouse and ask point-blank if he or she has gotten another message similar to the first one. If your spouse acknowledges receipt, express some disappointment that he or she didn't show it to you. Say that you want to see such messages. Then suggest that you want to get to the bottom of this and find out who is writing them. Therefore, if your spouse gets another message, he or she should initiate a correspondence with the intention of discovering the secret admirer's identity. If you are refused, ask your spouse if he or she is afraid that you'll find out who it is. If necessary, write a response with your spouse as you wait for the next installment. Whatever you do, don't give away your identity as the secret admirer.

8. Either way, by now you have established yourself as the secret admirer without the knowledge of your spouse. No doubt you will be asked your identity. Your wife may ask you, "Are you the guy who sits behind the photocopier and usually wears jeans?" Or your husband may ask you, "Are you the woman who rides the elevator up with me to the office every morning?" Don't divulge a thing. Be creative and keep your reader guessing. Turn the subject away from marriage. If you ask your spouse, "Do you have a happy marriage?" he or she will immediately know it's a setup. Rather, ask questions about your spouse, such as his or her tastes in music or movies. Don't get into anything sex related until way down the line.

9. At first, ask your spouse to share each missive with you. Ask to be shown the responses with the explanation that you are trying to uncover the secret admirer. But little by little, show that you find the whole thing erotic. Play games together guessing who it is who might be interested. Suggest names to your spouse so as to remove the suspicion from yourself. Turn the whole experience into something erotic. Talk about it while you make love. Ask your spouse what his or her intentions are with regard to the secret admirer. Ask your spouse what he or she would do if unmarried.

10. After the correspondence has been going for two weeks and at least six messages have been exchanged, tell your spouse that you no longer want to know what is in the exchanges. Say that not only have you grown comfortable with your spouse having a secret admirer, but you actually feel very excited about the whole thing. Mention that you would be even more excited if your spouse were to continue the correspondence on his or her own. Say you want your spouse to explore his or her erotic personality by writing freely and openly in the correspondence. Say that as long as your spouse promises never to meet the person in question—and keep it only as an e-mail affair—you're okay with it. Continue to talk about it whenever you make love. As you send more "secret admirer" messages to your spouse, become more daring. Ask your spouse about his or her fantasies and if he or she would ever contemplate an affair, and so on. Keep it going for as long as it lasts. And while chances are your spouse will *not* know that it's you, even if he or she does, this is a great erotic game that will stoke the fires of passion.

The secret admirer exercise works well with programs like Microsoft Network's Messenger Service, which now comes standard with Windows XP, as well as with AOL's very popular Instant Messenger Service. Just determine when your spouse will be surfing the Net or checking messages, and then have a window suddenly pop up with a new screen name that you will be using and that your spouse will not recognize. Instant messenger e-mail affairs can be even more erotic than having to constantly wait for the two of you to write to each other, and should definitely be added to your e-mail affair repertoire.

When initiating a secret e-mail affair with your wife, one idea is to hint that the author of the e-mails is someone you think she is attracted to anyway. But in that case, don't let it drag on for more than two weeks. Of course, you don't want to do anything that might get her hooked onto a man who is around the two of you on a regular basis. Also, make sure the man you claim to be is not married or seriously attached to another woman. Using the identity of someone your wife knows for your e-mail affair can be incredibly erotic because you can then gauge how she behaves around this man. Does she get all dressed up now when she knows the two of you are going to meet him for dinner? But make sure you are a part of it from the beginning. Your wife should write back to her admirer only with your knowledge.

There are few things that can transform a dull wife into a sexual creature like enabling her to believe that she is intensely desirable to many of the men that she knows and meets. You can honestly watch your wife change before your very eyes. Whereas before she may have been shy, now she walks and talks with immense self-confidence. Whereas before, she was reticent to talk openly to you about sexual issues, now her every word is impregnated with erotic meaning. And whereas before, she may have put scant attention into her appearance, now she stands before a mirror for half an hour in the morning, and wears bright clothes and silky underwear.

The Ten Commandments

of Kosher Adultery

SEVENSEVENSEVENSEVENSEVENS
EVENSEVENSEVENSEVENSEVENSE
VENSEVENSEVENSEVENSEVENSEV
ENSEVENSEV seven NSEVENSEVE
NSEVENSEVENSEVENSEVENSEVEN
SEVENSEVENSEVENSEVENSEVENS
EVENSEVENSEVENSEVENSEVENSE

Seducing
.AND
Sinning
WITH YOUR
SPOUSE

Woman wants monogamy;
Man delights in novelty. . . .
With this the gist and sum of it,
What earthly good can come of it?
— DOROTHY PARKER

Marriage is like the sphinx—a conspicuous and recogniz-
able monument on the landscape, full of secrets.
— NANCY COTT, PUBLIC VOWS

Love asks many things of us, including actions that seem
to be utterly counter to feelings of attachment and loyalty.
— THOMAS MOORE, CARE OF THE SOUL

Once, while visiting Miami with my family, an old classmate of mine took a few friends and me to a Miami Heat basketball game. I was in the midst of writing my book *Kosher Sex* at the time, so my mind was on numerous subjects other than basketball (which was never one of my passions anyway, my being about five feet and all). I sat scanning the room to see if I could learn anything from the couples that surrounded me, when a middle-aged couple sitting a few rows in front of us captured my attention.

Throughout the game, this man with graying hair on the sides of his otherwise bald scalp did not take his arm off the shoulder of the woman seated next to him. The first thing he did when he returned from buying some peanuts was to immediately sit down and put his arm back around her shoulder. He became something of a contortionist as he attempted to unshell his peanuts while holding a coke with his arm still close around the woman. When one of my friends noticed me staring at them, he said to me, "For three years I've been coming to these games and for three years I've watched that guy hold on to her through every single game. He never lets go. The whole thing is pretty weird."

On the drive home from the game, a debate erupted among my friends about the couple. Everyone wanted to know what the deal was with this man and woman. How could he be so obsessed as to have his arm around her for three hours at a time—consistently over three years—making this romantic gesture a priority, even before cheering for the game. Or, as one friend put it, "What could possibly be wrong with the guy?"

First, my friend Joey jumped into the fray. "The whole thing is simple. This man and woman aren't married. They're having a secret affair. It's his lover, not his wife. That's why he's so crazy about her."

"What?" I interrupted, "They're having a secret affair, *at a basketball game?* They've decided to conduct their clandestine affair at a stadium in front of fifteen thousand people and network cameras?"

Next, my friend Alan offered his two cents. "Shmuley's right. Of course they're not having an affair. Joey, you're an imbecile. Rather, I bet they are married. But she's probably dying. She's dying of some fatal disease. She probably has very little time to live, and that's why her husband is being so affectionate and loving. She might just pop off at any moment."

I turned to Alan. "Are you for real? She's dying. Over three years. At a *basketball game?* She couldn't find any more private place to expire than in front of the hot dog concession?"

Finally, I said, "Look, maybe the two of them are married, and he's in love with his wife?" There was a resonant chorus from the back of the car. All three said in unison, "Naah." And Joey said, "You're the one who's nuts. You think any husband is actually like that? In your love prophet dreams, baby."

I never did find out what the true story of the couple was (although I suspect that my simple approach was probably accurate). But more interesting was the reaction of my friends—all married men—who thought it preposterous, impossible even, that a married man and woman could sustain such intense passion in their relationship. Whenever I reflect on that story, I am still amazed. Not only have many of us lost the ability to be loving and romantic in our marriages, not only are we convinced that it is humanly impossible to sustain such intense attraction, but we are even prepared to assassinate the character of those few odd couples who do achieve this glorious feat.

So what was this couple's secret? How did he remain so intensely attached to the woman in his life? And once we identify the enigmatic quality, can we apply it to our own lives? The very first verse in the Bible reads: "In the beginning the Lord created the heavens and earth," implying that both were created equally by God, and thus both are holy and special; ". . . and God saw all that he had made, and it was good" implied that humanity is holy and good, and that makes human nature holy. So, rather than fighting human nature, we should harness it. Rather than being ashamed of it, we must try to understand it and use it to our advantage.

The Ten Commandments of Adultery

How many men have lost the potential passion in their lives by ignoring the wives in their own beds? How many men have lusted after strangers whose own erotic energy is not equal to that of their own wives?

Notice that the final commandment of the big ten Moses brought us expressly forbids men from coveting their neighbors' wives, which implicitly says that they should be coveting their own wives. So that this blatant tragedy does not continue, it is imperative that husbands stop lusting after strangers and begin to have affairs with their own wives. In order to do so, let's answer the question: "What are the essential ingredients for a successful adulterous affair, and why are they excluded from a marriage?"

Thus, with all due reverence toward the Almighty who gave us the original ten commandments, I now introduce my own version of the same, which the Creator—perhaps in an oversight—omitted at Mt. Sinai, but which nonetheless constitute the essential ingredients in every clandestine affair. I call them, "The Ten Commandments of Adultery," which are defined from here through the end of the chapter and put into practice in Chapters 8 through 16 as "Kosher Adultery." In those chapters I will show you how to transplant these erotic ingredients into your marriage and create a steamy affair with your spouse.

1. Adultery is first and foremost about sex.

Sixty percent of men and women who had affairs said that their number-one consideration was that they "had sexual needs that were not being met in their marriages." Adultery makes each participant into a desirable sexual object. It promises and usually delivers unimagined sexual pleasures. In adulterous affairs, attraction comes first and compatibility second.

Yes, there are adulterous affairs that grow to be deeply emotional and loving. But by and large, adultery is about great sex and is engaged in by both men and women who seek spice in their lives; an end to their everyday routines; and partners who appreciate their bodies and treat them as if they are the most desirable people on earth.

Unlike marriage, adulterous affairs are not bogged down by problems of housework, cleaning, children, and financial worries. As the responsibilities of marriage increase, as bills pile up, as children are born, and as jobs become more demanding, often a couple's sex life is put on the back burner. Passion is subordinated to the everyday challenges of life. Since sex is essential to the species but not to the individual, it begins to occupy a secondary role for most married couples.

Whereas marriages are usually founded on compatibility, shared interests, and shared values, adultery is predicated first and foremost on attraction. Illicit affairs are not based on a man or a woman having a common education or similar political outlook. No. Adultery is about a man feeling drawn illicitly to a woman as a sex object, and a woman being drawn to a man for the fire he can bring into her life, and she into his. Great conversation may ensue, but it takes a backseat role to great sex.

A poll in *People* magazine recently asked the question "If you were to be unfaithful, which characteristic would most attract you to a romantic partner?" The majority of respondents (33 percent) of both sexes answered "sexual attractiveness." Psychologist Shirley Glass, in her studies, found that sex scores as the highest justification for men's infidelity, while a 1998 *New York* magazine survey of over a thousand New Yorkers found that a man's priority in sexual partners is her "looks" (65 percent) and her body (65 percent).

In *The Dangerous Passion*, David Buss conducted a survey of wives and found that among the most highly rated aspects of potential male affair partners was that he should be athletic, strong, muscular, and physically fit—all characteristics of sexual attraction. In fact, he found that women often demand higher levels of attractiveness in an affair partner (seventy-seventh percentile) than in a husband (fifty-fourth percentile).

In Susan Barash's anecdotal account of wives' affairs, *A Passion for More,* one wife explained that she "did it for the most basic of reasons: It was for sex. Although sex was okay with my husband, I wanted to explore . . . I began to understand why I do it. I do it for the excitement and sex." Though perhaps another wife said it best: "The guy was an idiot but the sex was great."

In her definitive study on adultery (*Adultery*), Annette Lawson writes that "sexual fulfillment" was the most commonly mentioned benefit for everyone. Although most people interviewed for her study did not easily express their desire for sex—and their joy when they experienced it in the adulterous affair—the most common reason they gave on the questionnaire for having the liaison was that they "had sexual needs which were not being met."

Studies even show that wives who have affairs have much higher "sperm retention orgasms" from their lovers than from their husbands. This was measured by the amount of sperm collected after sex.

As Dr. David Buss writes, "When Heidi Greiling and I began to interview women about their affairs, one prominent theme emerged repeatedly: sexual gratification. In our very first study of women's perceptions of the benefits of affairs, women judged it to be "highly likely" that a woman would receive sexual gratification from an affair partner, making this the most likely of the 28 potential benefits in the initial study.

"When we asked women to evaluate which circumstances would be most likely to open them up to an affair, sexual dissatisfaction with regular partners loomed large. Some of their comments included: "My current partner is unwilling to engage in sexual relations with me." "Sexual relations with my current partner have been unsatisfying for a long time." "Sexual relations with my current partner are too infrequent for me." Moreover, women rated experiencing sexual gratification with an affair partner to be one of the most important benefits of an extramarital affair. Successful orgasms, in particular, seem important, as women rate these as more beneficial than merely receiving sexual gratification."

This is not to say that adultery is only about sex. It is to say that its *foundation* is great sex, and if a lover doesn't provide great sex, the affair usually ends rather quickly.

In Chapter 8 you will learn how to bring your sexual life with your spouse back to the foreground of your marriage, and to re-establish the centrality of lovemaking in your marital relationship.

2. Adultery thrives on delayed gratification, separation, and expectation.

In following Commandment One, a large part of the emotional intensity and sexual gratification of an adulterous affair is a result of the delayed gratification, the constant waiting and yearning to be with your illicit partner. Since you don't want your spouse to catch you, you are living apart from your lover, and you are in a constant state of expectation. There is this wall that separates you. You can't be together all the time. So you're anxious, yearning, lusting after your love. You gather steam pressure, repressed but collecting power. And when that rendezvous finally comes, oh boy! The roof blows right off! All that pent-up sexual energy and erotic fantasy that has been swimming around in your body and your brain comes to a head when you finally meet and fall into each other's arms, and you finally blast off to the moon like a hydrogen-powered rocket.

Is it any wonder that adultery involves such great sex compared to marriage where—because of its constant availability—there is no room for lust? To an extent, you will always want what you can't have. It is this element that is responsible for much of the erotic excitement of adultery.

I've mentioned earlier that adulterous partners who leave their spouses to move in together usually end up separating soon after. Once you get what you've been chasing, you aren't so hungry any more. While delayed gratification is a cornerstone of passion, instant gratification is its foremost enemy.

In her bestseller *How to Satisfy a Woman Every Time . . . and Have Her Beg for More*, Naura Hayden predicates her entire theory of lovemaking on a man learning to touch a woman for hours (or even one good hour), before he goes anywhere near her erogenous zones. He must avoid any overtly sexual areas so as to greatly heighten her desire. Then he should begin touching her sexual areas, for another long period as her desire becomes even greater, but still refrain from having sex with her. And only when she is truly aching with desire should they make love. There is much truth to this, and in a broader perspective, this principle must be brought into marriage.

In an adulterous affair you think about your lover all the time, and long to be with him or her. If you are a married man having an affair with a single woman, you become obsessed with her since she has a life of her own (she's not married to you, after all) and isn't at your beck and call.

The same is true in reverse: A wife who cannot have her lover in her bed at all times pines and aches for him constantly. As was so expertly portrayed by Diane Lane in the movie *Unfaithful*, she lives in constant anticipation and expectation of their next rendezvous. You become even more obsessed with the times that you cannot have sex with that person. You try to compensate for the void by playing out the affair in your mind. While you may meet only once or twice a week, you're constantly thinking about your lover. Your body cheats only twice a week, but you're committing adultery in your head all the time. You even tell yourself how you will make up for the lost time by having mind-blowing sex the next time you meet up. You map out all erotic things you're going to do to each other. You create the encounter first in your mind before it happens in reality. Your mind is indeed the part of you that is most invested in the affair. You prepare surprises that you can't wait to act out.

In Chapter 9 you will discover how to bring separation and renewal into your relationship, which will reinvigorate your marriage.

3. Adultery is replete with erotic obstacles.

Following from Commandment Two, we find that the great excitement that comes with adultery is dependent on "erotic obstacles"—things that get in the way of satisfying one's lust. That erotic obstacles are the soul of passion is something that

Judaism has known and taught for thousands of years, but is only now being understood in modern psychology.

For example, in a famous passage in the Talmud, Rav Chisda—who is marrying off his daughter to Rava, perhaps the most quoted man in all the Talmud—instructs his daughters to be careful throughout their sexual relations never to allow their husbands to advance to their nether regions too soon. In effect, Rav Chisda is advising his daughters on how to greatly heighten their husbands' and their own sexual pleasure. "[Rav Chisda] held a jewel in one hand and a clump of soil in another. He showed them the jewel, but did not show them the clump until they were suffering. Then he showed them."

Rashi, the Talmud's foremost commentator, explains that the jewel symbolizes the breasts, while the clump of soils represents the woman's genitals. Rashi writes: "When your husband has marital relations and holds you with one hand on the breasts and the other hand on 'that place' for your pleasure, show him your breasts to increase his appetite. But do not show him your vagina quickly so his appetite and desire will increase. When he is in pain, show him." (Shabbat 140b)

We often feel the same erotic obstacle being inadvertently slipped into a marriage with an argument. When husbands and wives fight, they often have great sex afterward because the argument created emotional distance, an erotic obstacle, that paradoxically makes them want to tear each other's clothes off once they stop fighting. As Tolstoy wrote in his story *The Kreutzer Sonata:* "Our arguments were terrifying . . . and so much more striking in that they were followed by equally incensed paroxysms of animal sexuality."

But while adultery is fraught with erotic obstacles (indeed, obstacles are what adultery is all about), marriage is all about sex on tap, and that instant availability makes married sex about as interesting as doing the gardening. In fact, some of the only erotic obstacles in marriage are negative ones like the fighting we just mentioned above.

In Chapter 10, we'll learn about essential erotic obstacles that are a key to passion in marriage. I'll give you some suggestions, and teach you how to invent your own.

4. Adultery thrives on secrecy, modesty, and mystique.

In addition to the "unavailability" we discussed earlier, a second highly important component of adultery is modesty and secrecy. It may sound strange, but part of the excitement of an adulterous affair is that only the two people involved know about it. In life, things that are hidden always retain their allure. Masked from prying eyes, they become mysterious. Things that are too public are quickly forgotten. Any museum worth its salt rotates its collection so that not all its paintings are available to viewers at any given time. If they are, what's to bring the viewers back?

The same principle lies behind the success of voyeuristic activities like WebCams and Web girls, which are more popular than straight-out pornography. It's one thing to see a woman naked, but it's quite another to see her naked when you're *not supposed* to see her naked. That's why all those sites make it appear as though the woman is going about her normal life; if you just happen to catch her undressing and taking a bubble bath, well, lucky you! Overexposure, however, breeds contempt. In adultery, when the secret affair becomes known to the world, much of the excitement begins to dissipate. Modesty and secrecy are essential.

In addition, those who are involved in adulterous affairs, however much we might condemn or despise them, carry with them an air of seductive mystique. Think of the great literary adulteress heroines: Tolstoy's Anna Karenina, Flaubert's Madame Bovary, Lawrence's Lady Chatterley, and Hawthorne's Hester Prynne. Being wanted by someone else in a sinful relationship bestows an erotic and mysterious quality on the object of desire.

It is essential, then, that we learn to use modesty in marriage as a central erotic tool, and that we comprehend the dangers of sexual overexplicitness. We must learn that modesty will lead a spouse to cherish his or her partner's body once again, and will create an environment of mystery and intimacy. Finally, we must discover and embrace how secret fantasies can bring highly charged erotic sparks into marriage. We'll learn all about this in Chapter 10.

5. Adultery thrives on irreconcilable tension and being off balance.

The thrill of the chase, the fear of getting caught, and not knowing when you'll next be able to see your lover all add to the excitement of adultery. To a degree, they keep the affair alive. You never have time to settle into a routine and stagnate. You are constantly on the move, setting up secret meeting places, tapping into your most creative resources to outsmart all those curious eyes around you, anything to keep your affair going.

It is a relationship that ultimately has no real solution, and thus it generates constant tension. Whereas marriage is about "settling down," adultery is all about "going wild" and doing crazy things you never thought possible.

Sally, a thirty-eight-year-old woman in counseling, told me: "I shocked myself as I started getting involved in my affair. My husband was the only man I had ever kissed. Then on vacation with a girlfriend, I met Ralph. After talking for an hour, he tried to kiss me. I pulled away. Yet, there I was a day later knocking on his hotel room door to kiss him. We made passionate love. I still can't believe it."

In Chapter 11 you will read how the natural attraction that even married people feel for other men and women outside the marriage—far from betraying the commitment of marriage—can ensure that we are constantly choosing our spouses anew. The anxiety caused by our natural inclination to promiscuity, set alongside our steadfast commitment to our spouse, guarantees that our marriages will never become stagnant or monotonous.

We'll also learn that too much trust in a marriage can serve to undermine the marriage. We'll examine how husbands and wives can create a new kind of trust, one that is predicated on the idea that they can at any moment cheat, yet remain committed and devoted because they believe in the integrity of the relationship, and not because their nature is not pushing them in that direction. We'll list some off-balance activities that husbands and wives can always practice, assuring them that they never become complacent about each other. You will also learn how to use to your advantage the natural tension that exists between wishing our spouses to be seductive and hypnotic (which makes them attractive to strangers as well), and yet wanting to possess them entirely.

6. Adultery is about intense jealousy and competitiveness.

The great majority of married women who enter into adulterous affairs do so not with single, but with married men. Peggy Vaughn (*The Monogamy Myth*) estimates that 80 percent of wives' affairs are entered into with married men, while Carol Botwin (*Tempted Women*) writes that "the overwhelming majority of wives get involved with someone else's husband . . . women feel that a married man is safer, less likely to pose a threat to their own marriages."

This is borne out by most of the anecdotal studies, in which, by far, the greater part of cheating wives' quotations about their affairs deal with married men. Thus, every time the couple separates after a rendezvous and returns to their normal lives, the woman knows that her lover is going back to his wife, so she lives in a constant state of jealousy of the other woman. She knows that she is the second woman in her lover's life, always a subordinate. When he goes on vacation, he does so with his wife and children, and indeed, he spends most of his time in his wife's company, and most of his nights in her bed.

The same is true of any man who has an affair with a married woman. He lives in a constant state of jealousy. Sure, he may be the one who has her swinging from the chandeliers in their hotel rooms (well, hypothetical chandeliers at least), but when the ecstasy is over, she puts on her clothes and goes back to the man whose name she bears. She goes back to cooking him dinner, sleeping in his bed, and raising his kids. Her male lover is driven crazy by this; he's insanely jealous at all times. But far from that jealousy being merely a source of pain, it serves also as the fuel for the affair's fire.

In addition, since every act of adultery involves a betrayal of marital vows, the adulterer's lover is always aware that the person he or she is involved with is duplicitous. This wife, for example, is always telling her husband that she loves him and she is swearing that she is faithful—only to leave home and embark upon a double life.

This knowledge that your lover is not faithful to his or her spouse leads you always to suspect that perhaps he or she is not faithful to you either; maybe you are only one of several extramarital affairs that this playboy (or playgirl) is juggling. At the very least you know that your lover has the potential for betraying you, just as he or she has already betrayed his or her spouse. This knowledge is painful, and stirs up feelings of intense jealousy. You have no security—there is no home, children, or even commitment to bind you—and thus you always fear being discarded in favor of someone else. Your lover may even choose to return to a monogamous relationship with his or her spouse.

Your jealousy makes you want to possess your lover even more, so you exert every effort to sustain your lover's attention. You always dress your best, speak lovingly, and act on your best behavior. Moreover, the fact that your illicit partner goes home every night to his or her spouse makes you intensely competitive. You must always perform (physically and emotionally) better than her husband or his wife. You always have something to prove. You become a master or mistress of the sexual act because you know that your performance is being rated and evaluated against a much more accessible standard. Hence, your performance never falters, and you get better and better. The pressure itself becomes a pleasure.

As Charles, a New York lawyer, once told me:

My relationship with Jordana was in a real rut. We were together three years and she was pressuring me to get engaged. The more she pressured, the more I just wanted to get away from her. Then on New Year's Eve we went to a party. She was wearing this silky little black dress. I watched from the side of the room as this cool-looking guy wearing leather pants with green tattoos all over his arms started to hit on her. Then she was dancing with him. He was pressing his body real tight against hers. The way he touched her in public was obscene. Suddenly, I started feeling something incredibly strong building up inside me.

It was a rage that I never felt before. I went on to the dance floor, grabbed her by her hand, and said, "What the hell are you doing?" We walked straight out of there, without even bothering to pick up our coats. When we got into the car, we did things that would have made Bob Guccione blush, all the way until the morning. The following day we got engaged.

In Chapter 12 you will learn about healthy jealousy and how indispensable it is in a marriage. You will discover that, if your spouse felt more jealous about you, the desire to possess you and his or her loving behavior toward you would increase. You will learn that, in truth, no one has any real security in marriage, and so you must always devote energy to earning your spouse's attentions. You will also find out how to think more competitively in marriage.

As a husband you will learn that your wife subtly compares your attributes to her gym trainer's body, her attorney's humor, and her shrink's patience. It's impossible not to. You'll learn how to use that competitive spirit in becoming a more passionate and erotic lover.

7. Adultery involves intense focus.

The points that I have already made about separation, expectation, delayed gratification, erotic obstacles, secrecy, and mystique all come to a point at the one most important element of an adulterous affair: the all-consuming focus that one has on one's lover. Lovers who yearn for each other are not distracted by anything; they think only about each other. When they are in bed together, they don't call up past images of other sexual partners to excite them. On the contrary, their passion is such that the world outside the bedroom has altogether ceased to exist.

Until now it was believed that the greatest love in the world is that of a parent for a child. But in the realm of adultery, women are prepared to follow their lovers to the ends of the earth, even if it means losing their children.

For example, I met with Natasha, a twenty-eight-year-old woman, who left her husband and four-year-old girl for her history professor at college. As she describes it: "Michael [her professor] has taught me more about life in our half year together than I learned in my previous twenty-seven. He makes me do things I've never done before, not just sexual, but even like visiting museums and going to the opera. There's no way I'm going back."

"But what about your daughter?" I asked. "Your husband is saying he's going to try and deny you visitation. After all, you up and abandoned your own daughter."

"Before finding Michael my daughter was my whole life. I lived through her because my marriage was so empty. My daughter is my life, but if I leave Michael I will die. There's no question about it. And then where will my daughter be?"

There is such fervor in affairs like this one that the individuals are ready to give away everything, including their beloved children, for their partner. Compare this to marriage, where parents often rank their children's needs above all else, even each other.

What inspires such intense focus in these relations? Marriage is casual, too casual, whereas everything about adultery is intense. In addition, the risks that lovers have taken to be together act as a catalyst to reveal their total sexual sides, and involve them in the relationship in a way unknown in marriage. United and impassioned by danger, they disclose their secret sexual fantasies to each other and let go of all inhibitions. Lovers in an illicit affair become powerful magnets to each other, attracting each other's complete interest.

In Chapter 13 you will discover the importance of sexual focus, how to rid yourself of all sexual distractions, and throw caution to the wind when you make love to your spouse. You'll be taught how, and when, to purge all inhibition in your marriage. Reading that chapter, you will never be shy in the bedroom again. You'll discover the technique of making your spouse your only sexual outlet, and the immense passion and satisfaction that this generates.

8. Adultery is about attraction.

Marriages today seem to be predicated primarily on compatibility and common interests. We may be sexually attracted to and excited by a person such that we desire to marry him or her, but we are readily prepared not to marry if we feel that we don't have enough in common, if our communication is bad, or if financial considerations are not favorable. Of course, commonality of interests is important, but it is never as important as the raw attraction between the masculine and the feminine. Only this nuclear force has the power to keep you happily under the same roof for the duration of your days. People simply have to be interested in each other as individuals and not just in each other's individual interests. The mistake of believing that first and foremost we must share common interests results in the sad fact that, as time goes on, the common interests take precedence over sexual attraction. Even though a couple may love going to the cinema together and will enjoy the same kind of music, they begin to drift apart. Marriage is first and foremost about being lovers, not music lovers.

In addition, there is the increasing homogenization of the sexes that is fast diminishing the raw attraction between men and women. Attraction is contingent on the idea that men and women are not the same—that they gravitate toward one another because of the magnetic attraction of polar opposites. Every man has had the experience of browsing through some items in a department store when suddenly a woman walks past him; they will lock eyes for an instant, and he is jolted and unsettled. It's as if a bolt of electricity passes through him and he's suddenly filled with a sense of aliveness.

The same is true of a woman who is exercising in a gym when an attractive stranger gives her a look from across the room. As David Deida writes in *Intimate Communion,* "A few moments of sexual polarity can cause the memory of your trip to the supermarket to linger in your mind for hours or even days. Total strangers can raise your body temperature, cause your face to blush, and make your heart pound. On the other hand, when sexual polarity is weak in our intimate relationships, we begin to feel that something is missing, and we often blame our partners or ourselves."

Now when's the last time this happened in marriage? When's the last time a husband was in bed watching TV before going to sleep, his wife walked into the bedroom, and there was a sudden change in the sexual polarity? Are you kidding? If anything, his wife walks in and gets scolded by her husband for blocking the tube!

The sexes are losing their sexual polarity by becoming unisex. Men and women are becoming increasingly indistinguishable to each other. But this process is especially expedited in marriage. A couple becomes functionary as the husband and wife struggle to pay their bills and raise their children. Who has time for the development of any specific femininity or masculinity?

Not so in an adulterous affair, which is run entirely on the basis of attraction. Lack of common interests is subordinated almost entirely to the physical lure posed by a seductive member of the opposite sex. And boy, do men and women ever make time to highlight their masculinity and femininity in an affair! Studies show that when women take a lover they suddenly start wearing lacy underwear and sexy lingerie, putting on seductive perfume, growing their hair longer, and dressing much more provocatively.

The same is true of the men. When they take a mistress they suddenly start going to the gym to work on their pectorals. One of the quickest giveaways that a husband is having an affair is that he suddenly starts exercising or jogging (sometimes he's running to her home). Heck, he'll even shower before having sex! When's the last time you heard a husband doing *that* for his wife?

It seems that in marriage, couples simply forget how to be sexy around one another. They pride themselves on having great communication skills and common interests. And sure, those are important. But that's exactly the same as what you have with a best friend, and marriage is not about friendship. It's about being lovers. Many affairs begin between a man and a woman who know nothing about each other. They go to bed together simply because they can't resist each other, not because they can't resist talking to each other. The animal magnetism of attraction is missing in marriage.

One of the most important things you will discover in Chapter 14 is the centrality of physical and emotional attraction in a marriage, and how the kind of compatibility that makes a marriage work comes from the fact that you and your spouse are opposites that are attracted to each other. A marriage is not successful simply because you both vote Democrat (which is aside from the fact that Republicans are better lovers anyway). You will learn how to accentuate your masculine and feminine properties, thereby heightening attraction to each other. You will also learn how the power of physical attraction can be employed to your benefit in resolving marital strife.

9. Adultery boosts the ego; as such, it is an act of re-creation.

Adultery makes people come alive; they feel as if they're born anew. Many people justify what they know to be a wrong move because of the need to feel rehabilitated after sharing much of their life with an uncaring, insensitive spouse. The fact that someone else shows such an immense interest in him or her makes a neglected husband or wife feel once again like the most desirable person on earth. When people are ignored or neglected, they begin to feel as though they don't exist. For many people an adulterous affair makes them feel alive again, as if they were re-created.

The other side of the coin, however, is equally as intense. After discovering her husband's infidelity, one wife described in Janet Alese and Martin Reibstein's book *Sexual Arrangements* stopped eating right, lost nearly ten pounds in two weeks, and started chain-smoking. She felt lost, confused, and hurt, "I wonder if I'll ever sleep again. I can't trust anything. I don't know what to believe anymore. I feel as if everything has just collapsed. Completely. A house of cards."

California marriage and family counselor Daphne Rose Kingman says, "Next to the death of a loved one, the ending of a relationship is the single most emotionally painful experience that any of us ever goes through." The end of a relationship resonates like a death. And thus, the endurance of a relationship should feel like eternal life.

Chapter 15 is dedicated exclusively to exercises you can use to make your spouse feel alive. We'll teach you how to bring exhilaration into marriage. Rather than experiencing the pain of a cheated spouse, by focusing extravagant love on your husband or wife, you can re-create him or her anew and bring novelty and freshness into your marriage.

10. Adultery is about danger, forbiddenness, sinfulness, and excitement.

I saved the most important commandment for last. Overwhelmingly, men enter into adulterous affairs simply because of the attraction posed by a new sexual conquest and a new body. The very familiarity of marriage can work against it, while the novelty of adultery has ensured that it has remained the most indulgent and erotic vice since the beginning of time. Just as buying a new car or a new dress always excites us, adultery offers excitement by affording the opportunity for something new and different, while marriage just offers more of the same.

But newness doesn't have to mean acquiring something new. It can come in the form of rearranging the furniture in the house, reupholstering that old sofa, repainting the car. It can also be achieved when you have lost an object, or thought you had lost an object, and you find it again. What this affords is a new opportunity to rediscover what you already possess; it brings excitement and newness to those things you take for granted because you have allowed them to become monotonous and boring to you through lack of effort on your part to renew them.

Passion, excitement, and newness are not empirical concepts, but mental ones. We all have the capacity to reinvent our spouses through the power of the mind. All eroticism taps into some primal, erotic fantasy. Think about the following: A man calls a phone-sex line for some excitement. A woman with a sultry voice answers on the other line. "What's your fantasy?" she asks. He gets hot just hearing her voice. In his mind he pictures a beautiful seductress, long legged and large chested, lying in bed in lacy underwear, all ready to service his needs. Of course, in reality he is probably speaking to a woman wearing a tracksuit, bored to death with her job, who puts up with horny men because, "Hey, it's a living." Do you see the power of fantasy? This man has a fantasy about what he finds attractive, and he superimposes that fantasy onto the woman he's speaking to.

Now, I'm not implying that the average wife is that far from the ideal, but given that husbands are not sufficiently attracted to their wives and too frequently compare them to false ideals, why can't the same principle apply? Why can't they transfer these fantasies onto their own wives? They can if they make the effort. A wife can become the ideal mistress that her husband finds so erotic, if he uses his mind.

Since sexuality and eroticism are cerebral, they can be easily induced with the proper techniques, as you will read in Chapter 16. The most important thing you will learn from this book is a proven method by which to constantly rediscover your spouse, guaranteeing more passion in your married life than you could ever experience with adultery. What—is that possible? Marriage even more exciting than adultery? Yes, far more.

Finally, adultery is above all else about forbiddenness, and nothing is as exciting as something that is forbidden. In the stable world that most of us in the West are lucky enough to enjoy, we have lost a sense of danger. Adultery seems to provide it. Adultery is taboo, and taboo is exciting. Just think about this for a moment. Nearly every man who has an affair describes the sex as the best he's ever had. Yet these men also speak of how different the sex becomes once they give up their respective spouses and move in together. Once it is no longer forbidden, it becomes too stale.

Charlene, a woman in her forties, said, "The sex was much freer because he wasn't my husband. I'm convinced that sex is much more exciting when you're sneaking it. You get pumping before you even begin. We'd go to his apartment . . . and we'd be having this amazing sex together. I think the sex with this man, without thoughts of one's day-to-day existence, made it thrilling. There is no mortgage, no car, no kids, and no alarm clock at 6 A.M. with a lover . . . Once I was divorced, I called my lover, thinking we'd be together. He said to me, 'I wouldn't date my best friend's ex-wife.' That was it for me. I had to move on."

Julie, who is forty-one years old, said, "The sex was hot and heavy, very passionate . . . we'd spend the entire day in bed at a motel. We did it for hours, having intercourse three times, at least . . . It was wonderful and I realized how unlike a marriage it was . . . We'd stay up all night sometimes, making love and drinking wine . . . [But] once we were no longer illicit lovers and reality set in, we didn't function as well."

Lilly, forty-four years old, had this to say: "The taboo side of an affair is what makes it attractive . . . I like the titillating aspect, the dance beforehand, the unsanctioned bit . . . I admit that I'd been curious and it was more interesting for me to see what it was all about" (Susan Shapiro Barash, *A Passion for More*).

These examples illustrate what everyday life shows, and what every teenager who is attracted to drug use knows: Forbidden things have a more enticing, erotic quality. Sin is exciting. The more forbidden something is, the more we seem to hunger for it. In no area is this truer than sex. Sexual attraction is greatly enhanced by the quality of forbiddenness. Desirability and sexuality are not contingent on aesthetic appeal or looks. Rather, it is all in the mind, which gravitates toward forbidden things like nothing else. In Chapter 16, you will learn how to sin and fornicate with your spouse—a very good reason to read on.

EIGHTEIGHTEIGHTEIGHTEIGHTEIG
HTEIGHTEIGHTEIGHTEIGHTEIGHTE
IGHTEIGHTEIGHTEIGHTEIGHTEIGH
TEIGHTEIGHT eight IGHTEIGHTEI
GHTEIGHTEIGHTEIGHTEIGHTEIGHT
EIGHTEIGHTEIGHTEIGHTEIGHTEIG
HTEIGHTEIGHTEIGHTEIGHTEIGHTE

COMMANDMENT
ONE
IN ACTION—
BECOMING A
Total
SEXUAL PARTNER

The first time I went to bed with him, I felt as though the world had stopped and I was a shooting star sending out enough light to illuminate the blackest of black holes.
—AN ADULTEROUS WIFE, QUOTED FROM THE HITE REPORT

Pursuit and seduction are the essence of sexuality. It's part of the sizzle.

—CAMILLE PAGLIA

People have relationships not because they want to feel safe—though they often think they do—but because they want to find out what the danger is. This is where infidelity can often let people down.

—ADAM PHILLIPS, MONOGAMY

Commandment One
Adultery is first and foremost about sex.

My friend James was mortified when his wife Linda began scrutinizing the Visa bills and uncovered several vague charges for "apparel" from an establishment in Kentucky. Her curiosity led her to call the bank and get the number of this strange establishment that had already cost them more than $400. To her surprise, a seductive female voice picked up the phone on the other end and asked, "What is your fantasy?"

Linda was furious when she quickly realized that her husband had squandered their hard-earned money talking trash to women on a phone-sex line. Not only was she personally insulted, she felt humiliated and inadequate. Was talking about sex with another woman even more exciting than actually having it with your wife? She confronted James and peppered him with questions such as, "What did you talk about?" and "Did you do most of the talking, or did the women?" but he was too embarrassed to answer any of them. She couldn't understand why her husband felt that he needed to have sex over the telephone. His silence infuriated her and, when the couple realized they couldn't resolve the problem, they came to me for advice.

James refused to discuss the issue until his wife left my study, which she did. With an agonized look on his face, he told me how he regarded Linda as a beautiful woman, but felt she was very shy about sex. She maintained that she had been raised in a very religious home and had never overcome her inhibitions about sex—even with her husband. "Sex is important to Linda," James said, "but not nearly as important as it is to me."

Yes, they could have sex whenever they wanted. But they could never *talk* about it. He desired to engage in sexual banter with his wife. When they were in bed together, he would use explicit language telling her what he wanted to do to her. She

enjoyed listening to what he was saying, but she couldn't reciprocate. James would get frustrated and, rather than making
love, they usually ended up fighting. James also pushed Linda
to tell him about her fantasies, and wanted her to know his.
Again, she was uncomfortable with the idea. Finally, in frustration, he began wasting their money on fantasy lines.

This story and countless others like it show how today's
husbands and wives are—or more precisely are not—sexually
involved with each other. They need to become total sexual
partners within their marriages. Countless stories of adultery
tell how a man and woman tried things they had never tried
before, pushed the sexual envelope to its extreme, and found
great fire and pleasure in doing so.

If a human being is like a grape, then adultery seems to be
the pressure that squeezes out the wine. Many people find themselves trying new things in their affairs, both sexual and not. Dr.
Frank Pittman, a psychologist from Atlanta, reports in his study,
Private Lies: Infidelity and the Betrayal of Intimacy, that an
affair is "three times more likely to be the pursuit of a buddy
than the pursuit of a better orgasm." In Annette Lawson's
Adultery, one man relates how "she [his lover] would make me
do things I had never done before. I went and visited cathedrals.
My life . . . has been enriched vastly as a result."

Adulterous partners have established the sexual supremacy
of their character over and above all other facets, something
that is usually not true in marriage. Husbands and their mistresses, wives and their lovers, not only have more sex with
each other than they do with their spouses, but think about it
more, talk about it more, and expose their deepest, darkest
fantasies to each other more. In short, adulterous lovers are
usually consumed with sex. It's the soul and life force of their
relationship. In *Women Who Stay with Men Who Stray,* Dr.
Debbie Then lists the following as some of the leading causes
of male infidelity: "[the desire for] more sex, more often, oral
sex . . . the thrill of a new body . . . and hearing a different set
of moans and groans." Yes, something as simple as wanting to
hear a woman shriek out loud in delight can lead a man astray
from the marital bed.

In her autobiography *Fear of Fifty,* Erica Jong relates how her third (and current) marriage seems to be succeeding where the others failed. She identifies one of the essential ingredients in preserving the sexual passion in the marriage as being her new habit of writing down her sexual fantasies and reading them aloud to her husband. Adulterous partners are obsessed with each other's erotic personality. They leave no stone unturned in trying to fathom the depths of the other's sexuality. How can we bring this obsession into marriage?

Repression Is Always Destructive

There is a mistaken perception that religion is opposed to sex. Not so in Judaism, which has always celebrated physical love between a married man and a woman. Judaism actually opposes sexual repression, believing heartily in the need for sexual expression. The Talmud proclaims that everything that God forbade in one area, He made permissible in another. So while he closed off other women to a married man, he gave him a sexy mistress in his own marital bed.

Sex in Judaism is seen as the epitome of Godliness, a transcendent and spiritual experience whose power can render two distinct souls into one indivisible flesh. The fact is that nothing on this earth can make a man and a woman feel closer to each other than making love—and that's why sex is so Godly. When a man and a woman make love, they emulate the celestial union of the masculine and feminine energies within the Godhead, as detailed in the esoteric secrets of the Kabbalah. Whether or not sex is moral and holy does not depend on the sex act itself, but rather on how humans go about doing it. For instance, sex can be unholy even in marriage—such as when a spouse thinks about someone else during the act or when a husband makes love to his wife—if you can call it that—when she is half asleep.

The Talmud provides one of the most life-affirming statements about sex found in any ancient religious text: "In the final analysis, a husband and wife can do whatever pleases them most," meaning that they should pursue sexual practices that excite them, discover new positions that turn them on, and engage in the kind of sexual talk that drives them wild. Rabbi Akiva, arguably the most famous sage of the entire Talmud, even said that a husband is obligated to be jealous of his wife. Jealousy is not only permissible, he said, but mandatory. So many husbands are not jealous of their wives because they have lost attraction to them and no longer feel very passionate about their wives as desirable sexual objects. Not so with Rabbi Akiva. In his opinion, a husband was obligated to see his wife as an intensely sexual creature who all other men want, and who may indeed want other men. He should jealously possess her by passionately satisfying all her needs so that she would never find herself in another man's bed.

Among the many verses in the Bible that are dedicated to sexual prohibitions—with the exception of abstaining from having sex during menstruation, which applies to all couples— virtually every one applies exclusively to extramarital sex, and not to sex between a husband and wife. There can be no greater illustration of the Jewish outlook on sex than one that purports the importance of focus and sublimation, rather than repression.

The same activities that are absolutely prohibited in an adulterous relationship are actually considered holy when done by a husband and wife. As we will explore later, modesty is an essential part of eroticism—but only to create the actual attraction. Once the power of attraction works and a husband and wife start making love, all inhibition must be cast into the furnace. The ice wall of sexual inhibition must be melted by the fiery inferno of wild marital sex. Couples have to light a sexual fire that burns out of control. In fact, that's one of the great purposes of marriage: to build a fireplace. If your house is freezing, you need to light a fire to warm it up. But if you light the fire in the middle of the kitchen, you will burn the whole house down. If you light the fire in a stone fireplace, however, you'll safely contain the flames. Once the fire is going strong, you'll want to stoke the flames to heat up the entire house.

The same is true of our sexual fire. If we light our sexual fire only outside the context of a loving relationship (for example, before marriage), it can burn the metaphorical house down and ruin our lives. Look at how many people have brought great pain into their lives because of sex, rather than pleasure. Just ask Bill Clinton. But once we marry and our sexuality is practiced within the confines of an intimate, monogamous relationship, there is absolutely no room for inhibition in our sexual play.

Being inhibited is a mistake made by both husbands and wives. To their own detriment, many couples—both religious and secular—refrain from becoming total sexual partners. Many religious husbands have come to me for counseling because their wives are modest both outside and inside the bedroom. They're used to missionary position sex and they feel dirty trying anything else. The problem is, this gives husbands and wives the excuse to find satisfaction elsewhere.

That's why husbands and wives need to learn from adultery about the importance of sex in a relationship. Why should a husband have to call a phone-sex line when he should be having phone sex with his wife? Why do husbands watch so many pornographic films while they're holed up in hotel rooms away on business? When men tell me this, I say, "Have you taken leave of your senses? Why would you compromise the intimacy of your marriage by watching slutty strangers when you and your wife can make an erotic movie together that you can take with you and watch when you travel?" Isn't it a tragedy that husbands and wives allow so many artificial barriers between them that make them strangers to each other—and then rely on strangers for sexual stimulation?

Carrie and Stuart, a couple living in London, had been married for six years when she had an affair while Stuart was away for a month on business in the Far East. Her husband was extremely distraught over her affair, but he forgave her, blaming himself for being away for so long. She went into therapy to figure out why she felt she needed the affair—only to fall in love with her therapist. She had a two-year-long affair with him. Her husband found out when one of the kids received a call from the therapist's wife, asking why this number had appeared twenty times on her phone bill that month.

This time Stuart was livid. He abused his wife verbally and

told all the neighbors what she had done. When he couldn't stand the sight of her any longer, he moved into a hotel and soon after they became formally separated. Twelve months later, he moved into an apartment with Agatha, a woman he met on an airplane, and they lived together on and off for a year. It was at this point that Stuart, a devoted father, started to feel that he and his wife should try to get back together in some limited capacity for the sake of the children. By now, his anger had subsided and he discovered, to his surprise, that he still had loving feelings toward his wife. He went home to find Carrie excited by his return.

The catch was that Stuart still hadn't given up Agatha, who lived in the next town and whom Stuart would go to visit and spend weekends with about twice a month. When Carrie insisted that he leave Agatha, he wouldn't hear of it. So Carrie let Stuart move back in, but refused to have sex with him. "Every time I think of him being with her, it just turns me off him."

I spoke to Stuart and it was clear he was not going to give up Agatha until he saw that the marriage was viable. "I don't trust my wife," he said to me. "She's hurt me too many times. What if I give up Agatha and then Carrie ends up running off with another man again?" I went to Carrie and said to her, "Look, you tell me you love your husband, and he says he loves you, too. But you both have a lot of baggage and he's not going to give her up. So, this is what I suggest. Tell him 'Okay, I understand that you're punishing me in some way with this other woman, and maybe I deserve it. I want you to make love to me, and I'm not going to insist that you give her up yet. But I am going to insist that you not kiss her. Kissing is something you save for your wife. It's just too intimate.' Hopefully he'll agree. Then you'll wait a month, and you'll tell him, 'Okay, no kissing her, and no telling her anything personal about your sexual fantasies. That you save for me. I'm your wife, she isn't. Just keep the sex with her impersonal.' The next month you'll tell him to remove another component of his sex life with her."

Carrie objected: "What's the point? Why am I doing this?" I replied, "You're doing it to win your husband back. You told me how much you want to get him back, but he's not going to give up the other woman just like that. Because after a while, you'll be the one who is his total sexual partner, while the other woman is the one with whom he has all these strange walls. And he'll gravitate back to you."

Don't Simply Have Sex—Be Sexual

Far from being a perfunctory act of procreation, sex is one of our strongest and most deep-seated instincts. But it is not simply that people need to have sex. Rather, they need to *be* sexual. Men and women need to think sexy thoughts, indulge in erotic conversation, look at sexy images and, finally, undertake sexual acts. People need to be sexual because it is what makes them feel most alive. Erotic thrills send an electric shock down our spines. They make us sizzle and tingle. Marriage should be the total solution for all these erotic needs. No man should ever have to go on the Internet and look at eighteen-year-old coeds in their skivvies. He should set up a camera in his own bedroom and view his wife as his secret WebCam girl. No woman should ever need to obsess over Russell Crowe's rock-solid chest or Brad Pitt's twinkling eyes to feel that she has romantic thrills in her life. Likewise, no wife needs to view the movie *Unfaithful* and think to herself, "What am I missing?" Because real excitement is having a man who gets your blood boiling by obsessing over your body, staring at you whenever you undress, and touching you under the table when you go out to dinner with friends. And it is a woman's husband who should be producing all these romantic thrills.

The best kind of sex is that which consumes us entirely, like a burning flame. This is why premarital sex—where one is conscious of being judged according to performance—can never offer the totally natural, relaxed fulfillment of married sex. Sexuality is not an ancillary dimension of human existence. Rather, it is a total statement of who people are and what they do. If a husband and wife are to be happy together, it is essential that they serve as total sexual outlets for each other.

I know a doctor who had a happy marriage and an "okay"

sex life with his wife, but still ended up committing adultery, which resulted in his wife leaving him. "What prompted you to do it?" I asked him.

He answered, "Well, it started one day at a medical conference. There was this speaker talking about the medical benefits of masturbation. I turned to a woman doctor seated next to me and made some witty remark. She laughed and we had a drink later, where we both spoke about masturbation. She told me how she had started masturbating as a girl of twelve years old, how many times a week she did it, how she hid it from her parents, and how it's the mainstay of her sex life now, since she doesn't have a boyfriend. Whew, what a hot conversation that was! I knew that if I didn't put the brakes on, I'd end up in her hotel room. So after two hours, hammered from all the whiskey, I still managed to pry myself away and go back to my hotel room alone. I wanted to be a faithful husband. But when I got back home, and my wife and I went on our weekly Saturday night movie run, I tried to talk to my wife about masturbation in the car. I asked her at what age she started to masturbate, how many times a week she does it, how it feels. She said, 'Would you stop? You're embarrassing me. What's come over you?' And I compared this reaction with that sexually free woman who had my blood pumping. So the next time I was in her city, I gave her a call just to have a drink, and ended up spending the night."

Of course, there is never a justifiable excuse for having an affair. The doctor is a scoundrel (or worse) for cheating on his wife. Nevertheless, the story does provide an important lesson: Why give a husband even a poor excuse? Sex and marriage are at their best when a husband and wife are sexual together in every possible way. This is the essence of adultery and the secret of illicit lovers: They always put sex first. They never allow their sex life to be subordinated to any practical consideration. The house is a mess—who cares? The guy is wearing an expensive Armani suit—just tear it off, she's worth it! The neighbors are going to hear shrill howls of ecstasy—let them call the police! To heck with them.

In sharp contrast, half the time husbands and wives have sex they're afraid that they'll wake the baby. A husband in

Australia complained to me that it's impossible to have sex with his wife because she's afraid that the kids will walk in. I called her up and suggested, "Can't you get a lock on the door?" She replied, "If we locked the door, then the kids might wake up in the middle of the night and cry outside the door, terrified that Mommy and Daddy don't want them." I told her, "I don't care if you have to make your bedroom into Fort Knox, just do it. Your bedroom is your love chamber, not the family sitting room. It's where the most intimate moments take place between you and your husband. It's not a place for the kids to hang out. Let them get used to crying outside the door and then going back into their own beds. They will not be scarred from the experience. Rather, they will thank you for it when they grow into healthy and independent adults themselves. The worst lesson you can pass on to your kids is to have them grow up witnessing two parents who bore each other."

I know an attractive young female pediatrician who, at twenty-six, was happy with her relationship with her boyfriend of two years when suddenly, on a shopping trip to London, she was seduced by a female friend who was ten years her senior. "At first I thought, 'What am I doing? I'm not gay.' I was appalled at myself. But when I thought about it, heterosexual sex just didn't compare. The main thing was that we talked so much during sex and we kept our eyes open and looked at each other. We weren't ashamed to say what pleasured us and to ask for it. I had never had that with a man. Every guy I've been to bed with, it's the same sort of routine, the same positions, and most of all, the same inhibitions."

Husbands and wives cannot allow their love life to be submerged under a thick blanket of reserve. They must endeavor to destroy or transcend any sexual reticence that separates them and to become complete sexual outlets for each other. Refraining from an adulterous affair is not sufficient. A couple will still be losing the opportunity to use sex for its most important purpose: binding husband and wife together. They will not become bone of one bone, and flesh of one flesh.

To be sure, nobody has the right to demand that his or her spouse instantly submit to every sexual need—especially when the other person is uncomfortable with certain activities. Rather, you must try to coax the sexual spark out of your spouse. You must tell your wife how beautiful and sexy she is, and how you're obsessed with her and her body. Foreplay must begin in the morning when you first wake up, not at night when you're about to go to sleep. Kiss her before you go, call her from work to say you're thinking about her. Vent your sexual thoughts to your wife at the end of the day when both of you get home. Tell her that you thought of the time the two of you made passionate love on the beach on your fifth wedding anniversary, and how the thought of her naked under the moonlight aroused you to the point where you had to come home and hold her. Make her feel desirable. Let her know how important passionate sex is to you because she simply drives you wild with her sexual appeal. Explain that you want to explore every sexual nook and cranny together so you can get to know each other in the deepest possible way.

A spouse should not be seen as one's business partner, housemate, best friend, psychiatrist, or confidante. First and foremost, a spouse must be a lover. Everything else is secondary.

Remember, part of Commandment One is to turn partners into desirable sexual objects. If our husbands and wives are totally absorbed with us sexually, if they can talk about sex with us, fantasize about sex with us, be sexually adventurous with us, look forward to trying every different position with us, act out fantasies with us—then there is no reason in the world that they should have to look for sex outside of the marriage. When everything else in a marriage becomes more important than sex, one partner is likely to stray, or both are likely to get bored and drift apart. Having children and buying each other beautiful clothes and jewelry are poor safeguards against adultery.

Marriage Comes First

How do couples turn partners into desirable sexual objects? Whether or not a husband or wife feels sexy depends largely on the spouse. A husband should never feel the need to look at *Playboy* centerfolds for stimulation. A wife shouldn't have to read cheap Harlequin romance novels to fill a void in her life. If a woman finds a romantic novel set in Venice inspiring, she must persuade her husband to hop on a plane at the next available opportunity so they may enjoy the experience together. And if it cannot be Venice, Italy, let it be Venice Beach, California, or the Venetian Hotel in Las Vegas.

It's the shared experience that counts. Men, go ahead and fantasize—but always about your wives. Men need sexual variety. But rather than fantasizing about the bikini who sat next to you on the beach, ask your wife, as you drive home, what she thought about the lifeguards. If she found them attractive or found herself admiring the guy on the surfboard, then go ahead and fantasize about your wife with that hunky wave-runner. And tell her that's what you're fantasizing about. She'll go wild with desire when she hears that you find her a seductive and insatiable mistress. Women, go ahead and get sentimental—but always about your husbands. Walk into the bedroom at night with some new sex toy and tell him you want him to try it out on you. Go online and buy one of the thousands of ointments that are made to be applied on a woman's nether regions, promising instant ecstasy and delight. Tell your husband you want him to massage it onto you. Even if it's a placebo, it will get both your juices going. Try to translate all your fantasies into reality by living out your dreams—together.

You may argue that this advice is impractical. After all, you can't just drop everything and take off somewhere at a moment's notice. But I ask you this: If you were at work and heard that the plumbing at your house went haywire and was flooding all the rooms, wouldn't you immediately run home? If your son got in big trouble with the principal at school, wouldn't you have to pick him up?

Well, why don't we do the same thing in marriage? When our home is in danger of physical destruction, we move heaven and earth to protect it. But when our marriages are in danger of dying the cold death of static boredom, we do almost nothing to save them. We're too busy. Hey, a hotel room in the middle of the day for the two of you is a lot cheaper than the cost of an illicit visit with a prostitute—and a heck of a lot cheaper than a divorce lawyer. Our marriages are the most important things in our lives, and we should, if necessary, accept financial loss and distraction from our careers to boost and salvage them.

If you were involved in an adulterous affair, you would find the time in the middle of the workday to run to an out-of-the-way hotel room to secretly spend some time with your lover. So why should marriage be any less spontaneous?

Exercises
BECOMING A TOTAL
SEXUAL PARTNER

1. Spontaneously call your spouse in the middle of the day and arrange to meet at a restaurant near a hotel for a quick lunch. Rather than sitting opposite each other, sit side by side in one of the booths. Keep your hands under the tablecloth where no one can see and surprise your spouse by touching him or her with daring abandon. Touch your spouse even as you order with the waitress right there in front of you (prop the menu up if you need extra cover). When lunch is over, slide your spouse a hotel room key under the table. Pay the restaurant bill as your spouse heads up to the room to make him- or herself comfortable. Meet your spouse upstairs in the room you have reserved for the elusive "Smiths." Bring some new sexual game, lingerie, lotion, ointment, or technique. Tell your spouse that this whole arrangement was made to experiment with this new addition. Spend an hour having heavenly sex. Tell your secretary to hold all calls until you return.

2. Read each other erotic literature. Even sexual studies like *The Hite Report,* which contains scores of personal stories, will do the trick.

3. Discuss your sexual fantasies with your spouse. A lot of people find it easier—at least initially—to write them down and read them, even if it's just bullet points. Or write them down and let your spouse read your fantasy to you. If you're too embarrassed, wait until you're both juiced up during sex and then drop the grenade. Out of the blue, start recounting your fantasies. Look your spouse right in the eye as you tell him or her all the details. That usually allows someone who was raised to be uncomfortable with sharing such illicit thoughts to be more open in sharing his or her secret desires. By telling your spouse your sexual fantasies, you make your spouse into a total sexual partner for you. And by hearing about your fantasies, your partner begins to see you as a sexual being who is creative and imaginative. You should be able to relate your fantasies to each other, and dress up in accordance with each other's wishes. It may seem strange at first, but in time you will find it easier, and the intimate passion and closeness in your marriage will increase immeasurably.

4. Go to a sexual novelty shop together and buy yourselves all kinds of sex toys. While it should be noted that I'm completely against pornography (because it undermines the intimacy between husband and wife and for other reasons discussed in my book *Kosher Sex*), I fully encourage the use of sex toys if married couples enjoy them together. While pornography has you both getting excited about strangers, sexual novelty will allow you to draw closer together as you experiment with playful sexual games. The novelty brings excitement, while the adventure helps to diminish inhibition. You'd be surprised at what delight a small pair of handcuffs can bring.

5. Start having phone sex. A wife can call her husband in the middle of the day at work and tell him how excited she is just thinking about him and how she wishes that she could have him, right there, right away, wherever she is. Or, a husband can call his wife and tell her what he's been thinking about doing to her at night. Phone sex is especially important whenever one partner travels. It's a much better alternative to the boring porn that hotel cable serves up. It might be a bit tricky at first, but the discomfort can make it that much more erotic. The physical distance is the perfect erotic barrier that creates desire and makes it easier to discuss fantasy than it otherwise would be when your spouse is sexually available to you.

6. Practice the tantric idea of having sex without climax. Try it for three days at a time. Hug, kiss, and engage in all kinds of foreplay—even leading to intercourse. But stop before climax. That means both of you. It takes discipline, but if you can contain yourselves, it will bring you to the heights of desire and eroticism. During the day, you'll still be hot for each other because climax and release haven't been achieved. These are ideal days to practice phone sex, even for a few minutes at a time. Talk about your lust that just cannot be satisfied. Practice heightening and maintaining your state of arousal, just as you would in an illicit affair where you aren't always available to each other to satisfy your lust. Pretty soon, if you stick to the program and abstain from climax, you will be delirious with desire for your spouse. Then, after three days, you can bring the whole thing to an ecstatic finish. After your break, resume your lovemaking sessions, trying to delay gratification further—maybe five days—until you're climbing the walls for each other. You'll then see that you don't even notice the attractive strangers that surround you, since you are so consumed with your lust for your spouse. Sounds impossible, but try it and you'll be completely convinced.

7. Sit down one night and talk to each other about three people you each encountered during the day—coworkers, friends that you both know, and so on—who you find particularly attractive. Explain why they attract you. Be careful not to hurt each other while doing this. Make it playful. Tease each other without wounding each other. Delight in the danger of the discussion. Whenever you say that you like someone for some reason, immediately relate it to your spouse. Point out to your spouse any of the stranger's sexy qualities that are identical, or at least very similar, to his or hers.

8. Call one of those 900 party lines, where lustful men and women, usually singles, are all on the line talking, trying to meet someone. But call it together. Excite each other as you talk openly about what turns you on, sharing these thoughts with each other, and the other anonymous chatters on the line. The presence of others—whom you cannot see and will never again encounter—will make the experience all the more stimulating. But don't be too explicit or compromise the intimacy of your relationship.

9. WIVES: Prepare erotic photographs for your husbands. Have a professional female photographer come over and produce beautifully erotic photos that your husband can take with him to the office and keep in his wallet. Download the photos on your computer, then send him a new erotic photo by e-mail. Set up a special account for him at Yahoo! or Hotmail that only the two of you can access. (*Important note:* Be careful not to send anything provocative to him at work, because there are serious sexual harassment laws protecting coworkers from offensive material being present in the work environment. Many companies have complete access to e-mail accounts and employees' computers, and are fully entitled to search them at their sole discretion. In some cases, this can lead to losing a job—which certainly is not beneficial to any relationship.)

10. Start traveling together. Husbands and wives find that liaisons on business trips are great ways to relieve pressure, revel in the joy of the forbidden, and get the ego boost of being attractive to a stranger. Spouses should therefore make a point of trying to travel with their partners as often as time and resources permit. Parents should get baby-sitters for the kids and explain to them that Mommy and Daddy love each other and need time away alone together. New locations are erotic and lead to great desire. New lovemaking arenas, like hotel rooms, are natural aphrodisiacs. And why should a husband or wife seduce a stranger when the couple can get hot and lusty with each other in a strange new exciting destination?

NINENINENINENINENINENINENINE
NINENINENINENINENINENINENINE
NINENINENINENINENINENINENINE
NINENINENIN nine INENINENINE
NINENINENINENINENINENINENINE
NINENINENINENINENINENINENINE
NINENINENINENINENINENINENINE

COMMANDMENT TWO IN ACTION— EROTIC OBSTACLES THAT LEAD TO Desire

The time away [from his wife] had a salubrious effect on their marriage and each visit home was a renewed honeymoon. . . . after seeing the children, they made love with a fervor reminiscent of their courtship.

—GAY TALESE, *THY NEIGHBOR'S WIFE*

That the man and woman were husband and wife, and the parents of the girl in arms there could be little doubt. No other than such a relationship could have accounted for the atmosphere of stale familiarity which the trio carried along with them like a nimbus as they moved down the road.

—THOMAS HARDY, *THE MAYOR OF CASTERBRIDGE* (1886)

Absence is to love what wind is to fire; it extinguishes the small, it enkindles the great.

—COMTE DEBUSSY RABUTIN

Commandment Two
Adultery thrives on delayed gratification,
separation, and expectation.

Ready and Willing for Sex

I discovered the expression "ready and willing for sex" in my early years at Oxford when I studied Judaism with a married couple in their forties who wanted to become more observant Jews. Ironically, that the couple had allowed themselves to become sexually incompatible led me to a greater understanding of the aforementioned phrase.

They had been married for only five years, but judging from their conversation, it was clear that much of the spark of their marriage was already gone. In addition, they were arguing more than ever before. One fight began when he started frequenting a health club to lose weight, and his wife told him jokingly that she didn't mind him getting personal training sessions from a big-chested woman in a tight leotard because "it would be a miracle if you got excited about anything these days." The husband took offense at the comment, especially since it was said in front of friends, and would not speak to his wife for days. He blamed her for not trying to look younger for him. "If you came with me to the gym maybe I'd get interested in you again." She in turn put the onus on him for never being romantic: "The next time I'll get flowers from him will be on my coffin."

I suggested to them that they could kill two birds with one stone. I advised this couple that if they wished to become more observant—and to reinstill passion into their marriage as well—they should institute a monthly period of sexual separation.

One of the central tenets of Jewish family living is what is known as the Jewish laws of family purity (in Hebrew *Taharas Hamishpocha*). The Bible mandates a period of sexual separation each month in marriage. Once a month, for the five days of menstruation and for seven nights thereafter, a husband and wife refrain from engaging in intimate relations. This precludes not only having sex, but hugging or sleeping in the same bed as well. At the conclusion of this interlude, the wife goes to a *mikveh,* or ritual bath—which resembles a small swimming pool—whose water is drawn from, and always connected to, a living spring. After her immersion in the *mikveh,* she reunites sexually with her husband.

Many have mistakenly understood these laws to mean that a woman's menses render her unclean and that is why she cannot be with her husband. The idea that a woman's natural body cycle could make her unclean is an insinuation that riles the sensibilities of most feminists, and rightly so. But this is not the intention of the law. A far more accurate understanding is that given by the Talmud itself, which argues that separation leads to increased sexual desire and prevents the boredom of familiarity.

Rabbi Meir used to say: "For what reason does the Torah say that a *niddah* (a menstruating woman) is forbidden to her husband for seven days?" Because otherwise he would be with her too frequently and thus become tired of her, and she with him. Therefore, the Torah said: "Let her be ritually unavailable for seven days (during which cohabitation is forbidden) so that she should become as desirable to her husband as when she entered under the bridal canopy" (T.B. Niddah 31b). This was a very keen insight made by the Bible 3,500 years ago about the human erotic mind, and no better mechanism for sustaining passion in marriage has ever been found.

As every husband and wife who has been separated from one another for twelve days should already know, the sexual reunion that follows is explosive. When your wife comes home from the *mikveh* and enters the bedroom, you jump each other as if you were still in your twenties. (Remember those days?) What separation does is repackage our old lovers in new lover's trappings. And while this is not a complete solution to the problem of how to restore lost passion in marriage, as we shall explore later, it is undeniable that observing the laws of Jewish family purity is extraordinarily effective.

Many historians and modern sociologists accurately attribute the traditionally strong and vibrant Jewish marriage to the observance of these ancient laws.

Many Jewish authors have described the monthly night of reunion as "a second honeymoon," but better, because it is one that recurs with great frequency. Jewish couples are in the habit of making this a very special evening. Many book a hotel room for the night and get baby-sitters for the kids. Others have candlelit baths together as a prelude to lovemaking. I even knew one couple that would make love that one night of every month in the spacious confines of their family SUV.

Jewish Law in Secular Lives

When *Kosher Sex* came out, I was amazed at how many non-Jewish couples started instituting the twelve-day period of abstinence. I was getting letters from pig farmers out in Yorkshire (well, almost—the point is, they were as non-Jewish as they came) telling me how wise they found this period of separation and the wonder it had brought into their marriage.

I decided to form a global "Kosher Sex Club" for all those who bought into the "abstinence makes the heart grow fonder" mentality. Then I got a letter from a woman out in Malaysia and we started a very interesting correspondence. She told me that she's fifty years old and is postmenopausal. "But that didn't stop me from kicking my husband out of our bed for two weeks every month just as soon as I read your book. Now he has to earn me. I feel like a prize again!" No doubt, I'm none too popular with this woman's husband, but if he really acknowledged what this was doing for both of their desires, he would thank me for introducing them to these time-honored Jewish observances.

Let's now return to the story at the beginning of the chapter and the expression "ready and willing for sex." After this woman had been to the *mikveh* for the first time, I asked her how she viewed the experience.

It was amazing. It was the first time in my life that I felt both spiritual and sexual. Before that night, I thought the body and the soul were always going to be in conflict. For two weeks my husband and I stopped having sex. Then, I went to the mikveh. *I immersed myself in the water, in the fetal position. It was like being back in the amniotic fluid. Before going home, I put on a colorful dress and applied my makeup, and underneath it all I wore my sexiest lingerie— all for my husband's benefit. I had to stop on the way home to fill the car with petrol. I could tell that all the men at the service station couldn't take their eyes off me. I felt that I was very desirable. But I could also tell that the reason wasn't only the way I was dressed. Rather, it was the way I felt about myself, and how I carried myself. After having been off limits for nearly two weeks I was ready and willing for sex. I was rife with lust. I was a woman filled with desire, whose hormones were running wild, who couldn't wait to get home and jump in bed with her man. I wasn't behaving at all flirtatiously with these guys and I really wasn't dressed immodestly. But I didn't have to be. The men noticed me nonetheless. And when I finally got home to my husband, I felt this energy pass between us. I'm not kidding. When he started touching me and took off my clothes, I even had this sensation of a metallic taste in my mouth, so tangible was the magnetism. We had really aggressive sex. I told him how all the men on the way home had looked at me, and my husband saw the same thing. I felt he really wanted me, for the first time in a long time.*

Abstention and Separation Build Sexual Energy

Sexual barriers, such as the twelve-day period of abstinence, build intense erotic desire. Human nature needs partitions in order to thrive and flourish. The love between a man and a woman should be a burning flame. But even a flame flickers. And so should the marriage. There should be two weeks of great sex, fire, passion, and romance. And then, just as our libido is beginning to weaken and we get into the fifteen-minute routine, rather than our sex life putt-putting along at this infirm pace, we must quit cold turkey. All of the powerful emotions generated in the two-week period of sexual play must now be transmuted from physical closeness into *emotional* closeness.

Psychologist C. A. Tripp supports this theory: "A person's sexual motivation is seldom aroused and is never rewarding unless something in the partner or in the situation itself is viewed as resistant to it. This resistance may be in the form of the partner's hesitance, the disapproval of outsiders, or any other impediment to easy access. . . . It is apparent that an erotic attitude does not develop toward a fully accessible partner (even one who's wonderfully complementary), but is aroused like a cannibal's appetite when a desired but somehow remote partner cannot 'be had' by other means. As anyone can see, sexual motives are especially stimulated in a person who feels an urgent need or intense admiration for the qualities he sees in a partner and wants to 'import.' Certainly there is much in sex that has to do with wanting, taking, and conquering, or otherwise possessing a partner, sometimes one who has as little as a single highly desired quality" (*The Homosexual Matrix*).

Jack Morin, psychologist and author of *The Erotic Mind*, also confirms the impact of erotic obstacles: "It was becoming clear to me that sex therapy's focus on the removal of impediments to sexual desire and arousal was far too narrow. Whereas modern sex therapy is anchored in the neat and clean model of sexual interaction that views barriers and inhibitions as unnecessary and unwelcome troublemakers, I was finding it impossible to ignore the fact that barriers seem to turn people *on* at least as often as they turn them *off*. . . . I had to admit the obvious truth: My ex-lover's unavailability had been a key ingredient of the overwhelming intensity that had held me in its grip."

In addition to the erotic barrier that abstinence provides, the separation also allows our libido to replenish itself. Studies show that the average husband and wife in America have sex about twice a week. Now that may not sound like it's so bad.

After all, that's 100 times a year, right? But search on and you will discover that the average sexual encounter in marriage lasts only about fourteen minutes at a time! So a grand total of about half an hour a week is dedicated to sexual encounters. That's it. Can you imagine how deprived you'd feel if you got only half an hour of television per week? Or had to walk out of a movie after your allotted quota of half an hour?

During the period of abstention, couples should now begin a period of verbal, rather than physical, exploration. They may feed off the closeness that great sex has provided, without the resentment that bad and uninspired sex provides. They must learn to talk and communicate, rather than rushing to undress each other.

Then, as the twelve days off progress and libidos are not fed, sexual appetites increase. You and your spouse will begin lusting after each other once again. But until the respite period is up, you can't even sleep in the same bed. So the lust increases. And still you can't even touch or hug. This becomes twelve days of orgasmic desire, building every day. Your coworkers blend into obscurity as you only have eyes for each other. Then, the night finally arrives, and fireworks go off in the bedroom. All the little things you remember from the first time you made love—details about your partner's body, the unique sounds he or she makes—become apparent again.

Michael, my sheepherding non-Jewish New Zealand friend whom I met when I was in Auckland (he came to a book signing, with wife, sans sheep), wrote to me: "It was the darnedest thing. We took your advice and decided to go the whole nine yards. We have the kind of double beds where you usually fall into the middle when you're making love. We separated them. And after about a week, I was horny as hell for my wife. But still she wouldn't let me into her bed. After ten days, I was spying on her when she got dressed in the morning and undressed at night. I watched her take showers. I was climbing the wall, mate! After eleven days, even my sheep started looking attractive. And finally, on the twelfth night, the trumpets were playing. Alleluia! Alleluia! A volcano exploded in our home. In the morning all the neighbors saw was a great big hole where the house used to be."

The natural cycle of a woman's body indicates this need for abstention. Wives make love to their husbands for two weeks at a time, and then their period arrives. It's the body's own signal that it is time for a break. Most women feel uncomfortable having sex while they're menstruating. According to *Network,* a family planning magazine, it is often seen as "dirty," "unclean," and, in many developed societies, taboo. Of course, we said earlier that the Bible says none of those things. *Menstruation is not dirty.* Rather, it's the body's natural proclamation that for a period in the month the time for sex has ceased. It's time to create intimacy in other, nonphysical ways. Studies show that many couples refrain from sex during menstruation simply because it does happen to be messier. Clearly, the body is telling us that it needs borders and separations. And the male psyche tells us the same thing. It tells us that when a woman's body is available to her husband at all times, he becomes as excited about her as he is about a newspaper he's already read or a movie he's seen twice over.

The Melding of Fire and Water in Marriage

Marriage is not designed to be passionate at every second of every moment. If it were, we wouldn't ever leave our beds. We'd get nothing done. The successful marriage is indeed where you and your partner are both lovers and best friends. But since one of these roles requires fiery love, and the other a watery love, they cannot coexist, at the same time. Water extinguishes fire.

Hence, you need to have two weeks of being lovers, followed by twelve days of being friends, which also follows the natural cycle of the body and the brain. Marriage needs hills and valleys, and not everything can appear new all the time. But you do have to have two fiery weeks every month or you will begin to bore each other and drift apart. The twelve abstemious days of a month actually strike a very good balance in contrast to the two passionate sexual weeks. They serve as periods when a couple can develop the nonsexual dimension of their relationship, and improve their communication with each other.

But if you go more than two weeks a month without at least a strong breeze of physical engagement, if not an outright earthquake of sexual encounters, you must refer to the other guidance in this book. It should be very difficult to abstain from sex with your spouse for those times, let alone not sharing the same bed. But that is the point. And trust me, the benefits are immensely rewarding.

Yes, it is absolutely possible to induce with your spouse a perpetual state of expectation, of the same kind that keeps adulterous affairs alive and exciting, even though you share the same house and the same bed nightly. If you are Jewish, I strongly recommend that you begin to observe the laws of sexual abstention in their entirety and not only separate, but go to *mikveh* after the twelve-day separation period is over.

The actual laws that govern this period are easy to follow, and many short guides about them have been produced. The best are *Waters of Eden,* by Rabbi Aryeh Kaplan, and *A Hedge of Roses,* by Rabbi Norman Lamm.

If you are not Jewish, I suggest that you institute a period of abstention and separation in your marriage for at least the five days of menstruation and for as many days thereafter as possible, up to a week. I'm aware that most couples will not go so far as to move out of the marital bed. But still, in this period of sexual abstention you must really abstain, and that means resisting any form of sexual release, not just coitus. Allow your sexual "steam" to build up. Don't engage in oral sex, don't masturbate, and don't look at pornographic magazines or films with explicit sexual imagery. Let yourself become an obsessed sexual being, lusting after your spouse with the gusto of a man or a woman incarcerated. Then, on the appointed reunion night, make the earth move.

You will also find that you treat your spouse far more kindly and argue less during this period of pent-up sexual excitement. Closing off all other sexual outlets and allowing your sexuality to build up—all the while knowing that the only person with whom you can release this powerful buildup is your spouse—will lead to a real feeling of dependency. You need your spouse. You think about him or her all the time. You long for that fantastic night of reunion that is just a few days away.

Ralph, a friend who had a lot of petty squabbles with his wife, told me that when he masturbates less he argues with his wife less. That makes perfect sense. Without self-satisfaction as an option, Ralph needs his wife for gratification, not a brief time in the shower. Let's face it. If a single guy wanted to get a woman at a bar to go to bed with him, would he be a gentleman and buy her a drink, or would he pick a fight with her?

It is well known how prisoners released from jail react upon seeing their first woman after years of incarceration. To them, she is an enchanted princess—irrespective of how she compares with other women he has seen. Just the fact that she is female makes her precious.

I have a close Mormon friend who, true to the traditions of the church, did not have sex until his wedding night, which wasn't easy since he married at thirty-three. The wedding was to take place in California, and his student friends at Oxford all joked that the Californian authorities would prohibit him from conducting the wedding there for fear that he and his bride, who was also a virgin, might awaken the San Andreas fault and have the whole state fall into the Pacific.

You, too, can achieve a cataclysmic encounter. The secret is in the separation.

Exercises
THE JEWISH LAWS OF PURITY AND YOUR MARRIAGE

In the final analysis, the most effective way of making your spouse feel and appear new to you is for them to actually *be like new*. A period of sexual and physical separation leads you to rediscover your spouse as a totally new sexual partner. You discover the feel of your partner's skin anew, the smell of your partner's body anew, and his or her sexual response anew. You yearn to be reunited with your spouse, which transforms him or her into a lover and your marriage into an illicit affair. You long to be together in much the same way that two forbidden lovers think always of each other, and pine for the next period of embrace. So sexual abstention for short periods of time every month provides for a period of reunion—a "honeymoon" if you will, every single month.

Here's what you need to do:

1. Abstain from all forms of sexual contact for a period of between five and twelve days per month. Take this seriously. Keep even pecks on the cheek to a minimum. The reward is commensurate with the sacrifice. The more you go cold turkey now, the more you'll get hot stuffing later. (And if you guys abstain from sex during the twelve days, I promise to abstain from bad puns.)

2. During this period, refrain from any other form of sexual outlet or gratification, including and especially masturbation. Guys, that also means get off the Internet porn stuff. No excuses that it came to you through junk e-mail. The delete button is just as easy to use as it is to double-click the mouse button.

3. If possible, sleep in separate beds for this period of time, so that every aspect of your physical love is appreciated when you reunite, from simply holding each other to snuggling up next to each other in bed. If you don't have separate beds, then go to opposite ends of the bed. But remember, no cheating. If you feel you can't trust yourself, ask one of the neighbors to move in during the twelve-day period and stand guard over the two of you with a shotgun during the night. If you feel inhibited allowing the neighbor to join you in bed, then simply erect an electrified fence in the bedroom separating you from your spouse.

4. During the period of abstention, don't dress and undress in front of each other. Go to the bathroom and change. Make your spouse hunger to see your body again. Make your spouse long for a sneak peek. Wives may benefit from a well-placed piece of lingerie left out in the bedroom, as a tempting glimpse of what is to come with reunion. Husbands should not leave their undergarments lying around, unless they *want* their wives to run off with another man.

5. On the last night of the twelve-day separation, wives should go to a *mikveh*, a ritual bath, as a symbol of their renewal and rebirth. The wife dips completely naked in the pool and re-emerges as an erotic being ready for passionate lovemaking with her husband. There are *mikvehs* in every major American city in the United States. Many are like exclusive spas, with whirlpools, saunas, and professional hairdryers. Others are simply the warm, soothing pool and the long hot bath you immerse yourself in for at least an hour before the pool. Either way, approach it as you would a day spa, and commit to your attendance.

6. If you're not Jewish, or the strict religious stipulation of the bath is beyond you, you should nevertheless soak for at least an hour in a bath to heighten your senses and magnify your feminine beauty. If you have the resources, go to a pool and dip totally naked, feeling the warm water against you. If you do not, then transform your own tub into a ritualistic bath, complete with scented candles, smoothing body soaps, and scented bath salts. When you get out, you should radiate a soft glow.

7. When you return home (or exit your steamy, scented tub), dress in your sexiest garments. I've learned from years of counseling couples that although most wives own lingerie, they rarely have occasion to use it. Soon they're donating it to puzzled volunteers at the Salvation Army. This is the perfect night to use your lingerie. Go for it. Put effort into your presentation, and don sexy undergarments. This is your night. Make the most of it.

8. Plan your night of reunion in a special hotel, or at least send the kids to a friend's home. Better yet, go away for the weekend. Just think—every month you will be guaranteed not just another single wedding night, but a few days of the most exciting and passionate sex you can experience.

9. For really intense thrills, keep the honeymoon quality of the *mikveh* night going for a couple of days by refraining from actually climaxing in sex. Use all the erotic energy generated to get you to prolong the things you normally rush through, like kissing, massaging, and touching each other, or even just staring at each other's nakedness. If you have to use a clock the first few times, no problem. Focus on foreplay—touching and massaging—lasting at least two hours before any climaxing follows.

10. The morning after your "reunion" night, try to have a lie-in together (sleep late, stay in bed) for at least an hour or two. Talk to each other about how much you missed each other's bodies and what made the previous night special. And if you're tempted to repeat the previous night's performance as a result of the conversation, then enjoy your encore.

TENTENTENTENTENTENTENTENTENTE
NTENTENTENTENTENTENTENTENTENT
ENTENTENTENTENTENTENTENTENTEN
TENTENTENTE ten TENTENTENTE
NTENTENTENTENTENTENTENTENTENT
ENTENTENTENTENTENTENTENTENTEN
TENTENTENTENTENTENTENTENTENTE

COMMANDMENTS THREE AND FOUR IN ACTION— CREATING
Friction

I am happy now that Charles calls on my bedchamber less frequently than of old. As it is, I now endure but two calls a week and when I hear his steps outside my door I lie down on my bed, close my eyes, open my legs, and think of England.

—LADY ALICE HILLINGDON, FROM HER JOURNAL, 1912

Affairs are loaded with romanticism, morality, mythology, and intense emotions. They're not really about sex, but about pain and fear and the desire to feel alive. They're also about betrayal.

—EMILY BROWN

We are ever striving after what is forbidden, and coveting what is denied us.

—OVID

189

Commandment Three
Adultery is replete with erotic obstacles.

Commandment Four
Adultery thrives on secrecy, modesty, and mystique.

A couple whose wedding ceremony I conducted invited family and close friends to their beautiful bridal suite in the elegant Claridges Hotel in London for drinks after their wedding reception. After about an hour had passed, I started saying in a loud voice, "Boy, is it late, and am I tired! I guess we'd all better be going now." Turning to the other guests, I encouraged our departure. "Okay, here we go. We're all going now. We're getting our coats now. We're all walking out the door." The others finally took the hint. Heck, it was this couple's wedding night, not a frat party. But just as everybody was leaving, the very beautiful bride began to cry: "Oh, please don't go yet. I can't believe the wedding is over." Her new husband tried to comfort her. "What's wrong, darling?" With tears rolling down her cheeks, she said, "I don't want to take off my wedding dress."

Of course, she meant that she had waited her whole life to be a bride and didn't want the occasion to end. But I couldn't help but contrast her statement with the jokes my friends and I used to make in the rabbinical seminary about the weddings of our older colleagues. You see, we didn't have sex before marriage. So there we'd be, singing near the wedding canopy as the bride and bridegroom were escorted by their parents to the *chupah,* and we used to whisper jokes about the bride and groom having to be chained to their seats at the reception in order to stop them from sneaking upstairs to the bridal suite to jump on each other in bed and rip each other's clothes off.

Now, compare that to this young woman who was upset that her friends were *leaving* the bridal suite, and you can see how confused I was. How do you think her husband felt hearing this? You see, this couple had been living together for two years prior to the wedding. They separated just one day prior to their marriage. How new or special could their wedding night possibly have been?

But this response was tame compared to Roger and Elyssa, friends of mine from my time as a student in Australia, who lived together for six years before Elyssa finally pressured Roger enough to agree to get married. On their wedding night, they celebrated by watching all three installments of the *Airplane* movie series. As Elyssa explained it at a dinner party, "We both love to laugh, so we decided to spend our wedding night watching terrific comedies. We had the best night of our lives, laughing for hours in each other's arms." Now Roger and Elyssa may not need any lessons in laughter, but they could sure use some immediate advice from an expert sex counselor. Indeed, studies show that many newly married couples have come to loathe the wedding night because of its heightened sexual expectations, which usually fall far short. Since so many couples have had bucket-loads of premarital sex, the wedding night naturally loses any special sexual relevance for them. It ends up being a burden to newlyweds, who are expected to have memorable sex, but would rather relax or watch TV instead.

Then there was Jake, who was married for seven years. We went out to dinner occasionally, and I provided a listening ear to his talk about his marriage and his outlandish views of relationships: "I don't care what you've written, Shmuley. You're not the sex expert. I am. Your expertise comes from books and hearing people's problems. I experienced it all myself. I've *shtupped* hundreds of women. Hundreds. When I was at Oxford, within three minutes of meeting a woman I would nonchalantly slip into the conversation that I was a Rhodes scholar, and it was all over right there. You could practically see them salivating. It never failed to work. . . . But to actually get them into bed, I had to get out the telltale romantic candle. . . . I had this one candle, which I'd use over and over again. I could use it on ten women before it burned down too low and became a fire hazard. I was set. Once the candle was lit, they would be thinking, 'Wow, this guy's not only a genius Rhodes scholar. He's also a romantic.' I'd put it out in a few minutes because I needed it for the next girl the next night. And women are stupid. If you've got a bit of money, or they think you're going to make some money, they'll do anything. So I would *shtup* them and move on. And each one thought I was in love with them. And now I'm married and I'm like a caged animal. I see these beautiful women every day. And I'm going crazy. I love that part of their body, the small of their back."

At this point a girl walks over to *me* at the restaurant, and asks me if I will sign her book. She glances at Jake, who, in his mid-thirties is an attractive and successful-looking man. Jake leans over and whispers. "Do you see? If I was single, I'd have her in a second. I'd tell her she's so beautiful that I wanted to be with her, and she'd be putty in my hands."

I sign the young woman's book and we return to our conversation. "But why can't you make love to your wife? Why lust after all these other women?"

"That just shows how ignorant you are of women, Shmuley. After a woman has a baby [Jake's wife Samantha had given birth to a girl the year before], they're not interested in sex anymore. When they decide they actually *want* a baby, then sex is amazing. You can do whatever you want to them. You can screw them upside down. They want you to push hard inside them because they want to get pregnant. They love sex. But the second they have the baby, they go completely off sex." I start to protest, but he cut me off. "You wouldn't know, Shmuley, because you're the lucky one who has seven kids," he said. I manage to slip in, "thank God" and he continued: "But all my friends tell me the same thing. Their wives aren't nearly as interested in sex as they are, and they go crazy. Everybody knows that women don't like sex. Once or twice a month is fine with them. But any more and they complain they're too tired."

"Maybe you're the one who is boring and your wife doesn't want to make love to a guy who thinks that foreplay is a type of golf club."

"Not a chance," he protests. "When I was in my twenties I developed a process of seducing a woman into its own art form. No woman could resist my charm. I knew exactly what to say to make their heart stop, and then I'd add a couple of silly things about how beautiful they were to make their underwear drop. But when women have a kid, they become boring moms."

"So why did you get married?" I ask.

"Because I fell in love," Jake admits with a sigh. "But I have to tell you that when I got married, part of me died. That part of me that has this fire for women, this endless lust for women, just died. It's not there any more. I can't act on it, and it's dying."

Are We Bored with Sex?

I've recounted two stories of people—one a woman, the other a man—both of whom felt that getting married was an end rather than a beginning. And, indeed, if an American Demographics study from February 1998 is to be believed and Americans are having sex just once a week, then who can blame them?

One of the great modern fallacies is that we are an over-sexed society. If that is true, it is true only in a visual sense. Seventy percent of the Internet is supposedly used for pornography, and flesh and nubile bodies shoot through our screen on cable TV every hour of every day. A 1999 to 2000 study by the Kaiser Family Foundation reported that two thirds of the programs on television contain sexual content. And it gets worse: The study also found that, during prime time, the proportion rises to three out of every four programs.

If you go to the movies, you cannot escape it; the study found that 89 percent of movies contain sexual subject matter. We see it everywhere, every day. Representative Mike Oxley, of Ohio, primary author of the Children Online Protection Act of 1998—passed overwhelmingly by the House and Senate—announced that over 600,000 Web sites contain sexual material, while a report by the Committee on Government Reform, Special Investigative Division, also found that the popular file-sharing services, such as Napster and Kazaa, are even more insidious. A casual search for "Britney Spears," which could have been initiated by any teenybopper minor, returned over 70 percent pornographic films and material.

The generation that now nears its forties, overindulged in overt sexual images and sexual experimentation before marriage, is under the assumption that nobody ever gets bored with sex. Here, I don't only mean bored with the same sexual partner, I mean bored with sex in general. Ours is such an oversexed society in that we think we can never get enough of it. But this is a far cry from the truth.

In my third year as rabbi at Oxford, a male and female student who had been seriously going out together for over half a year, broke it off abruptly. "We have quite literally screwed the life out of our relationship. We had sex at every possible moment, several times a day. It finally sorta just petered out," one of the partners said.

Less Is More

All around the world, people are getting bored with sex. From magazines to movies, flesh and erotica are out; all the truly great love scenes in movies seem to be a thing of the past. One fine Sunday morning in 1995 I was reading the London *Sunday Times* when I came across a bizarre story about how Britain's porn magazines were dressing their pinups in order to increase sales. The *Sunday Times* reported that *Penthouse* magazine, "the men's magazine that was the first to bare all, is asking its models to put their clothes back on. Skin, it seems, is no longer in.'"

What led to this sudden exercise in modesty? Did the proprietors of these magazines become born-again Christians, as Larry Flynt once famously did? No, it was nothing quite as profound as that. It was simply a business decision. The report went on to say: "The plunging sales of 'girlie' magazines have led to a catharsis in Britain's publishing industry. . . . *Penthouse* once boasted 500,000 readers; now it claims 120,000 a month. . . . The number of naked women is being reduced in favor of serious features. . . ." Ever hear of a porn magazine that boosts its subscribers by putting clothes on their models? Hello? Can anyone tell us what's going on?

It gets worse, though, for Bob Guccione. In April 2002, a front-page feature in the business section of the *New York Times* reported that *Penthouse* is nearly bankrupt and may even be taken over by the banks that have lent it money. (Talk about acquiring new assets!) Guccione tried to stymie the downslide in subscriptions by offering ever more explicit sexual images. Those worked for a time, but subscriptions still continue to fall.

So, what really killed *Penthouse?* To be sure, the accessibility of free Internet porn—as well as the privacy it provides—has hindered magazine sales as much as anything else. Men know they don't have to spend money if nude pix (and movies) can easily be downloaded; better, they don't have to face the embarrassment of bringing the magazine up to the register, as in that famous scene in Woody Allen's film *Bananas.*

Yet, this just proves my point. At one time men were content to look at images of naked women for that quick erotic thrill. They would hold the magazine centerfold in their hands, turn it in all kinds of different directions to maximize the thrill, and move on to the next image. But then they became desensitized to all that exposed flesh and it became boring. To retain their interest, there were only two things that could be done. The first was to show them sexier and more explicit scenes, which could work only for a time until they even became desensitized even to that. Guccione tried that; however, he was unsuccessful in the long run. The second vehicle, the Internet, accomplishes all of this even faster and easier than print. Since a man's sexual attention span can be measured only in nanoseconds, the medium is perfect for him. As soon as he gets bored with the naked woman he's looking at, all he need do is click on the accompanying link for a completely new image. Either way, a magazine has no chance, limited as it is by the number of images.

But imagine that. Modern men have lost their ability to look at a centerfold in a magazine and remain transfixed for even a few minutes. They need a newer and quicker hit to avoid falling asleep.

Here's another example. Remember the days when Madonna was the world's number-one sex symbol? She was so hot that she even did a book called *Sex* (1992), which sold 150,000 copies on the first day, and by week's end, over half a million copies total at $49.95 each. The book came plastic-wrapped so that you couldn't peek at it in the bookstore. You had to buy it.

Shortly afterwards, Madonna did a major motion picture with Willem Dafoe called *Body of Evidence* (1993). The so-called plot is that the character played by Madonna is accused of killing her wealthy lover with too much rough sex. But whatever the movie lacked in substance, Madonna was supposed to make up for with her writhing body. So who would have expected that the film would be the biggest box-office bomb of that year, costing $30 million to make, and grossing only $12.275 million at the box office. The reason? With Madonna's book, we've seen it all already. There's nothing left to discover.

At the outset of the sexual revolution, it was assumed that the more sex poured into a society, and the easier sex became to obtain, the greater the interest would be. Of course, this ran completely contrary to everything we know about every other area of life. It is specifically the scarcity of things that makes them precious. If the streets were lined with diamonds, the stones would be worth no more than granite. Sex, like so many other areas of life, can suffer from overkill. And this is especially true of sex, where the erotic thrills lie in its shadows. Sex thrives when covered behind veils and curtains, which is why a body clad in lace and lingerie will always be more exciting than naked flesh.

Society has become complacent about sex. Its explicitness has caused sex to lose its mystique. A wife catches her husband with another woman and he apologizes, but cannot understand why she is so hurt. "It was just sex. I didn't love her." *Just sex!* And what he means, of course, is that it was something totally casual, like a back rub or a foot massage. In the modern vernacular, sex is now nothing more serious than the harmless (we hope) exchange of bodily fluids.

One of the great challenges of modern-day living is to

re-establish the parameters that separate the casual from the intense. Life needs center points of intensity. All human undertakings must be understood not as casual and arbitrary, but as purposeful and meaningful. Otherwise, they prove pointless. Purpose makes things passionate and imbues them with a flood of intensity.

When you acquire money unearned, or accidentally, such as by winning a lottery, you are never as respectful as you would be if it had come through hard work. If a man and woman truly believed that they were chosen for each other by heaven, and that their marriage was preordained, they would be passionate about making it work. But it's the arbitrary quality of today's relationships that rob them of fire. So many husbands and wives are under the impression that if only they had not stopped at the pizza store that day and *accidentally* met the person they eventually married, they wouldn't have gotten married. Is life really a great big game of chance? And, if so, does that mean that our children are likewise an accident, an unintended byproduct of a chance encounter?

Today, when so many people speak of having accidentally married the "wrong" person, how can they ever be excited about making their marriages special? Lack of purpose sucks the intensity out of our marriages and makes them casual. Our attitude becomes, "If it works out, then great. And if not, then it was an unfortunate mistake. I married the wrong person. Too bad I went to Ziggy's party that night all those years ago."

"Meant to Be" or Meaningless?

Do you remember the days of junior high school when we would end a puppy-love romance with a "sorry, but let's just be friends note" written on a torn sheet of paper?

Well, one Monday morning a man named Arthur did this to his wife of nineteen years when he gave her "a divorce letter." The letter, at least neatly typed, was lawyerly and matter-of-fact: "Dear Edna, I am no longer happy to be married to you. I can no longer deprive myself emotionally or sexually by staying in this relationship. I am very fond of you, but I no longer love you. I plan to move out by Thursday of next week." The letter ended by saying, "Please make sure to change the air conditioning filters every four to six weeks or the dust will destroy the motors."

I called Arthur up and asked, "Are you some kind of loon? What kind of man writes a letter like that to his wife?"

"What did I do wrong?" he protested. "The letter was very polite."

I was taken aback. "Arthur, are you really asking me why it's wrong to inform your wife by way of polite letter that you're divorcing her and she should remember to change the air conditioner filter?"

He got angry. "I married the wrong woman and I'm politely correcting a mistake."

"Well, maybe that silly conclusion that you married the wrong woman can explain the utter heartlessness and lack of passion in your letter. If you screamed at your wife that you want a divorce, even *that* would be better. At least you would *feel* something. But your conviction that you erred in the woman you married manifests itself as a man prepared to leave his marriage with absolutely no emotion." The casualness of it all was breathtaking—and heartbreaking.

Then there was Larry, a super-smart young student who came to Oxford at the tender age of seventeen. A child prodigy, he had been very sheltered by his mother. He came to our L'Chaim Society on Friday nights and started becoming friendly with a German girl named Charlene. They went to movies and student plays together on Saturday nights.

Larry didn't quite comprehend that there was something romantic happening. He thought it was just a friendship until one night, in the middle of a conversation in Larry's room with both of them sitting on the bed, Charlene suddenly stood up, unbuttoned her blouse, took off her bra, and placed the garments neatly on his desk. Larry turned red and fled the room. He didn't come to Friday dinner that week. I had heard from a mutual friend what happened and suspected that Larry was avoiding Charlene. I called him up and asked him if he was embarrassed to see her. In an uncharacteristic display of anger, Larry said to me, "I'm not embarrassed, I'm mad. She . . . she *stole* something from me. I always had this dream that the first time you would do something intimate with a woman it would be incredibly intense. But this was so damned casual. There was no magic, no wonder. She undressed as if I was one of her female roommates."

He felt that he had been cheated; the line that separates the casual from the intense had somehow been blurred that evening. The first truly intense experience he was meant to have had become something commonplace, as if it were nothing special at all.

Modesty Preserves Intimacy

Judaism has long advocated the need for modesty in society: in the way people dress; the way they speak; and even the way they think. While many thought that the purpose of the laws concerning modesty was to minimize the attraction between the sexes, the exact opposite was true. It was to sustain the attraction between the sexes and guarantee erotic thoughts between men and women in marriage. God help married couples who *don't* have erotic and dirty thoughts about each other. Modesty is necessary to enhance sexual excitement and heighten interest. It's the perfect erotic barrier, and is necessary to the vitality of relationships.

Indeed, modesty in Jewish thought is a panacea and not just a way to dress. Everything that is precious in our religion is always hidden away so as to retain an attractiveness and fondness for it. There is an intrinsic relationship in Judaism between holiness and discreetness. The Torah (scroll of the Law) is placed in the Synagogue in a special chamber at the front of the Synagogue, closed off first by a curtain, then by doors, then by the Torah's mantle. When Moses first encounters God at the burning bush (Exodus 3:6), his reaction is to hide his face from the burning bush. Likewise, the prophet Isaiah describes (Isaiah 6:2–3) what angels look like. He says that each of the angels, as they chant "Holy, Holy, Holy is the Lord of Hosts, the whole earth is filled with His glory," has six wings. While two of the wings were used to fly, four of the six wings were used to cover the faces and legs of these angels. Where holiness exists, modesty, discreetness, and attractiveness also exists.

Rabbi Nachum Amsel, in *The Jewish Encyclopedia of Moral and Ethical Issues,* expresses this idea as follows: "When someone possesses something special, such as jewelry, it, too, like the Torah, is hidden away and brought out only for special occasions. If it were worn daily, the jewelry would no longer be considered special. . . . How most people treat their precious jewelry, that is, keeping it hidden except to show off on rare and appropriate occasions, should be expanded into a general attitude about how men and women should treat all their precious possessions, such as their talents, beauty, intelligence, and bodies. The sublime ideas behind modesty, then, demand that we do not publicly flaunt anything that people admire. Like jewels and the Torah, these should be preserved only for special and appropriate occasions." Our bodies are no different.

Judaism does truly admire physical beauty. However, like any another special quality, it should not be shown off with revealing clothes except on special occasions, which Judaism defines as in the bedroom with one's spouse. Sarah, Abraham's wife, remained in the tent when strangers came to visit, despite the fact that she was exceedingly beautiful. Western culture tells husbands to "show off" the beauty of their wives. Yet, because Sarah stayed inside the tent, the Talmud calls the beautiful Sarah modest. This is what Psalms verse 45:14 means by stating that honor is paid to the princess who remains hidden. Of course, in modern times this should not be interpreted as an injunction for women to remain out of public life. I have long been an advocate of women competing and succeeding in nearly all the male professions, with certain undignified exceptions like the longest belch or belly-flop competition. But they should endeavor to do so without compromising their uniquely feminine gifts of mystery and modesty. For instance, women need not make the lame male mistake of having to brag about their achievements. Their accomplishments should speak for themselves.

Learning Modesty from Michael

This is something that I especially learned from my friendship with Michael Jackson: Reducing public exposure increases interest. When we ran our Heal the Kids initiative together—in which we demanded that he appear at many public events to promote the need for nurturing relationships between parents and children—he would always lecture me about how he should never be overexposed. He told me that the secret to his longevity in the public eye and on the charts—aside from his obvious talent—is that, unlike other stars that jump at every opportunity to host an award show or appear at a Hollywood political fundraiser, he is careful about what he accepts. He told me countless times that that is why he does not do interviews—except on the rare occasion every few years.

Now, this is interesting. Any of us who had witnessed Michael's singing (and especially dancing) talent might be of the opinion that it's better to crank out as many albums as possible, and dance on as many television specials as possible before you grow old and your legs and voice become weak. But Michael was insistent that this was everyone else's greatest mistake. I remember once that he and I were watching part of an MTV music special together, all about a young music starlet. The level of access she gave MTV into her life was extraordinary. Michael turned to me and said, "I give her five years and nobody will want to hear from her again." Now, one might argue that Michael takes this to a bit of an extreme. But in a world of overexposure, perhaps the temporary antidote is extreme hiddenness.

In *Hidden Power,* Kati Marton writes of the mystifying hold that Jackie Kennedy held over America for more than forty years: "Jackie's father, 'Black Jack' Bouvier, was a handsome scoundrel who shared tales of his bad behavior with his daughter. . . . She listened carefully to his admonishment never to reveal too much of herself. Preserve the mystery, he instructed her." Marton further adds: "Jackie understood the value of scarcity. She made each public appearance count, carefully stage-managing her looks, saying little, allowing the mystery about herself to grow. She was soon on the covers of more movie magazines than Elizabeth Taylor."

Although I am certainly not the first to make the point, it is also highly likely that, in addition to their extraordinary music, the reason The Beatles have lasted so long has much to do with their breaking up just at the peak of their greatest success. Even as a kid growing up in the 1970s, I remember the public hunger for them to reunite, which paradoxically fueled incredible interest in their music—a phenomenon that continues to this very day.

Modesty and mystery are also necessary to *preserve intimacy,* and not to prevent sin, which is a common misconception. If every part of your body is public, there are no private spaces left with which to share an intimate moment. People shouldn't lock their houses at night to prevent someone from gaining entry. Rather, they should lock their houses to protect the contents of their homes. The emphasis should be on the preservation of that which is precious, not simply on the prevention of that which is sinful.

The same is true of relationships. A person should act and dress modestly not to prevent intrusion from the outside, but to preserve what is on the inside, that is, the precious ability to maintain an intimate relationship. An intimate moment is one in which two individuals invite each other into their private space. Not just a private room, but *a private part of themselves.* If every bit of ourselves has already become public property through lack of modesty, what part of us remains preserved for an intimate moment? Today's lack of emphasis on modesty has meant that our intimate selves have become like a secret told to too many people. It still may be exciting news, and a lot of people may be interested in hearing it—until it gets stale. In no way is it personal or private. Like a film negative that, when exposed to the light, loses its color, sexuality and our bodies lose their allure and suffer diminished intensity after a while. The human body is intended for exploration *within* marriage. It is this exclusivity that makes the body a treasured gift rather than a public playground.

Explicitness Kills Romance

Speaking of The Beatles, do you remember their 1964 song "I Want to Hold Your Hand"? Can you imagine a song today glorifying the simple joy of holding a lover's hand? Today we would expect lyrics more along the lines of, "I want to do you and then move on to an entire football team, all while a WebCam broadcasts the pictures live to the Net, baby!" Virtually none of The Beatles' lyrics could ever make it into rap. They're too tame and way too romantic.

In an earlier generation, there were many expressions of love outside the bedroom. This was the meaning of romance. A couple would hold hands, cuddle, or just walk together in the moonlight. But in today's society, where noninvolved men and women kiss and hug for ten minutes at a time as a form of greeting—and total strangers dance intimately at clubs, becoming one flesh on the dance floor rather than through marriage—what is left to a couple as an expression of affection besides the bedroom? Sex has become one of the only intimate acts left to a man and a woman to express affection, as the other, more subtle exercises have lost their uniqueness. And even sex is rapidly losing its potency as an exclusive expression of love. Husbands and wives now have only about one or two truly erotic zones on each other's bodies that are usually covered and that can still generate excitement when suddenly uncovered. But what a waste of the rest of the body, which possesses equal erotic potential.

While in Amsterdam with my family for a weekend a number of years ago, I decided to put this theory to the test. Was it true that in a place of extreme sexual explicitness, small acts of affection once considered magical, like holding hands, would be phased out? Specifically here, in what is probably the most sexually explicit city in the world (with the possible exception of Bangkok), would people's sense of romance be deadened—killed off by women sitting in neon windows advertising their wares, looking bored and distracted?

On a Saturday afternoon, the Jewish Shabbos, I sat in the window of our hotel room, looking at a busy shopping thoroughfare below. In five hours of gazing, I searched for couples who might be holding hands. Did romantics still exist?

I saw only five—out of 5,000, perhaps. I was hardly surprised. Why would something as simple yet romantic as holding hands maintain any excitement in a city where women put on shows whose content no decent author would describe? (Not that I saw them, but so my friends tell me.) Why waste time on petty romance when you can go straight for the kill and immediately have sex? In Amsterdam, men sit in bars watching men and women perform the most adventurous sex acts for their own edification. So, are they excited about it? No! *They are bored to death.* The proof is that when you ask the men who attend these shows, "How could you?" their response is, "Relax. It was no big deal." They sit and order Dutch beer and roll a couple of leaves made from Colombia's finest—all legal mind you—while watching the show.

I remember seeing an article in *Newsweek* magazine a number of years ago that told the story of a long-running French nudist colony, which was now witnessing a rebellion amongst the offspring of its founders. Many of the founding members of the colony were troubled that their kids were wearing clothes at the beach. (Talk about disappointment!) One of the girls explained why: "If I don't wear a bathing suit at the beach," she said, "the men don't even look at me."

Many of my American friends who visit topless beaches in Europe—which are mostly outlawed in the United States—feel the same way. For the first few days their attention is caught by every mammary gland that passes. But after a few days they're skipping stones and throwing rocks at trees trying to knock down coconuts. Anything is more interesting than the glut of bare bodies. And the undeniable proof to this truth is the fact that the two most common activities on a beach are falling asleep and reading a book. So how sexy can all these beaches be? Few men would argue with the fact that seeing a person partially hidden from view is far more exciting than seeing that person openly displayed. This theory is behind the immense success of companies like Victoria's Secret, whose provocative window displays are as much for the benefit of the men as they are for the women who shop in their stores.

A healthy society is one that is completely alert sexually, and recognizes that if women *and men* don't dress modestly, they will become desensitized—and less attractive—to one another. If men and women, whilst socializing and otherwise engaging with the outside world, put up a curtain that separates their inner selves from everyone else, they will be able, at other times, to lift that curtain to allow someone else to enter their private space for intimate purposes.

Don't Let Your Sexual Steam Leak Out

In *Doesn't Anyone Blush Anymore?* Rabbi Manis Friedman tells the "steamboat" story. Soon after the steamboat was invented, a captain brought his boat downriver and stopped at a small village in Europe to show it off. He was fascinated by his new toy, and tried repeatedly to impress the simple peasants with the loud boom of his foghorn. Over and over again, the captain stoked the engines, got up a big head of steam and sounded the horn. But when the time came to show how the boat ran, it wouldn't budge. He had used up all his steam on the foghorn.

The metaphor here translates as such: If we waste our sexual energy as we go through life and let it leak out, we are left without any when we actually need it. If we are sexual when it doesn't count, we won't have any steam left when it does. If we dress in an explicit and provocative way when we are not in a sexual situation, then our bodies may not pose the same erotic attraction necessary later on, when we actually desire to create a sexual situation.

Amazingly, people who have had adulterous affairs understand this a lot better than faithfully married couples. A mistress is careful to show her body only in unique situations and when she looks her very best. She's conscious that her body is the principal reason for the affair, so she doesn't trifle with the merchandise. She makes her body into a work of art, always making sure that her lover earns the right to see it and sees it under the most erotic of circumstances.

And then there's the issue of the marital bedroom. Some couples give their guests a tour of their home that includes a glimpse into the bedrooms. The bedroom is no big deal. It's just another room in the house, like the dining room or the living room. Anyone can come in. The kids can come in at night to sleep there as a matter of routine. Friends get to tour the closets. Heck, it's no big deal.

But can you imagine a man and a woman who are having an affair pointing out to their friends the room where they have sex? "Yeah, come on in, Bob. Be careful not to trip on the whips." Come on. They keep their love chamber and everything inside it a secret. The whole thing is cloaked in mystery, and that's what makes it so exciting. In Jewish thought, a couple's bedroom is a holy place where no one but the couple ought to trample.

Overexposure Dulls Passion

Two months after I arrived at Oxford, a young Jewish couple asked me to officiate their summer wedding at St. John's College. This was to be the very first wedding I had performed. I had no clue what I was doing, but what the heck, I thought. How hard could a wedding be? And if I messed up, the worst-case scenario would be that their children would be born bastards. Nothing more serious than that. I told them no problem, so long as we had six classes together in which they would discover the rudiments of Jewish living. We studied kosher food, the Jewish festivals, the Sabbath, and the synagogue service.

When it came to the Jewish sexual laws, I told them that Jewish law maintains that husband and wife dress and act modestly with each other. If a wife is not preparing for a sexual or intimate encounter, she should be wearing a night-gown—not parading around the bedroom nude. The bride-groom hit the roof. "I don't mind you telling us what we should eat and when we shouldn't work. But are you seriously advocating that we should be inhibited around each other after we marry?"

"Look," I replied, "you can disregard this advice. But if you do, you face the nightmare scenario." (I then had an organ play the "Dead Man's Waltz," perfectly cued, in the back-ground for effect.)

The bride got nervous at hearing this and asked, "Uh, Rabbi, what exactly is the nightmare scenario." "The night-mare scenario," I continued, "is when, after you marry, your husband is in bed watching TV, you come in and undress for bed, and he continues to watch television." She shuddered.

This nightmare scenario plays itself out in bedrooms across America every single night. Carla Rice, a leading researcher and educator in "body image" issues, has found that 80 to 90 percent of adult women are dissatisfied with their bodies. Many even undress in the bathroom, because they feel they're not beautiful. Another study, published by the Society for the Scientific Study of Sexuality in its *Journal of Sex Research,* shows that over a third of women in rela-tionships experience self-consciousness over their body image during sexual intercourse. And what is the cause of this shame? Why, husbands who never impulsively look at their bodies. If he's not looking, it must be because there isn't much worth looking at, right?

Judaism insists that husbands and wives avoid parading around each other naked—not for any puritanical reasons, but so that they don't become bored with each other. Overexposure leads to dullness. Modesty, on the other hand, leads to newness, discovery, and the ability to be excited about the subject. Men and women who are in affairs retain a strong interest in each other's bodies because it is a prize they don't normally get to see or enjoy.

One of the great secrets of adultery is that two lovers never grow bored with each other, since they are never overexposed to each other. They don't live together or share the same bedroom and they undress in front of each other only when they wish to have sex. Thus, they always cherish each other's bodies. Modesty, therefore, is one of the principal avenues by which we can turn our marriages into illicit affairs. In marriage it should be no different, with husbands and wives choosing to undress only with the intention of creating moments of passion and intimacy.

A Moment of Darkness

There is also a way of making love that heightens sensation and secrecy. That is, occasionally making love in the dark.

We can all identify with nutritional deficiency. There are impoverished countries like Sudan, whose inhabitants, our human brothers and sisters, suffer material and nutritional deficiency. We see heartbreaking pictures on television of people in Third World countries suffering from severe lack of food, drinking water, and clothing—things that we consider basic. Westerners are assured, by these devastating images, that we lack for nothing. We are surrounded with material comforts, and feel nothing essential is missing from our lives.

In truth, however, while we thank God that we do not suffer nutritional deprivation, we do suffer from *sensual deprivation*. We promote the sense of sight to the exclusion of all others. We are poorer as a result.

This is the age of television and the spotlight. However, the images on our television screens are very limited and restrict us to one specific locus. Gone are the days in which a woman's natural aroma (as opposed to artificial perfume-induced scent) could drive her husband wild. God gave men and women five senses by which they can enjoy each other, five sticking points that join two strangers together as one flesh. The providers of phone sex alone seem to understand the erotic nature of the human voice, and it is something that married men and women today scarcely appreciate.

The Ancient Talmudic Rabbis Say, "Make Love in the Dark"

In the same way that the body has material needs, it has sensual needs. Hugging, lovemaking, and sensual stimulation are not a luxury, but a *necessity* of the body. I believe that the modern age is causing our bodies' terminal, sensual deprivation. Our bodies may be healthy, but they are hardly alive, becoming more and more like unfeeling stones.

Instead of feeling closer after lovemaking, most couples experience a sensual disconnect. They've made love, but when it's over they don't stick. This is because they are only firing on one cylinder; they are making love only with their eyes. Today we promote the sense of sight to the virtual exclusion of our other senses. Lovemaking has consequently become much more of a visually passive, rather than an experientially sensual, endeavor. This is the age of the Internet, magazines, and television. A man or woman's looks determine a person's attractiveness in its entirety. Gone are the days of simple appreciation, say, for the erotic quality of sound and the human voice, or the uniqueness of an individual's scent. Even the sense of touch no longer sends us to the moon and back. The proof is the number-one complaint from wives—that their husbands have no clue as to how to make love to them. They have all become air-traffic controllers in bed, having to give their husband directions. "Turn right, turn left, descend, descend." The intuition men once had has been lost. Hence, he touches her without *feeling* her. No inner vibration is communicated. They make love while remaining apart.

Another tragic consequence of the promotion of looks is that we are more inhibited than ever before. We all feel deficient in our appearance, and thus we undertake every artificial enhancement to try to look better. Deep insecurity has become commonplace in most relationships as women feel they have to lose a few more pounds and men feel that they have to glue hair to their balding scalps in order to remain lovable.

That's why married couples have to start making love more often in the dark rather than with mirrors on the wall and all the lights blazing. All couples should "observe a moment of darkness." Immersing ourselves in a moment of darkness, or shutting out the sense of sight and the vast "noise" of light, allows all the other senses to be fed.

Overexposure

Desmond Morris, the famous social anthropologist and author of *Manwatching,* observed that almost all fast-food restaurants use bright lighting. This is because customers, feeling vulnerable and exposed while eating in this light, will finish their meals and leave sooner, clearing the way for another diner. By contrast, expensive restaurants that make their money not by volume but by customers staying a long time and purchasing several expensive courses are dimly lit, often by candlelight. This way the people feel comfortable and are likely to settle in for a long, drawn-out meal.

We have way too much light in our relationships. Light shows people's flaws so that they feel exposed and vulnerable. Notice that darkness is something that we experience in three dimensions. Darkness is something palpable. In complete darkness, you actually *feel* the darkness. This is because it heightens the senses and brings all those things it conceals to life.

When couples make love in the dark, they can surprise each other by touching each other in places that are least expected and all the more exciting to each other. That's half the excitement of sex—lying back and being pleasured by your spouse, never knowing which area he or she is going to tackle next. The anticipation and element of surprise greatly heightens the erotic mood. Hence, darkness is the perfect place to entertain the fantasy in a relationship. It invites the mind—our principal sexual organ—as a participant in sex.

Making Love in the Dark: Step by Step

The best way to reinvigorate a marriage is to have at least ten minutes of complete darkness every night. In the same way that countries commemorate the loss of military heroes with a moment of silence, couples around the world should institute a universal moment of darkness, every night in the bedroom, when they surprise each other by trying something completely new in bed, which will leave them gasping for breath and crying out for more.

Each and every light in the bedroom should be extinguished. Revel in the sense of delight that touch, sound, even rates of breathing bring.

Be strong. Be weaned off the light.

Secret Exercises I
PRACTICE MODESTY TO INSTILL PASSION

Alter your perception of each other and give your marriage an aura of secrecy by doing the following:

1. WIVES: Do not let your husbands see your naked bodies at all times. Don't parade around the bedroom nude; do not wander the room completely naked looking for a pair of stockings as if your body was simply functional and commonplace. Even if it takes a bit more effort to cover, do it: Grab a robe, slip on pants and a T-shirt—the reward will be worth the effort.

2. Practice not allowing each other to see your naked bodies for the twelve days of separation that we discussed earlier. Undress seductively, but in such a manner that your spouse can't see the actual "goods." Change your clothing as if you were changing at the beach, with a towel around you, and the like. Let your spouse hunger for your nakedness. Don't worry about your spouse thinking you're a prude. Your spouse may tease you about suddenly becoming a nun or monk, but remember, the sexiest erotic jokes are all about nuns.

3. Always show your body in the best possible light. This means two things. Try to always maintain your attractiveness to your spouse by exercising and maintaining high standards of hygiene. Always try to look fresh and alive. Getting a good night of sleep can do wonders for your complexion.

4. Bring secrecy into your relationship. Do sexual things together in public that don't compromise modesty but do enhance passion. In a restaurant, touch each other under the table. On an airplane together, put the blanket between you and stroke each other's magic spots under the blanket. At the movie theater where it's dark, you can really go to town. Become experts at pleasuring each other secretly, just like two participants in an affair would do. Learn how to fondle each other in public with your heads turned in opposite directions so that no one would ever know what you're doing. Practice receiving pleasure without giving it away with your facial expressions.

5. Make love in the dark, where sounds and sensations are heightened when they're out of the glare of the light.

Secret Exercises II
MAKE YOUR WIFE INTO A SECRET WEBCAM GIRL

1. Make your wife into a secret WebCam girl. Spy on your wife as something secret, mysterious, and modest. First, go to a Web site and order a Web-controlled secret video camera:

- *www.panasonic.com/consumerelectronics/gate/ cameras.asp* (KX-HCM10: $499.95)
- *www.stardot-tech.com/netcam/?source=overture* (Stardot Netcam: $499)
- *www.securityideas.com/ax21netcam1.html* (Axis 2120: $985)
- *www.pelikancam.com/cgi-bin/pelikancam/wbe.htm* (Webeye E104: $1,150)

Preferably, get two cameras or even three, if you can afford them.

2. Sit your wife down and teasingly and playfully tell her that you're going to make her into your secret WebCam girl. Say something like, "Honey, I got these online cameras and now everything you do is going to be impregnated with erotic overtones. I'm installing them all over the bedroom and your dressing room. You're not going to know where they are and I'm not going to tell you. When you put on your bra in the morning, I'll be able to see it even if I'm at work. If you get horny during the day and decide to stimulate yourself in front of the full-length mirror, I'll be watching. If you take a sensual bath at night and run the warm water over your silky legs, that's right, I'll have access to it from any computer in the world on my own special Web site that I'm building."

At this point your wife may call the men in the white suits and have you locked up in a rubber room with a rubber jacket. Don't take any notice. This is *her* version of an outlandish sex game. She's responding in kind. Don't be disheartened. But seriously, she may at first resist the idea. Explain to her lovingly that she has no choice in the matter. Say, "There's no way you're going to stop me. You're right that I'm crazy. I'm crazy about your body and I need to see it, especially in the moments when you think no one is looking. I know how badly you need to touch yourself and dress that gorgeous body in the sexiest clothes. But your body is mine and I'm going to see it." Hopefully, with these loving words, she will tear up the committal papers and have you released from your rubber room. Now that you're free, it's time to get to work.

3. When your wife is out, install the cameras in your bedroom and bathroom. Install the software in a way that you can get online on your secret Web site and watch your wife from any location around the world, especially when you're on a business trip and far away from home.

4. Your wife is now your WebCam girl. Spy on her as she gets dressed in the morning and as she gets ready to go to bed at night. You can even call her and have phone sex with her from your hotel room when you travel, and watch her actions as the two of you have an erotic conversation. At the end of each day, tease her about the things you saw her doing. You'll discover that your wife can blush, just like a virginal young woman who is experiencing sexual thoughts for the first time.

5. As you help your wife get over her initial inhibition about the cameras, especially by complimenting her on how gorgeous her body is and how you can't take your eyes off her ("I can't get any work done anymore. I'm staring at my WebCam girl the whole day."), encourage her to put on a daily show for you. Let her use her imagination about what she would do if the workmen outside her bedroom could watch her get dressed and undressed every day, or take a shower.

6. Tell your wife that you gave the URL to a stranger, telling him that this is a great Web site of some sexy, voyeuristic woman who wants guys to see she's hot. Tell her that you arranged for the face to always be blocked out, so no one can identify her, but not the body. See how this affects her actions. Of course, *don't really do it*. You're not that insane, at least I *hope not*. And if she gets upset, tell her the truth, that this is all an erotic game to excite the two of you.

7. Leave the cameras up for as long as your wife feels comfortable with them, or as long as you retain interest. When it's over, move on to the next erotic game and sell them to the neighbors who sadly are on the verge of divorce.

ELEVENELEVENELEVENELEVENELE
VENELEVENELEVENELEVENELEVEN
ELEVENELEVENELEVENELEVENELE
VENELEVENE eleven EVENELEVEN
ELEVENELEVENELEVENELEVENELE
VENELEVENELEVENELEVENELEVEN
ELEVENELEVENELEVENELEVENELE

COMMANDMENT FIVE IN ACTION—
ATTRACTION TO
Strangers

Nobody bothered to tell you what marriage was really about. . . . You expected not to desire any other men after marriage. . . . Then the desires came and you were thrown into a panic of self-hatred. . . . How could you do that to your husband? Did anyone ever tell you that maybe it had nothing to do with your husband?

—ISADORA IN ERICA JONG'S *FEAR OF FLYING*

CHRYSIS: You would not have thought [that he loves me] in that insane fury that overcomes him when I but walk in the shadow of another man.

AMPELIS: He must be crazy about you. If he weren't, he wouldn't have become excited when he saw you with another lover.

—LUCIAN, *DIALOGUES OF THE COURTESANS*

He knew that between him and her there could be no secrets, and therefore he had decided it was his duty; but he did not realize the effect the confession might have on her. . . . On entering her room he saw in her sweet, pitiful, tear-stained face the irremediable sorrow he had caused. . . . She said, "Take them, take these dreadful books away!"

—*ANNA KARENINA* BY LEO TOLSTOY;
LEVIN SHOWING HIS SECRET DIARIES TO KITTY, HIS FIANCÉE

217

Commandment Five
Adultery thrives on irreconcilable
tension and being off balance.

One of the vagaries of being human, or so it seems, is that we learn to appreciate things only once they are lost or about to be lost. Otherwise, we take them for granted. As something starts slipping out of our hands, we suddenly recall its preciousness. It's amazing how, sometimes only when husbands and wives experience separation in marriage and yearn to be reunited, do they remember how dear they are to each other.

In the wake of the tragic events of September 11, 2001, I paid attention to the now-famous conversations made by husbands and wives, who knew they were doomed to die, and their spouses back at home. Men and women of all different persuasions, trapped in the upper floors of the Twin Towers, called their loving partners to say chilling goodbyes. The amazing thing about all of this is how, in virtually every case, the words were nearly identical.

- Stuart T. Meltzer, thirty-two, who had begun his job at the World Trade Center only a month before, called his wife from the 105th floor of the first building shortly after it was hit. He said to her: "Honey something terrible is happening. I don't think I am going to make it. I love you. Take care of the children." (*The Boston Herald,* Sept. 13, 2001)
- Kenneth Van Auken worked on the 102nd floor of the World Trade Center, and here were his last words to his wife: "I love you. I'm in the World Trade Center. And the building was hit by something. I don't know if I'm going to get out. But I love you very much. I hope I'll see you later. Bye." (*Larry King Live,* Sept. 12, 2001)

- Melissa Harrington Hughes was in New York attending a conference and was staying at the Marriott Hotel on the 101st floor of the north tower. When the plane hit several floors below, she left an answering machine message for her husband in San Francisco, California: "Sean, it's me. I just wanted to let you know I love you and I'm stuck in this building in New York. A plane hit the building or a bomb went off, we don't know, but there's lots of smoke and I just wanted you to know that I love you always." (BBC News, Sept. 13, 2001)

And from the doomed planes . . .

- Brian Sweeney, thirty-eight, was a passenger on Flight 175 that crashed into the south tower. He left a message for his wife, Julie, on their answering machine: "Hey Jules, it's Brian, I'm on a plane and it's hijacked and it doesn't look good. I just wanted to let you know that I love you and I hope to see you again. If I don't, please have fun in life and live your life the best you can. Know that I love you and no matter what, I'll see you again." (*The Boston Herald,* Sept. 13, 2001)
- Businessman Thomas Burnett, of San Ramon, California, called his wife Deena from United Flight 93. He told her, "I know we're all going to die; there's three of us who are going to do something about it. I love you, honey." (Associated Press, Sept. 13, 2001)

When you think about it, this is incredible. Since more than half of all American couples divorce and/or are unhappy with their marriages, surely there would be a couple of people who would have called and said, "I'm trapped on the eighty-sixth floor and there's no way out. I'm calling to tell you before I die how I'll never forgive you for cheating on me in our fourth year of marriage." Or, "These are the last moments of my life and I want you to know that I live them out in misery because you have made me so unhappy for so many years."

How is it that every victim, in his or her last moments in

this life, remembered only the happier times? Of course, it's because the good times are much more powerful than the bad. Even the tiniest spot of light has the power to dispel much darkness. The only thing these husbands and wives remembered in their last moments of life were the loving moments they shared together.

That's why, paradoxically enough, every marriage has to have a slight but recognizable element of possible loss. This is an important and profound insight too often overlooked by misguided marital experts who argue, unconvincingly, that trust and communication are the most important ingredients in a marriage. It turns out that the opposite is true. The specter of possible loss must loom large if we are never to fall into the soul-destroying pit of complacency and taking each other for granted. The same is true of war and death. The most common thing an American soldier says as he's dying in the battlefield is, "Tell my wife I love her." Of course, a lot of these same soldiers, in Vietnam, were running around with prostitutes in Hong Kong and Bangkok just a few days before. But in that quintessential moment of loss, all they wanted was their wives.

As I've stated in the first chapter of this book, too much trust in a marriage will destroy a marriage because the participants no longer have to work on pursuing each other. They can just take each for granted. Passion thrives between two people for whom there exists an element of danger—even potential tragedy, like the possibility of one leaving the other for another man or woman.

In his classic *Principles of Behavior Modification* (1969), Professor Albert Bandura elucidates the concept of "intermittent reinforcement" in relationships. We all know what "positive reinforcement" is in relationships; it's where good behavior is rewarded with good results. You do something in a marriage, like establish trust, that later leads to greater intimacy and love. So you keep on building trust. Your action has had a positive impact, thereby reinforcing itself.

But there are ways where *intermittent* reinforcement can be even more powerful, such as when one's actions within a relationship are only rewarded *sometimes*. The rewards are not guaranteed, they are only occasional, thus snuffing out the possibility of a routine setting in, and inviting the element of surprise. When things are only good in a relationship, it can lead, paradoxically, to routine and boredom. Conversely, if things are consistently awful, there is no compelling reason to remain in that relationship. The idea of intermittent rewards, therefore, stimulates a greater investment on our part into the relationship because it holds out the possibility of something marvelous being just around the corner. We are held in constant suspense. We get captivated, even addicted, to the thrill that is just outside our reach and we spend our energies continuing to chase it.

Adultery, as opposed to marriage, seems to possess this component. The rewards in adultery are erratic and unpredictable. A wife may be sitting at home preparing for a night of the most passionate sex at the apartment of her lover. Just as she is about to leave, her own husband comes home and announces he's going to be watching the ball game at home because his buddy Jason's big screen TV is broken.

On other occasions, just when the wife settles down to watch some mind-numbing TV, her husband's flight attendant mistress calls him and says, "I have a four-hour layover here in town. Quick, come to the Marriott by the airport and we can have a few hours of backbreaking sex." It's the unpredictability of the rewards that lead the addiction to the affair because the lovers never know what's going to be just around the corner. The element of surprise is central to the affairs, thereby heightening erotic longing and expectation.

The ancient rabbis of the Talmud understood this insightful lesson and commanded humans to learn to lead every day of their lives as if it were their last. If we could not lose everything at a moment's notice, how else would we learn to appreciate what we have? Married couples take each other for granted because *they can afford to do so,* reconciled as they are to the eternity of the relationship, unencumbered by any outside threat. When there is nothing but trust in a marriage, it means that you can treat your wife with marked indifference, and still have no fear that she'll get fed up with your neglect. She's your wife. She's not going anywhere. End of story.

Real trust in a marriage is something different altogether. *It's where you trust the principles of love, rather than the commitments of your relationship.* It's where you have confidence in the fact that if you treat your spouse like a desirable, sexy creature, then you will fulfill emotional and erotic needs and she will remain committed. Real trust in marriage is not about trusting your wife's *heart,* but rather her *nature.* Her heart is a burning fire, looking for love and sexual bliss wherever she can find it. Her feminine nature dictates—as nearly all studies have shown—that a woman who has great sex with her husband and is the object of his romantic affection will hardly ever cheat. But if you ignore her and show greater interest in who is playing quarterback for the Minnesota Vikings than in her, she might just end up in someone else's arms, rather than yours.

Amazingly, one of the greatest hopes for reinvigorating marriage with newness and freshness comes from the very side of human nature that is directly responsible for adultery: our attraction—even after marriage—to other men and women. Is it wrong, then, for a husband or wife to be attracted to other people? To an extent, the question is irrelevant. It is simply a fact that even while we are fully and utterly in love with and devoted to our spouse, this does still not preclude us from noticing other men and women, and at times harboring an irresistible attraction to them.

Loyalty of the Mind

Does it betray a lack of love for one's spouse if one feels attracted to other people, if he or she resists acting upon such interest? I am not asking whether it is reasonable for one to notice that other people are attractive. Rather, is it acceptable to allow oneself to be attracted to other men or women besides one's spouse? Is it excusable if one's flesh heats up as a result of pondering the sexuality of someone outside the marriage? Is it acceptable to want to commit adultery, so long as one never actually does it? Can you lust after strangers and still be devoted to your spouse?

One of the most frequent complaints that women voice is that when their husbands take them out for dinner, they're focused on every pair of legs that passes by, rather than on them, in what bestselling author and talk-show host Dennis Prager calls "the male radar-tower syndrome." The average male instinctively homes in on every female who ambles by. It's true: A man may enjoy a wonderful relationship with his wife, but this doesn't mean that he is not attracted to other women—sometimes strongly so—even while he is in the company of the woman he loves.

Excessive behavior of this nature is, of course, unacceptable, and wives justifiably find it insulting. I strongly maintain that men must do their utmost to transcend, not their natural *attraction* to women, but their compulsion to ogle and want to connect—visually or otherwise—with other women, and focus their sexual interest on their wives.

If anything, you (male reader) must let your natural attraction to women lead to greater passion about your own wife. *Always notice when other men are attracted to her and ogle her.* Stare at her and the responses she elicits, rather than at the waitress or the barmaid.

Yet our actual attraction to others is an undeniable phenomenon, and warrants closer scrutiny. It seems almost unfair that although we can be so totally in love with our spouse, we are still so aware of the sexual appeal of others. Why is this, and how can it be used to our advantage in marriage?

The Tension Between Good and Evil

Those people who endeavor to lead meritorious lives will notice that even if they have overcome the desire to perpetrate a dishonorable, unrighteous, or dishonest act, it becomes only marginally easier to choose good the next time round. It takes nearly the same amount of effort to choose good on each and every occasion. Take giving to charity, for example. No matter how much you give, it's always a challenge to part with money that you have worked so hard to earn, although the resulting pleasure is usually equal to the sacrifice.

To be sure, the great medieval Jewish thinker Maimonides maintained that humans have two natures: the first inborn; the second acquired through repetitive action and habit. The more frequently you do something good—even amidst fierce inner resistance—the easier it becomes to repeat the act until it becomes ingrained in your nature. And yet the struggle will always remain. In other words, you can never actually *become* a good person. You may be able to behave as a good person, but you can never rid yourself permanently of your selfish nature. Doing the right things requires active choice on every occasion. It never becomes automatic. Being good involves being constantly engaged *in the act of becoming good*. It is a continuous process.

Another great rabbi and mystic, Shneur Zalman of Liadi, said that while there are some saintly people who seem to be born with a higher propensity for good, they are extremely rare. The rest of us normal "battlers" have to work on being good every day of our lives.

But this seems highly unfair. Why can't we make one choice at the age of twelve or thirteen to lead a good life, and remain that way for the rest of our lives? Why must these choices be made continually? Why did God make it all so difficult?

The *Zohar*, the Bible of Jewish mysticism, provides the answer: God's desire was for goodness to be an active part of our life, not just a one-time decision we made in our adolescent years. Judaism does not believe in man making one choice of good over evil, which lasts forever. What God desires is not *righteousness*, but *struggle*. He wants us to *wrestle* to do the right thing: to engage in a daily fight to choose good over evil; charity over selfishness; compassion over judgmentalism; love over hate; and fidelity over adultery. God and goodness prove far more glorious if good is chosen repeatedly rather than just once. God wants us to be engaged in the act of *choosing* goodness. He wants it to be a pivotal part of our lives. Choosing goodness must be a *daily* activity, not something confined to our past.

Getting Married Every Day of Our Lives

In a similar vein we may say that the reason God created us in such a way that we feel attracted to other men and women—notwithstanding our love and loyalty to our spouses—is so that we have the opportunity to express the most sublime level of love: that which comes about through *constant choice.* Having to actively choose our spouse from a never-ending pool of candidates makes our commitment fresh and passionate.

In a best-case scenario, attraction to others while being married provides the best of all possible worlds. We get to be committed to our spouse without any plans of betrayal. But we also get to have all the benefits of being like two kids dating who have not yet made a serious commitment. The person we're dating has plenty of other suitors interested, so we better make the effort to win over each other's hearts. Couples should never have to rely on a single statement of fidelity under the wedding canopy or at the altar. Rather, our commitment is dynamic, constantly being reinforced and strengthened. The strong marriage is not built on complacency, but rather on the statement that "I love you and choose you ceaselessly. Not just once, long ago, but every single day."

A wife might consider it a great compliment if her husband said to her, "You should know that I am not at all attracted to other women; I don't even notice them, only you. Not because you're beautiful or virtuous, but simply because for me there is only *one* woman in the world. You." But far more flattering would be the proclamation, "There are many very beautiful, attractive women whom I encounter daily. I see them on the subway, I pass them by on the streets. They're all appealing and desirable. But none of them could hold a candle to you. I choose you because you are special in this world and the most beautiful woman I have ever met." A wife with a husband who possesses this attitude gets to win a daily beauty contest.

When a woman remains steadfastly loyal and in love with her husband, despite finding other men attractive, he can really feel special. He is not simply *alone,* but he is *unique,* in a class of his own. He understands that his life with his wife is continually renewed with ever-present vigor. She loves and chooses him *constantly.* Choosing one's spouse constantly expresses the depth and intensity of the relationship. The most sublime way of telling someone, "I love you" is "I have *chosen* to make you mine, and I go on choosing you daily. I am never complacent about my love for you and my need to *do* something about it."

If a husband and wife, separated by a business trip, were to find no necessity to struggle to remain faithful in heart, mind, and deed to each other, what would this say about their marriage? Of course, it would mean that their marriage is very secure, but not necessarily passionate or alive. They got married long ago and now find no need to invoke the memory of each other while away, since they are never tempted by anyone else. It's another way of saying that their libidos are dead.

The husband or wife who naturally feels an attraction to a business associate must have recourse to the loving memories of a loyal spouse waiting at home in order to remain faithful. A husband or wife must take his or her spouse and marriage everywhere he or she goes. This requires no small effort, but the rewards are great: The result is a marriage of the highest quality, in which one's spouse is continually affirmed as being chosen, rather than merely being established once and for all as "the wife" or "the husband" and taken for granted from that point onwards. This is a beautiful insight into relationships that one may cull from Jewish religious thought.

Once a man came to see me and told me he was a sex

addict. "Whenever I travel on business, I end up with a hooker or some woman I pick up from the bar. I want to be better. I love my wife and I want to start being faithful. But I'm an addict. Can you help me?"

"When you travel on business, does your wife sometimes accompany you?" I asked him.

"Yes," he said.

"Well, when your wife is there in the hotel room with you, do you often tell her, 'Just one second honey. I'm calling a hooker and I'll be having sex with her in the twin bed over there. And as soon as it's over, we'll go out to dinner, okay? In the meantime, you can watch TV or something.' Do you ever do that?"

"Do you think I'm insane?" he asked me. "I may be a sex addict, but I'm not a lunatic."

"My God it's a miracle," I called out. "You're cured. You're saved. When your wife is with you, you are cured of your addiction to other women. Now, just understand, that you and your wife are one flesh. Wherever you go she is with you, even when she's not with you. Capice? Understand? Wherever you travel you should be thinking about the feel of her silky skin, the aroma of her beautiful hair, the sound of her loving voice as she moans when you touch her. If you do that, you'll be cured of your addiction because your wife will always be there."

Marriages thrive when couples notice who is attracted to their respective spouses. The need to win them anew brings the thrill of the chase back into marriage. Husbands should notice how, when they double-date with friends, the guy on the other side of the table is attracted to their wives. If she bends over to pick up a fork, he will usually give a little glance to notice her form even better. If he sees her from the side, he may be looking at her bra strap which suddenly becomes visible. If she's walking in the cold, your friend may notice how your wife's breasts are suddenly showing through her clothes. The key is, he's always looking at her. To him, she's new and unconquered, and therefore erotically exciting.

Learn to renew your interest in your wife through the eyes of strangers, rather than being dependent on strangers yourself in order to feel sexually interested. One husband, who has been happily married for fifteen years, agrees: "In fact, I find myself turned on even more when making love to a woman who I know is sought after by others."

Exercises
HOW POTENTIAL LOSS CAN HELP US APPRECIATE OUR SPOUSES

1. Close your eyes and imagine your own death. It may be painful, but let's face it, we all think about this on occasion. But this time, think about it in great detail: Who would be most affected by your demise? Can you see your own funeral? Who looks the saddest? Whose face is devastated by emotional trauma? That's right, it's your spouse. Now picture that face perfectly as he or she absorbs the full blow of your eternal absence. Can you see the extent of their pain? Let it hurt you to see how much your spouse loves you and is going to miss you. Not only will this increase your appreciation of your spouse, it ensures you will never take it for granted. In many counseling sessions where I have asked men and women to do this, husbands and wives who were fighting one moment earlier were suddenly in floods of tears.

2. Now, take this "visual death" experience further. Imagine your spouse slowly recovering, over a period of months subsequent to your death. If you are a husband, imagine your wife slowly beginning to date again. (Wives, envision a similar scenario with your husbands.) At first it's really hard. She misses the only man she ever really loved. But life goes on and her friends and family, trying to help her rebuild her life, fix her up on a blind date. Maybe they even set her up with your former best friend who is now single. Imagine that. At first she is very quiet on the date— shy and introspective. Later, on subsequent dates, she begins to open up. She is beginning to enjoy male company again. She feels comfortable with the big strong man sitting across from her who listens intently to everything she says, as she pours her heart out over her grief at your sudden loss. At the end of the date, he takes her home in his car. Before she gets out of the car he tries to kiss her. She instinctively pulls back. "I'm not ready yet," she says. "I still feel like I'd be betraying my husband."

A few months pass by—remember, you are still in your fantasy and time moves fast—and she is now laughing with him at picnics in the park. Occasionally, she cries in his arms, which he welcomes because it gives him an opportunity to feel her firm and warm body without any of her usual resistance. They stroll hand in hand on the lakeside. He is slowly moving in for the kill. All these months of comfort have made him crazy with lust for your wife.

One night, he picks up your wife from her home, and hands her two tickets to Barbados. "I couldn't go away with you alone," she tells him. "I mean, I'd love to, but who would stay with the kids. And besides, I'm still not ready." "I'm not taking no for an answer," he tells her authoritatively. He then literally whisks her off her feet and carries her into his car. "I've made all the arrangements. Your mother is moving in with the kids and I've paid for a nanny to help her for all the days we'll be away."

At the hotel in Barbados, during a beautiful midnight stroll accompanied by warm waves splashing against their feet under the exquisite moonlight, he suddenly grabs your wife and lowers her onto the soft, warm sands of the beach. Her heart is pounding for him. She offers some token resistance, but really her desire is that he ravish her. She's been lusting after him even more than he's been lusting after her. Slowly, he takes off every last stitch of her clothing, from the lacy black bra she bought specially for the occasion, to the garter belt and stockings she once put on to help celebrate your big job promotion. She is lying there, as naked as on her wedding night, and they are about to consummate their mutual desire, when, suddenly . . .

You wake up! That's right. *Wake up*. Get out of your dream state. Your wife is about to be ravished by another man. Now come back to life. Bring your marriage back from the dead. Go and claim this sex goddess, because she's yours and you're the one she really wants, if only you would stop dying in front of the TV. You need to make passionate love to her in the privacy of your own beach bedroom.

TWELVETWELVETWELVETWELVETW
ELVETWELVETWELVETWELVETWELV
ETWELVETWELVETWELVETWELVET
WELVETWELV twelve ETWELVETWE
LVETWELVETWELVETWELVETWELVE
TWELVETWELVETWELVETWELVETW
ELVETWELVETWELVETWELVETWELV

COMMANDMENT
SIX
IN ACTION—
Jealousy
IS ESSENTIAL

My wife's jealousy is getting ridiculous. The other day she looked at my calendar and wanted to know who May was.
—RODNEY DANGERFIELD

In the man, jealous aggression tends to concentrate on the partner. The woman more frequently extends the aggression to the rival and third parties!
—DANIEL LAGACHE, *LA JALOUSIE AMOUREUSE* (1947)

The "Green-Eyed Monster" causes much woe, but the absence of this ugly serpent argues the presence of a corpse whose name is Eros.
—MINNA ANTRIM, AMERICAN WRITER (1901)

Commandment Six
Adultery is about intense jealousy and competitiveness.

Susanna, an attractive twenty-two-year-old woman, served as secretary to a well-known professor at Oxford. She had been the professor's doctoral student a year earlier, and when she finished her doctorate, the pair had worked so closely together and grown so fond of each other, that she accepted a job as his assistant. This made the professor's wife, Marjorie, unsettled and jealous. She had a strong and loving relationship with her husband, but she felt increasingly uneasy about his dependency on the lively, young assistant. Susanna unwittingly exacerbated the situation by making Marjorie feel that she was subordinate when it came to the office. Marjorie would call to speak to her husband, and Susanna would tell her that the two of them were in a meeting and could not be disturbed.

In addition, Susanna insisted on accompanying her boss to nearly all his lectures and meetings. She was always the life of the party when the professor and Marjorie had dinner parties. With time, Marjorie came to loathe Susanna. Not wanting to disrupt her husband's work, she called me to ask me if I thought she was being unreasonable. I told her I would have a word with Susanna, whom I happened to know.

We sat down in a coffee shop. I said to her, "You know, you are a remarkably talented young woman. You're attractive, super bright, and have a dynamic personality to boot. Other people have gifts different from your own—subtler, more introspective gifts. Marjorie is one of those people. Sometimes, when God gives you many talents, you have to know when to allow them to shine a bit less brightly, so that other people, with equally potent but less noticeable gifts, can be allowed to shine as well." I then suggested to Susanna that if she would fade a bit more into the background when Marjorie was in the office and when she was a guest at her home, the relationship with her boss's wife would be much better. "A woman has the right to be the queen of her home, and it's a right that you should not deny her. Every woman wants to feel that she is foremost in her husband's life. You have a large enough heart, Susanna, to act magnanimously and indulge Marjorie's legitimate needs."

Susanna immediately became hostile and defensive. "I'm here to do a job, not to enter into some jealousy vortex. I am always nice to Marjorie. If she has a problem with me and her husband working together, well then, that's *her* problem. I have little time or respect for jealous women who have no self-esteem. I'm a woman who is completely confident and I don't understand women who are jealous. My boyfriend is rich and handsome, and he has these two female assistants who fawn over him all the time. But I never get jealous. If he wants me, he has to come after me. I'm not going to pursue him with jealousy. I feel that I'm a prize and I therefore have no reason to feel insecure. Marjorie should just grow up."

"Well, that's easy for you to say now," I responded, "When you're young and beautiful and have your whole life ahead of you. But imagine that you're married to your boyfriend ten years down the road, your relationship with your husband in marriage is a bit more routine than it was when the two of you were dating, and you're a bit older and a few more lines appear on your face. Maybe you even have the added responsibility of kids. Suddenly, a vivacious young woman appears in your husband's life and seems, with every passing day, to be replacing you more and more. Are you sure you would be just as secure?"

She was adamant that she would. "This is a silly discussion. You're talking to the wrong person. Go talk to Marjorie and tell her to stop making her husband's life miserable. If she feels badly about herself, she should go to therapy rather than take it out on me and him."

Susanna is among those who see jealousy as something bad, a betrayal of personal insecurity—a sign that he or she who harbors jealousy is an unconfident loser. In her mind, she was superior to Marjorie because she had overcome the backward and primitive emotion of jealousy.

There is nothing new in this approach. It is a common mistake that has been made by even some of the greatest intellectuals of the twentieth century. Celebrated philosopher Bertrand Russell, one of the foremost advocates of open marriage, set out to purge jealousy from marriage. He established an arrangement with his wife whereby they could each have any lover they wished and they would even tell each other about it afterwards. Indeed, Russell wrote his wife long letters divulging the sexual pleasures he regularly shared with other women.

Justifying his arrangement with his wife, Russell wrote (from *The Autobiography of Bertrand Russell*): "A man or woman who has been thwarted sexually is apt to be full of envy; this generally takes the form of moral condemnation of the more fortunate."

Things changed for Russell when his wife, Dora, had a child by another man. He left her, later commenting: "My capacity for forgiveness, and what might be called Christian love, was not equal to the demands I was making on it. . . . I was blinded by theory." Their daughter Kathleen Tait pithily remarked about her parents' strange marriage: "Calling jealousy deplorable had not freed them from it . . . both found it hard to admit that the ideal had been destroyed by the old-fashioned evils of jealousy and infidelity."

Vilifying Jealousy

Of all the human emotions, jealousy is the most misunderstood and the most maligned. Margaret Mead, as cited by Dr. David Buss, referred to jealousy as "undesirable, a festering spot in every personality so afflicted, an ineffective negativistic attitude which is more likely to lose than to gain any goal." Eastern religions have gone even further in denigrating jealousy, with Zen Buddhists maintaining that "jealousy is the dragon in paradise; the hell of heaven; and the most bitter of all emotions."

To be sure, living with a spouse who is psychotically jealous can be one of the most unpleasant and soul-destroying experiences in any relationship. I have counseled many couples in which one partner is irrationally jealous and ruins the life of the person he or she claims to love, as well as the life of the marriage.

There can be no doubt that jealousy is one of the most powerful emotions known to humankind and is as harmful as it is beneficial. One of the great novels and film adaptations in recent years, Michael Ondaatje's *The English Patient,* romanticizes adultery in a completely unique way. Readers and film audiences alike were swept away by the passion between the two lovers (played by Ralph Fiennes and Kristin Scott Thomas) such that they cheered with joy when they were together and cried during their separations. Yet . . . what about the poor cuckolded husband who, raging with jealousy, lost his life (and, ultimately, his wife's as well) crashing down in an airplane? Suddenly he had seen his wife in a new light and went completely out of control to defend her—at a tremendous cost.

On an even graver note closer to our reality, sexual jealousy on the part of adulterers, their spouses, their lovers, or their rivals accounts for one third of all solved murders in the United States every year! In Texas in 1974, a man was found innocent of murder when he killed his wife and her lover when he caught them in "flagrante delicto" in bed. The law maintained that "a reasonable man" could hardly contain himself in the face of so intense a provocation.

In *The Dangerous Passion,* Dr. David Buss quotes a thirty-one-year-old man who stabbed his twenty-year-old wife to death: "She said that since she came back in April she had [slept with] this other man about ten times. I told her how can you talk about love and marriage and you have been [sleeping with] this other man. I was really mad. I went to the kitchen and got the knife. I went back to our room and asked: 'Were you serious when you told me that?' She said, 'Yes.' We fought on the bed, I was stabbing her. Her grandfather came up and tried to take the knife out of my hand. I told him to go and call the cops for me. I don't know why I killed the woman, I loved her."

Doesn't all this show just how potent the emotion of jealousy is? Can you imagine harnessing it from its destructive nature and using it to instill fire and passion in relationships? Can we not see that a lack of jealousy betrays a lack of love? If you don't wish to possess your spouse, it's because, in your opinion, your partner is not worth possessing. Not being jealous of your spouse is the equivalent of putting your spouse out for a garage sale, as yesterday's goods. You're not jealous because you don't think there's anyone interested in your spouse, or because you, yourself, have lost interest and you're just praying that someone will come and take him or her off your hands.

Indeed, in my counseling sessions with couples, one of the fundamental ways I examine whether there is any hope for them to overcome their current animosity or distance is to find out whether or not they are jealous of each other showing affection to strangers. I often have them visualize divorcing their spouse, and then bumping into them three months later while out on a date with a strange man or woman.

I say to the husbands, "How does it feel to see your wife in the arms of another man, exchanging pleasantries with you, asking how you're doing since the divorce, as you watch her passionately attached to another man." Sometimes a husband will tell me, "I feel relieved. Thank God someone took her off my hands and she's not my problem anymore." When I hear that, my heart sinks because it often indicates a loss of love. But more often than not, I hear, "I have to admit, it hurts a lot." It is then that I spring into action because I know that there is an underground spring of love between this couple than can be unearthed and brought to the surface.

I have always been intrigued by the emotion of jealousy. Indeed, so important is this emotion that it is the only one mentioned in all of the Ten Commandments, where God commands us: "You shall not covet your neighbor's house; you shall not covet your neighbor's wife, or male or female slave, or ox, or donkey, or anything that belongs to your neighbor." (Exodus 20:17)

Yet, trying to find insightful studies about jealousy is difficult, if not impossible. This is one of the reasons that I decided to write a book about the emotions, called *Kosher Emotions* (1999). The neglect of jealousy as topical matter for serious researchers is said to be due to the fact that jealousy is not a "primary emotion." Rather, it's a mutt hybrid of other, more primary emotions such as sorrow, fear, and anger. Others dismiss jealousy as an emotion altogether. To their minds, jealousy is nothing but a manifestation of other, more serious problems, such as a general lack of maturity, neurosis, or psychosis. It would of course follow that men and women who possess high self-esteem, a highly developed sense of emotional maturity, and great psychological balance never have any feelings of jealousy. As Mark Twain once wrote in *Letters from the Earth* (1909): ". . . among human beings jealousy ranks distinctly as a weakness; a trademark of small minds; a property of all small minds, yet a property which even the smallest is ashamed of; and when accused of its possession will lyingly deny it and resent the accusation as an insult."

Jealousy is not only an essential part of any romantic partnership, it is a significant factor in determining the longevity of the relationship. Eugene Mathes of Western Illinois University proved this in a remarkable study in which he took a sample of romantically involved, yet unmarried, men and women and asked them to complete a jealousy test.

After seven years had elapsed, he contacted the same people to discover the status of their relationships. It should not be surprising that 75 percent of the couples had broken up, while a healthy 25 percent had eventually married. What was surprising, however, was that the jealousy scores for those who had eventually married registered a very high 168, while those who had broken up registered a significantly lower 142. The study bears out what everyone feels in their heart to be true—that jealousy is one of the prime indicators of the *degree* of a couple's love.

The easy dismissal of jealousy belies our everyday reality. Indeed, one might even argue that it is specifically intellectuals who are so suspicious of emotion in general—which to their minds leads to subjectivity and a clouding of the truth. By extension of this logic, these same intellectuals would be loathsome of the strongest emotion of all.

Love Doesn't Work in Duplicate

Throughout my interviews with women who have had extramarital relationships, I was startled that so many of them could carry on an affair for years at a time and still not have their husbands find out. Worse, in many cases the husbands would simply turn a blind eye, showing no jealousy amidst all the evidence staring them in their faces. But in subsequent questioning as to the nature of this strange phenomenon, it turned out that in nearly every case it was because the husband, himself, had a woman on the side. In many ways, the wife having an affair released him to pursue sex with the woman he really felt passionate about.

We should not find this discovery to be particularly startling. Indeed, as we've already established, the main reason that wives have affairs is to due to an emotionless and sexless marriage—and the neglect they experience from their husbands. Often, this is because the husband has already transferred his erotic interest to a woman other than his wife.

But the same is true for women who were having an affair. They generally felt little or no guilt for having the affair, nor were they jealous of their husband's affairs, once they had started one of their own. The reason? You can't love two people at once. And once a woman has become infatuated with another man, her husband's affair is not the cause of jealousy, but rather a relief that allows her to pursue her own pleasure.

Your Spouse Is More Desirable Than You Think

One of the things that perplexes me most about married people—primarily the husbands who begin to lose interest in their wives, sometimes to business pursuits and other times by focusing attention on other women—is just how attractive and desirable their own partners are. In so many cases, not only would other men give life and limb for the woman whom the husband is ignoring but also, even more bafflingly, the woman whom the husband now pursues is rarely comparable to his wife in beauty, intelligence, or in personality.

This happens frequently among celebrities. The list is long, but to name a few: Billy Joel and Christie Brinkley; Bruce Springsteen and Julianne Phillips; Mick Jagger and super-model Jerry Hall; Kevin Costner and his ex-wife Cindy; and of course Tom Cruise and Nicole Kidman. Some of the men in this group were even caught having affairs with women who, objectively speaking, were far less attractive than their own wives. In fact, it is such a common occurrence that a group of women formed a support group twenty-five years ago, the Hollywood Ex-Wives Club.

So what's happening here? This answer is simple. Although the husband's wife is very desirable and attractive, *he has stopped noticing.* The novelty has worn off and he is there-fore out hunting new game. While the woman's husband may be a loving and decent man, he is often loving and decent to everyone but his wife. She begins to feel listless and bored and homes in on more exciting men who make her laugh. This is not so surprising. Just as we can become immune to the beauty of our home and our good fortune at having a fine job and living in a rich democratic Western country, we can become indifferent to the people who mean the most to us.

As time wears on, we begin to take them for granted. That's why the tale of adultery seems so pathetic. It usually involves husbands and wives playing out their fantasies with strangers, while strangers play out their fantasies with these same husbands and wives—all in a vicious circle of adultery. In nearly all the adultery stories you hear in which both the hus-band and the wife are having an affair, what is so interesting is that both are reporting that they are having the greatest sex ever with their illicit partner, and their illicit partner—as opposed to their married partner—finds them sexy, desirable, youthful, and passionate.

But couldn't they have found the same passion and excitement with each other? If the husband had made his wife feel sexy and desirable, could he also have elicited from her a deep sexual response? But, unfortunately, the routine of marriage and the predictability of the relationship blinds husbands and wives to each other's attractiveness. They become so used to each other that they just blend into the background.

The Vagaries of Mate Value

There is something else as well. Every man or woman in a relationship has what psychologists call a "mate value." Calculating mate value is an inherently shallow and destructive game. But when we begin feeling dissatisfied in a relationship, it's an exercise we engage in almost subconsciously. Determining mate value is as easy as summing up people as an "eight" or a "ten." For example, in our current society that idolizes external beauty, Heidi Klum or Gwyneth Paltrow would be regarded as a "ten."

But what happens when an "eight" marries a "ten"? Elaine Hatfield and her fellow researchers at the University of Hawaii found evidence that proves the patently obvious: The more desirable partner in a relationship is much more likely to stray. And those who are in relationships with men or women whom they perceive to be more attractive and desirable than themselves live with an acute sense of anxiety and insecurity, amidst the awareness that their partners may be attracted to strangers who have a higher mate value than themselves.

To be sure, mate value is not only calculated in the quality of physical attraction. Rather, money, success, celebrity, education, and pedigree all play a part in this shallow and superficial game. From a very young age, women learn that their beauty is a commodity with a price on it that can be traded in for, say, a very wealthy husband who can have them live in a castle with an unlimited spending account. Many women fall into this trap, the paragon of which would be *Playboy* Playmate and model Anna Nicole Smith who married an eighty-nine-year-old billionaire and traded in her life and reputation for a few hundred million dollars. But that also explains why a husband who may be wealthy or famous may begin cheating on his wife when she ages, or actually trade her in for a younger model, because her mate value has decreased. The same would be true of a beautiful woman, say a supermodel, who dumps the man in her life the moment he is not as successful as he once was, as appears to have possibly been the case between super-magician David Copperfield and his fiancée, supermodel Claudia Schiffer.

The same is, of course, true with regards to divorce. How often do we see Hollywood couples divorce or break up when one of the two partners' careers takes off while the other's remains stagnant? Think of Madonna and Sean Penn; Julia Roberts and Lyle Lovett; Bruce Willis and Demi Moore; Dennis Quaid and Meg Ryan; and Emma Thompson and Kenneth Branagh.

While there are, of course, many individual cases where women are ostensibly more desirable than their husbands, in general it is the men as a gender that have much higher "mate value" than the women. The women can remain focused much longer, so they are usually much more involved in the relationship by their very nature. And here their makeup works against them. Being much more involved in the relationship actually gives them a lower mate value, since they are the ones more anxious about the relationship faltering. They will demonstrate greater insecurity and anxiety, especially as they get older. Just look at how many successful men dump their wives for attractive younger women:

- Michael Douglas left his wife Diandra after twenty-two years and is now with Catherine Zeta-Jones (twenty-five years younger).
- Neil Diamond divorced his wife Marcia after twenty-five years and was soon reported dating women half his age.
- Clint Eastwood started his trend of infidelity twenty-five years ago by allegedly cheating on his wife with teenage starlet Jill Banner, after which he finally abandoned his wife of twenty-six years for leading actress Sondra Locke. He quickly dumped Locke, and just recently, at the age of sixty-seven, married thirty-two-year-old Dina Ruiz, a television reporter.

Psychiatrist Dr. Eugene Landy has seen this time and time again: "Older men choose young lovers, young sexy nubile women to satisfy their fantasies. When men are older, they may have achieved success, but they've lost the power of youth, and having a young, attractive girl on their arm makes up for this loss" (*The Underground Dictionary*, 1971).

Once a woman feels that her position is threatened—that her partner might leave for someone else—she cannot help but experience pangs of jealousy. She inevitably becomes the living fulfillment of this horrible prophecy, unavoidably ending up having lower mate value than her husband. This is exacerbated by the unfair but undeniable fact that as men grow older, they become more desirable since they are climbing the ladder of success, making more money, and having increased power and influence. But women, as they grow older, become less desirable because their beauty begins to fade.

So, are men therefore destined to always flaunt their innate mate value over women? Are we fated to see the never-ending statistics of men being three times more unfaithful than their wives, seven times more prone to fantasize about other women while in bed with their wives? Does human instinct tragically predict our inability to close this growing discrepancy with studies like these reported in *The Dangerous Passion* by psychologist David Buss, who discovered in a survey of 1,000 men and women: "Men reported desiring eight sex partners over the next three years, whereas women reported desiring only one or two. In another study, men were four times more likely than women to say that they have imagined having sex with 1,000 partners or more."

The answer to this conundrum is a deeper understanding of female sexuality and the need for husbands to equalize the growing disparity over mate value by utilizing jealousy. Women, as we have noted throughout this book, are orders of magnitude more sexual in their nature than men. They crave sex not from a superficial hormonal side of their personalities, as men do, but from the deepest level of their heart and soul. They desire to connect emotionally and intimately, with flesh pressed against flesh and every pore of the body opening between them and their lover. Thus, when men's natural proclivity to stray and ignore their wives begins to kick in, thereby enhancing their own mate value because they are less dependent on their wives, something equally remarkable kicks in—namely, the wives' innate desire to connect with a man who finds her desirable.

Suddenly, these same wives who are ignored by their husbands begin fantasizing about other men, flirting—at first fairly innocently—with other men. They are also subtly sending out signals of how lonely they are to other men. The men, of course, pick up the signals and notice. Since men are so competitive, nothing is as thrilling as having someone else's woman interested in them. And men especially love rescuing a damsel in distress. It makes them feel like heroes, messiahs who bring salvation. It makes the chosen man feel better than the other guy. Hence, sex with a married woman always has a very high degree of eroticism attached to it. And this unquenchable desire on the part of the wife to have her sexuality and lust for intimacy break free, is the great equalizing force in terms of mate value. Now the husband gets reinvested in his wife, since he has to pursue her all over again. Her innate longing for other men—and other men's longing for her—create the erotic distance needed to re-energize his libido in her direction. All it takes is for a husband to notice this. But many husbands remain blind to it. That's why it is our primary purpose in this book to create scenarios where this equalization and the wife's desirability to other men can be highlighted.

The same is true in reverse. Husbands who carry with them *the possibility of adultery* with other women equalize their "mate value" with their wives, who may have moved ahead of their husbands in terms of mate value by landing a big job, being discovered as an actress, or having become highly desirable to a powerful man. When this happens, husbands who may have been boring to their wives up to that point suddenly become attractive to them all over again. This was the essential story behind the controversial movie, *Indecent Proposal*, which we cited earlier. Demi Moore plays a pretty, but ordinary wife. Her mate value suddenly soars when a billionaire businessman gets interested in her. Her husband becomes incredibly jealous, but he still cannot win her back. It is only when he lets go of her at the end of the movie—and opens the possibility of connecting with another woman—that his wife suddenly becomes interested in him again and wants him back.

No one is attracted to someone who is beneath them. Attraction has to be parallel or upward, never downward. And "mate value" is determined by the forces of the market—supply and demand. When a wife or husband is in demand it raises that person's mate value. Hence, this concept of a spouse being desirable to strangers is crucial.

To be sure, there are other ways to equalize the "mate value" between men and women and guarantee long and abiding partnerships. We could, for example, change societal values by which men and women are rated. For example, one of my great sporting heroes is St. Louis Rams quarterback Kurt Warner. I admire him not only because of his excellence on the playing field, but, more importantly, because of his deep-seated religious convictions that are at the center of his life. Hardly a game passes when he doesn't start and end the game by attributing all glory to God and denigrating his own skills and expertise. But he wasn't always a success. In fact, his athletic career was incredibly pathetic until recently. In fact, his biography on the official team Web site describes him as "defying odds" to reach the NFL in the first place.

Now, with a Super Bowl ring on his finger and myriad awards and team records under his belt, his "mate value" has absolutely skyrocketed in just a few years. Now, should that affect his marriage to his wife Brenda? In many cases it would. But what we see instead on television and at his public appearances is how utterly dependent he is on his wife and the incredible strength of their marriage.

How have they managed to beat the odds of sudden success and remain a happy, well-adjusted couple? The answer seems fairly obvious. Kurt Warner is a devout Christian. As such, he has a different values system than most Americans. He does not rate his wife based on the amount of lines on her face or how she compares with the St. Louis Rams' voluptuous cheerleaders. Rather, he values her infinitely as the love of his life; she's the mother of his children and the woman who stood by him when the whole world rejected him as a loser.

There can be no doubt that injecting more religious values into our society would help equalize the disparity in "mate value," as would reducing popular culture's incessant emphasis on money, youth, and beauty. Having said this, the answer lies not only in changing the external conditions that influence the marriage of a man and a woman, but addressing the internal mechanisms of the relationship itself. The use of jealousy and the possibility of adultery is the great equalizing factor in mate value and would render the couple impervious to outside threats. This should work for all men and women, regardless of values system, degree of monetary success, or religious affiliation.

Unfortunately, men are so incredibly caught up in their own lives, so sure of their conviction that their wives are unattractive drones who would never be desirable to other men, that they usually learn just to look right past them rather than doing anything about it. The average man who has already hooked onto other women—whether in full-blown affairs or just in fantasizing, flirting, or drawing emotionally close to them—is so oblivious to his wife's needs and nature that he will rarely realize her growing attraction to other men and other men's growing interest in her. But rest assured that it happens. Women intrinsically crave intimacy and sexual satisfaction. Even when they consciously suppress those desires, these needs are still simmering strongly beneath the surface.

There isn't a woman on earth whose husband has lost interest in her that hasn't developed some sort of fondness for a guy like the pharmacist, or the tech guy at work, who shows her an interest and hints that he thinks she's special. Unfortunately, the husbands never inquire about these petty attachments that their wives forge. If they did, they would nip the attraction in the bud, and more, they would find their own desire greatly heightened by this realization of their wife's allure. They would, ultimately, begin to pursue their wives again. Yet is it really surprising that husbands don't notice this when an astonishing 54 percent of husbands never even realize that their wives are having affairs—even when the affair has gone on for years at a time? In fact, the number one way that husbands discover that their wives are having an affair is through the wife finally confessing it to her husband, usually out of guilt or fear of getting caught. Could you imagine that? Your wife has become some other guy's mistress, and yet you don't even know about it, such is the level of your neglect and indifference!

When it comes to women, the opposite is true. Nearly all women discover that their husbands are having an affair. The husbands don't reveal it; they're not that crazy. Rather, they are caught red-handed. The wives begin to notice that he dresses up more, that he is more concerned with his looks, that he suddenly starts going to a gym, that he disappears and gives unconvincing stories about where he has been, or even that he starts doing his own laundry to hide the evidence (always a dead giveaway because what husband would *willingly* do his own laundry?).

Dr. David Buss and Todd Shackelford, et. al., explored this in a 2001 study published in *Journal of Marriage and Family*, and ended up with more than 170 "clues" to a husband's infidelity. Among the most prevalent (*besides* actually catching him in bed!) was the scent of perfume or odor of sex or changes in sexual pattern, personal appearance, or daily routine. Another big indicator cited was sudden new interests, such as a sudden obsession with classical music or theater. Whatever the means, wives seem to be particularly in tune with a man's sexual faithfulness.

But the men seem utterly oblivious. Read any book with interviews of women who have had affairs, and nine times out of ten you will discover the wives saying that their husbands had no clue until the wife revealed it to them. From this study, Dr. Buss notes that, "women seem more finely attuned to the subtle emotional changes in their husbands that might betray a change in emotional commitment." One wife found particular satisfaction in using the marital bed, with her husband still clueless: "I changed the sheets and everything, and then that night—oh, it was amazing really because he wouldn't speak to me. I'm in Coventry at the moment you see, and I could lie there just thinking, 'Oh, you don't know, you don't know the half of it!' Cuckolded he was and in his own bed" (*Adultery* by Annette Lawson).

Jealousy Rekindles Passion

Did you ever have the experience of rummaging through old clothes you wish to donate to charity and chancing upon an old outfit that has lost its appeal? A close friend who is helping you notices the outfit and says that it is lovely, and that if you are throwing it out anyway, she would like to keep it. Suddenly, you're not so sure that you want to get rid of it anymore. Your friend's appreciation for the garment has reawakened your own interest in it as well. But why? Just a moment ago you were adamant that you didn't want it. You were going to throw it out! Ah! But that wasn't because it didn't suit you. You wanted to get rid of it because it was old *to you,* and you had grown bored with it. But to your friend it is brand new. And her excitement about it—coupled with her desire to take it away from you and make it her own—reminds you of just how nice it really is. Suddenly you want it back. The moment someone else shows an interest in your spouse, you are immediately reminded of how special that person is and you want him or her back. It is *jealousy* that reminds you.

We must expend every effort to remind ourselves constantly of how precious the people with whom we share our lives really are. Although jealousy is often destructive, it can also be turned to good. Rather than waiting for the breakdown of a marriage, one must induce a perpetual state of jealousy, burning brightly but not too brightly, which will ensure that each spouse will do everything he or she can to please and impress his or her partner—not just in a crisis, but continually. But, I cannot emphasize too much the importance of not confusing jealousy with unfaithfulness.

No marriage could last without a husband and wife being fully confident that as long as they try their darnedest to earn their spouse's affections, their husband or wife will remain loyal. If a wife really had to worry about what her husband was doing out late at night—and vice versa—both would be miserable, particularly if they went to great lengths to try to please each other. By jealousy in marriage I do not mean that each spouse *deliberately* seeks to make his or her partner jealous, or flirts with other people at cocktail parties and the like. Rather, a husband and wife should always be *conscious of the interest shown to their spouse by members of the opposite sex.* The fact is that other men will stare at your wife, and other women will look admiringly at your husband. Others appreciate his or her sexiness and attractiveness, even if you don't.

Jealousy in the Workplace

When I lived in England, I was once privy to an argument between two of my closest married friends—Henry and Paula—again, over the issue of hiring a secretary. Henry's secretary had resigned and he was very sad to lose her. His wife, who worked in the same company in the publicity and public relations department, helped him scour all the employment agencies in search of a suitable replacement. One day, a woman's resume that seemed too good to be true came through the fax machine. In subsequent interviews with Henry, she proved to be the perfect candidate. He wanted to hire her instantly.

But Henry's wife objected, and told him that in no circumstances would she allow him to hire her. The woman was young, very attractive, and dressed highly seductively. In her first interview she even came with two of the middle buttons in her blouse open, exposing her bra. The wife insisted that she knew that type of woman, and that she had left her buttons undone intentionally. Henry and his wife had a huge argument over the matter. She called me in tears, and in mid-conversation, he grabbed the telephone and told me that he is a generous husband and father, allowing for his wife's extravagant tastes. "But someone's got to pay all these bills, and I need an efficient assistant in order to be successful enough to do so. This woman is perfect, and I am not prepared to give her up just because of my wife's irrational jealousies." He was adamant. "Let my wife go and see a psychiatrist. I am not giving up this secretary."

Of all the irrational elements to be found within the behavior of a spouse, jealousy is the most troublesome. Many husbands and wives are utterly unable to deal with their spouse's jealousy, and treat it as something that betrays a deep character flaw in their spouse—something that they must "work at, or it will destroy our marriage." They rarely consider the possibility that perhaps—regardless of whether or not their spouse is justified in insisting that they not speak to "so and so"—maybe they should abstain, just to preserve the peace of the marriage and keep their spouse happy. No, this jealousy has got to change and the husband or wife will just have to accept it.

The flaw in this thinking is that it will *not* change. The fact is that the confident and flirtatious way that some men and women speak to our spouses, and the way in which our spouses respond to them, just rubs us up the wrong way, and it always will. To be sure, I always insist to husbands and wives who experience raging jealousy that they must express this to their spouse, but they must do so in a controlled and loving way. It is when they can no longer express it in a calm and reasonable manner, and have exploded with little provocation many times, that they must then turn to a professional counselor to deal with their rage. But it is not the jealousy itself that is unreasonable. It is the anger that accompanies it. A spouse has a right—even an obligation to be jealous—of his or her partner.

This attitude that "my spouse is being irrational and therefore I will not accommodate that behavior" is predicated on the idea that we are obliged to conform to the desires of our spouse only if they appear to us to make sense. That is a grave misassumption. Love is not always rational. Marriage is not always cogent. But the vow is, after all, "for better or worse."

Instead of the immediate dismissal that jealousy is "irrational" and "petty," ask yourself: Why is it that your spouse feels so insecure? Have you hurt him or her significantly in the past? Have you had an affair? If you haven't, maybe you have shown too much attention to someone in the past and given your spouse cause to be jealous. Or maybe you simply haven't shown your own spouse *enough* attention. Maybe your spouse feels neglected and unloved. Maybe your spouse feels that he or she is no longer attractive *to you,* so that any close association you have with a member of the opposite sex makes your spouse feel insecure. Something, however subtle, is causing your spouse to be uncontrollably jealous. The issue must be worked on together and reconciled.

I firmly advocate that the jealousies of one's spouse must be accommodated, tied as they are to the spouse's essential masculinity or femininity. Your husband is jealous of the close association you have with your male yoga teacher because your husband is a man. Don't ask him why. That's the way men are. And it's a good thing they're like that because it is that aspect that allows them to take you under their wings, affording you intimacy, security, and passion.

If you truly think that he's being irrational, then discuss it with him. Try to make him see your point of view. Talk about it constantly. A healthy marriage is one in which the principal object of discussion is the marriage.

But if he simply won't come around, then find a different yoga class. Your husband, along with his seemingly irrational desires, should come first. To be sure, I advocated earlier that we must use jealousy to heighten passion. But this is only when the marriage has a strong element of security and the couple can use jealousy playfully. It cannot be used when a marriage is on a rickety foundation from the beginning, in which case it will only exacerbate tension. It's useful when a husband and wife have achieved a strong and passionate attachment, and have a wonderful and amazing sex life, such that they can *playfully* tease each other about attraction to strangers as a way of stoking the fires of their attraction and never allowing the embers to burn out.

Similarly, as I told my friend in the previous situation, your wife's jealousy obviously results from her being your wife. That's the way some women are. She wants you to herself and feels insecure when you will be spending more time in your office with a woman whom she feels does not respect your marital commitments, than you will be spending at home with her. To be sure, your business is important. But your wife is *more* important. Accommodate her on this request; don't tell her to stifle her essential femininity and the love, and by extension the jealousy, that she feels toward her husband.

The Bond of Trust

The healthiest resolution to the problem of jealousy is that of trust. Now, I do not mean to trust completely in the solidity of the relationship or in your spouse's fidelity and commitment to you, for those kinds of trust are the surest route to complacency. Rather, it is about trusting in the principles of love—that when a woman is satisfied sexually and has a husband who is a romantic, she will not have an interest in cheating at all. Nearly every study ever conducted bears that out. Conversely, when a woman is wise enough to never allow her husband to grow bored with her and always remains somewhat independent and just outside his reach, he will be much more concerned about keeping her faithful than in pursuing extramarital liaisons himself. Above all else, trust means trusting in your spouse's commitment to work on the relationship and ensure it never degenerates to the point where both of you will be seeking out adventure in someone else's bed.

Ironically, one of the things that married men and women can learn from adulterous men and women is the need to embed more trust in a relationship as the primary means by which to purge a marriage of inhibition. One of the key elements in adultery is trust. Two lovers trust each other not to betray one another, not to abruptly end an affair for which so much has been risked, and not to two-time each other with other lovers that will make the situation radically more complicated. That's one heck of a lot of trust for two people to share, especially when their entire relationship is based upon both being duplicitous.

But just think of the rewards of that trust. Because this unfaithful pair put so much faith in one another, they have no inhibition in their relationship. Nearly every adulterous affair has stories of wild sex—for example, tales of men and women joining the mile-high club in the lavatory of a jumbo jet. Even nonsexual things push the envelope, with many men and women involved in affairs reportedly trying new things that they would not otherwise have done, like going to art exhibitions, learning ballroom dancing, and learning to cook Thai cuisine.

By trusting in the principles of love—and by incessantly feeding a marriage with affection and attention—we gain the best of both worlds: the constantly reinvigorating knowledge that the people we are married to are wonderfully attractive to others, coupled with the flattery that notwithstanding that desirability to others they *choose* to remain steadfastly loyal to us, in every way, because their emotional and sexual life with us is immensely satisfying. This is what adulterous lovers enjoy. Amidst the tenuous and unpredictable state of their relationship, they trust each other with their compromising secrets even more than they trust their own spouses. This trust helps them to maintain their passion and devotion.

Put your spouse first in all matters. Make your spouse feel that amidst your natural attraction to strangers he or she never has to worry about your being interested in someone else. Marriage deserves no less.

Exercises
INCORPORATING
JEALOUSY

Below are radical techniques *that should only be done if absolutely necessary*. They are not normally advisable, since there are some risks and they have the potential of compromising modesty. I liken them to a defibrillator, and the powerful electric charge used to restart a stopped heart. Radical action becomes necessary, and a strong burst of electricity becomes a means by which to save a person's life—but do it regularly and you could electrocute the marriage.

The same applies to marriage and relationships. If a husband and wife have come to the point where they feel utterly uninspired with one another, they must then undertake serious action that displays each one as attractive and exciting. They must at times use the intense shock therapy of jealousy and envy in order to jolt some intensity and passion into their marriage.

1. HUSBANDS: Always notice the looks and stares that strangers give your wife. Sometimes, make distance between you and your wife to allow yourself to notice it. For example, make going out to the supermarket an erotic experience by going into the store ten minutes after her. Watch her get into a short conversation with the male deli attendant. Watch from a distance as they chuckle together. Go with your wife to a friend's party and cut her loose for some of the evening. Let her mingle and see what she gets up to (within reason, of course). When you return home at night, relive the experience. Talk about it. Ask her what men told her and what was going through her mind. And let passion overtake you.

2. HUSBANDS: If and when you're feeling particularly bored with, or turned off by your wife, take it even further. These may be extreme measures, but worth a try in extreme circumstances when the passion in the marriage is all but gone. Go to a local bar together, but get there half an hour after your wife. Sit apart from her, and each should embark on a mission to speak to members of the same sex about each other. The wife should ask the woman sitting next to her what she thinks about the man in the distance (her husband). Let him then start speaking to some of the other men there and ask their opinion, in a disinterested way, about the woman at the bar (his wife). He'll see firsthand how appealing and sexy they find her.

3. WIVES: A wife should do the same with her husband. Speak to other women and hear the way they find your husband masculine and sexy, because undoubtedly there will be some who do. Every time a husband or wife hears from a stranger how attractive his or her spouse is, interest is renewed.

4. COUPLES: Check into a hotel together, but get your wife to check in an hour before you. Let her come across as a business executive on her own for a conference. Watch her amble about the lobby meeting people. Tell her to strike up some conversations with everyone from the bellboy to the bartender. Just "friendly conversation." But *aha!* Women on their own are never treated by other men as merely friendly. Your wife need not—and should not—be a tease. There will inevitably be some men who will offer things like bringing her some extra shampoo, giving her a complimentary drink, or showing her a bit around town. Afterwards, when you both end up in your room, have her share her experiences. The same is true of flying on planes together. Occasionally you should sit apart and let your wife get into a conversation with the sexy Italian sitting by the window.

5. COUPLES: Together, arrange for the wife to call a male photographer to come over and take some nice pictures as a gift for her husband. Of course, nothing immodest or too racy. This is a married woman and her body belongs to her husband, not another man. But it will be interesting to watch your wife being directed by a strange man to do all kinds of poses, innocent ones, and it will be even more interesting to watch your reaction. Of course, the subsequent photos can be highly stimulating as well and will well justify the expense.

6. HUSBANDS: Get your wife to go to evening classes—pottery, art history, French lessons—any area in which she can interact with other men and come home and tell you all the gossip of what's happening in the class. In the meantime, you stay home and watch the kids. It gives her a night out, makes you wonder what she's up to, establishes her independence, and makes you yearn for her to return home with all her tales of erotic interest.

7. HUSBANDS: Occasionally, when you go to a concert or the theater together, choose not to sit next to each other. Sit two rows behind your wife. Have her strike up a conversation with the guy sitting to her right. After the intermission, sit next to each other. It's always interesting to see the other man's reaction. He might show some jealousy. Then you'll truly recognize that you have a prize for a wife. These are all great games that husbands and wives can bring into their marriages to bring back erotic playfulness. It also allows them to tease each other when they get home about how the evening went. There is precious little playfulness in marriage; the more we bring into it, the more exciting it's going to be.

8. The final exercise offers even more radical shock treatment for husbands who really are growing bored with their wives. First, you'll need some background information.

The March 4, 2002, *Time* magazine reported on the growing trend of male nannies—known as "*mannies*"—in the United States. According to the article, "they are most sought after by a growing cadre of single mothers, many of whom want a daily dose of male energy around the house for their kids. But the trend is also being sought by dual-income couples in which the father travels a lot or is older and less equipped for, say, a pickup game of tackle football. Ellen Leans, a married mother of three boys . . . whose husband used to travel frequently, says the three male nannies she hired have helped make up for her weaknesses."

What the article doesn't focus on is how this might also make up for her *husband's* weaknesses. It's usually the wives who have to put up with lecherous husbands eyeing the young nannies that move into the house to look after their young children. Wouldn't it be good for marriages if there were a sudden role reversal? What if the husbands had to worry about their wives always being around some hunky young "mannie" who is not only strong and gorgeous, but nurturing and does housework to boot?

Time quotes actor Mandy Patinkin, "who raves about the two male nannies he and his wife Kathryn Grody hired." Mr. Patinkin admits to feeling jealous, not about his wife, surprisingly, but about the role of father that was being usurped by the mannies. "Then I quickly realized that I'm going to be a dad in my own way."

Now for the exercise: If you are one of the many husbands I increasingly encounter who expresses little or no attraction for his wife, hire a "mannie" right away. Go for an Adonis: tall, muscular, with a fabulous tan, but kind, gentle, and accommodating. In short, the "perfect man." Under the wife's supervision, have him play baseball and touch football with your kids; or suggest activities that your husband hasn't done with them, like going to the zoo or a playground. If the "mannie" is game and your budget allows it, ask him to do manly stuff around the house: gardening, fixing things, lifting heavy objects, etc. Make sure to fill your husband in on all of the details, especially if your husband is tied up at work or on a business trip. Make sure to also tell him what a lifesaver the mannie is and how your life is immeasurably better since he entered it.

A note of caution: *Tell the mannie his job is bound to be cancelled at any moment.* When the husband discovers any of these innocent "mannie" activities, he is sure to fire his rockets to the moon with jealousy and, when he gets back, he may demand his immediate termination. And good! While this could cause the husband a lot of anxiety, worry, and even pain, it is certain to reinvigorate his erotic attraction to you. And the pain of jealousy is a lot better than the 'walking dead' of a husband and wife living within a morbid marriage or erotic indifference. It's also a lot less painful than divorce—for your spouse, your kids, and you.

THIRTEENTHIRTEENTHIRTEENTHIR
TEENTHIRTEENTHIRTEENTHIRTEEN
THIRTEENTHIRTEENTHIRTEENTHIR
TEENTHIRTE thirteen ENTHIRTEEN
THIRTEENTHIRTEENTHIRTEENTHIR
TEENTHIRTEENTHIRTEENTHIRTEEN
THIRTEENTHIRTEENTHIRTEENTHIR

COMMANDMENT SEVEN IN ACTION— Intense FOCUS

Most men, even when they have some affection for the other woman, are able to keep an affair from taking over their emotional lives. This is in direct contrast to women, who tend to become consumed. In letter after letter, case history after case history, wives confessed that their heads were totally occupied by their lovers.

—CAROL BOTWIN, TEMPTED WOMEN

If you surrender completely to the moments as they pass, you live more richly those moments.

—ANNE MORROW LINDBERGH, AMERICAN AUTHOR AND AVIATOR

I never married because there was no need. I have three pets at home which answer the same purpose as a husband. I have a dog which growls every morning, a parrot which swears all afternoon, and a cat that comes home late at night.

—MARIE CORELLI, SCOTTISH AUTHOR AND POET

Commandment Seven
Adultery involves intense focus.

Blocking Everything Out—Except Sex

Separation, expectation, delayed gratification, anxiety, erotic obstacles, secrecy, mystique, and the perception of your spouse as a total sexual partner all contribute to the real power of an adulterous affair: power that is contained in the mesmerizing focus that one has on his or her lover. Lovers who yearn for each other are not distracted by anything; their passion is such that the world outside the bedroom has ceased to exist. And that's why they're always making love and connecting.

The intensity of the focus on each other is indescribable. In *A Passion for More,* author Susan Shapiro Barash quotes a woman named Melanie, who describes her adulterous affair: "We made love everywhere. We did it in his car and when we went bike riding. We did it on an airplane and in the back of a movie theater. We even did it once in one of those ski bubble things as we went up a mountain. We would touch each other in crowded bars. Wherever we were, we did it. We couldn't keep our hands off each other."

Now, how many married couples could say the same thing? Here's another woman describing her affair: "It's the best high in the whole world. If people could sustain this euphoria, there'd be no need to have liquor, drugs."

Until now, it was believed that the greatest love in the world is that of a parent for a child. But, as I've mentioned earlier, women are prepared to follow their lovers to the ends of the earth, even if it means losing their children. In addition, lovers take risks that reveal their total sexual sides, something unknown in marriage.

Adulterous lovers become total sexual partners. Their focus on each other is so intense that it blocks out *everything else.* They not only have sex, they *talk about it, dream about it,* and *fantasize about it.* The focus is *complete.*

As Louise DeSalvo writes in *Adultery:* "Soon, you discover that it's not the sex that glues things together, it's the talking about the sex—about whether you're going to have it, about when you're going to have it, about how good it's going to be when you have it, about how good it was the last time you had it, about whether you should stop having it, about how you can't stop having it, about whether you can live without having it."

The general rule in life is this: Cohesion and unity of our personality generates happiness. We human beings are generally content and pleasured when we're focused on where we want to go, and content with what we want to be. Happiness is always associated with a feeling of contentment, an inner serenity that is the direct product of having all of our faculties cohere under a single canopy.

By contrast, unhappiness and depression are caused by internal fragmentation—when you are waging an inner war with yourself. Depression and unhappiness are the direct result of sensing that our innermost convictions cannot translate themselves into outermost actions. When the human personality feels pulled apart by uncontrollable forces, when we are no longer masters of our own destiny, when we become thermometers rather than thermostats, or when we cannot be what we deeply desire to be, those are the casualties of this inner war. That's why so many marriages end up fraught with unhappiness. The couple loses control of their love for each other as the everyday pressures of life destroy them: raising kids, paying bills, satisfying bosses, and just trying to keep afloat.

On the other hand, even when faced with the phenomenal confusion sown by adultery and all the competing forces that need to be satisfied in order for an affair to take off, its immense intensity somehow manages to focus the man and woman involved to such an extent that they feel they just can't let go. They sense they are totally in sync with their desires. They want pleasure, and they're getting pleasure. They want romance, and they're getting romance. They want someone who makes them feel alive, and they get it in spades. They desire an intense sexual thrill, and their lovemaking sessions become like rocket fuel that launches them to the outer limits of the solar system. United and impassioned by danger, they disclose their secret sexual fantasies to each other and let go of all inhibitions. They become like laser beams that emit an extraordinarily powerful light.

We earlier discussed how monogamy runs completely against the grain of human nature. We may now understand the centrality of sex in marriage and the need for couples to have the most passionate intimate lives possible (a) if they are to remain together for the long haul, and (b) if they are to remain faithful to each other. The idea of using adultery to rekindle passion in marriage is important only if you truly understand how important a good sex life is to marriage.

But nowadays, people don't like hearing this. Most people today feel that sex is not one of the loftier pursuits of humanity, and is even somewhat degrading. When I used to tell my students at Oxford that once upon a time people actually married because it was the only way they could have sex, they looked at me in horror and astonishment. A student once stood up during a lecture I delivered and said, "Of all the superficial, silly things I have ever heard, to tell us we should marry for sex. My God!"

I responded incredulously: "Superficial and silly? Is that what sex is to you?" Of course, that may be what it has become. But the Jewish religion sees sex as the ultimate form of knowledge and union. Indeed, the Bible has no word for sex other than knowledge, as in, "And Adam came *to know* his wife Eve, and she conceived and bore Cain" (Genesis 4:1). Sex where a man and woman remove, not just their clothing, but their defenses, and expose, for the first time, their soft underbellies. Sex is man and woman naked of all artifice, stripped of all pretense.

The problem, of course, is that today sex is not a form of knowledge. Studies show that approximately one third of American singles have sex on the first or second date of their budding relationships. Yet, in most cases, even months later their emotional vulnerabilities do not manifest. I have always maintained that, aside from the obvious hormonal impetus to do so, another prime reason men and women jump into the sack is actually to *subvert* intimacy. Terrified as they are of true emotional cohesion, they use physical closeness as a substitute for emotional closeness. Rather than allowing sex to serve as the physical glue to cement an existing emotional bond, it is used to create a deeply unfertile ground from which no healthy emotional fruit will ever grow.

Today a man can have sex with a woman, see her on the street the next day, smile at her, and keep on walking. Sure, there is a brief moment of awkwardness. But the man and woman both work hard to overcome it. After all, it was only sex, right? But sex is the most intense experience we have in life, and should be the thing that we all look forward to most in our marriages. It has the power to make everything else appear insignificant. If a husband and wife have a good sex life, then the fact that dinner isn't ready on time just doesn't matter that much. Conversely, if things don't work well in the bedroom, you can rest assured that they won't work well in the living room either. Unfortunately, most husbands and wives lack the level of intensity that would so narrowly focus them on one another such that nothing else would be able to intrude.

Marriage Is Different from Friendship

Sex is certainly not the only important thing in marriage. But it *is* what transforms a friendship into a marriage. Whenever acquaintances make the ridiculous proclamation—which has sadly become all too common—that "my wife [husband] is my best friend," I respond, "Really, you had children with your best friend?" They think about the remark and they then agree that it is inappropriate. You are not husband and wife when you simply share a home or apartment. That's called being roommates. Nor are you husband and wife when you merely share a bedroom. That can still be a platonic friendship. You are specifically husband and wife when you share *the same bed,* make love, and become *the same flesh.* The strong *motions* of sex are meant to unite you with the even stronger *emotions* that are generated.

A major trend in the United States is the celibate marriage. This is built on the idea that no marriage can really preserve its passion, and that makes people hung up on the sexual problems in their relationships.

So, who needs sex in marriage at all? Just focus on the really important things, like going to art galleries together, discussing Vivaldi, listening to music, providing each other with comfort and security, baking lasagna, debating politics, and so on. *But these are the activities you share with everybody else.* That's not marriage. Marriage is sharing one bed, and becoming orchestrated together emotionally and especially physically, as an indivisible unit. It's having children together. Sex is definitely the most important element of a marriage, certainly in its first twenty to thirty years—and even well beyond. A couple who still feels very close and loving in old age has engendered that closeness by virtue of the passion they shared earlier in life, even if, due to physical considerations, their sex life has now dwindled or even terminated. The threads of attachment that were created from the pleasure and celebration of a passionate sex life are enough to cement a man and a woman in blissful union for the duration of their days. Sex is the only thing that can truly keep a man and woman together over a long period of time. And a good sex life in particular is the only thing that will guarantee that they remain faithful to each other.

This is why, according to the Jewish religion, a cessation of sex between a young and healthy couple is seen as a functional termination of the marriage and the strongest possible grounds for divorce. A celibate marriage is nothing more than a relationship between best friends: The two people involved may feel closer to each other than to anyone else on earth, but they do not experience the intense passion that only sex brings to a marriage.

Achieving Sexual Focus

Put your spouse in situations where you will notice the natural attraction that others have for him or her. Use jealousy to your own advantage by placing your spouse in environments where his or her sexuality will stand out. Whenever a member of the opposite sex speaks to your spouse, watch his or her eyes. You will realize that person sees an attractive man or woman in your spouse.

Remember, if you aren't excited about your husband or your wife, it is not an intrinsic fault of the spouse. Rather, it is because to you your partner has become too familiar. The men and women who attract you more than your spouse are not necessarily more handsome or beautiful; even if they are, this is not the source of the attraction. It is rather their newness and the unexplored possibilities that they present that make them appealing. The proof is that just as you are looking with envy at someone to whom you are not married, others are looking at your spouse in very much the same way.

What you are doing in effect, then, with this methodology is using other people's eyes through which to perceive your spouse. The advantage of this is that in their eyes your spouse is new, and thus your partner becomes new to you as well.

In order to keep their sexual lives together happy, passionate, and comfortable, the first thing couples need to do is minimize all forms of distraction.

Exercises
ACTIVITIES THAT
SHARPEN YOUR
FOCUS

1. Get rid of the TV sets in your bedroom immediately. Do it. No turning back. There is no greater obstacle to a couple's concentration on each other than having a television in the bedroom. You can even chart the gradual death of the sex life of the American couple with the growing saturation of TV. Sex between married couples was three to four times a week in the 1940s and '50s, then tapered off, commensurate with the total domination of TV, to twice a week in the 1980s and '90s. Now, as I said earlier, according to American Demographics, it has fallen to the pitiful state of just once a week. Would we have expected anything different, with better and funnier late night TV than ever before, and with the proliferation of VCRs, DVDs, and the Internet?

Let's admit the truth: Jay Leno, David Letterman, and Conan O'Brien have destroyed our sex lives. We all think it is we who laugh at *them*. But if they could peer right back at us into our bedroom, it would be they who would be laughing at *us!* Let's revolt against them by throwing them out of our bedrooms. Watch them in the living room, but not in your love chamber. It is simply not fair when a man has to compete with the likes of Tom Cruise or Brad Pitt, or a woman finds herself pitted against Britney Spears or Gwyneth Paltrow. Even if it's a *Simpsons* cartoon, or something absolutely nonsexual, why should you bring such a terrible distraction into your bedroom—the sanctuary in which you should be focusing solely on each other? Put the TV back where it belongs, in the store where you bought it, or at the very least in the living room. Television viewing, just like pornography, separates husband and wife because it means focusing on the images you are looking at and not on each other.

2. Try your hand at role-playing, and not only when in a sexual situation. Try playing yourself as a teenager, and have your husband or wife approach you at a high school dance. I know it sounds corny, but even if you laugh, you'll feel turned on. Use such game playing (and this is the *good* kind of game playing— no mind games or manipulations) to learn things about your spouse that you hadn't previously known, and had never really thought to ask about. For instance, you might ask your wife when she first started having sexual feelings. (No need to ask your husband that. For men it starts at conception.) But sexual exploration of your spouse is a great way to stoke the fires of lust.

3. Create your own unique set of game rules that are individual to the relationship you have with your spouse. For example, one couple told me how they took pictures of their various body parts (the innocent ones—that is, their arms, legs, ears, feet, toes) and then mixed and matched them with other photos they were able to get off the Internet and other places. They then played the game of whether their spouse could identify their knees, their earlobes, their fingers, their neck, etc. Only you can decide what the rewards are for these games. The nice thing about little things like this is that by doing so a husband might suddenly find that his wife's arms or legs really are erotic and then, presto, he has more than just three erogenous zones on her body to turn him on.

4. If you have to, live more modestly rather than knocking yourselves out in order to earn money, thus never having time for each other. Notice that couples in adulterous affairs couldn't care less about things like money. In the hundreds of interviews I conducted with men and women involved in affairs, they told me about the amazing sex they had and the beautiful places they visited clandestinely. What they almost never talked about is the gifts they gave each other. Gifts pose too much of a risk. (Remember Clinton's gifts to Monica, like *Leaves of Grass?*) Rather, they give each other the greatest gift of all, sexual passion and intense focus.

5. Alter your locations of lovemaking to those that force you to focus (moving cars are out). I don't mean hotel rooms, either. Do things that heighten your awareness of everything that is happening in the situation, because you might get caught. For example, drive to an empty golf course late at night and make out under the palm trees. (It helps if you're in Miami for that one, while if you live in Hackensack you can use your vivid imagination and make believe that the highway overpass is rainforest fauna.) Every passing headlight will increase the thrill. You'll hardly be thinking about the meeting with the clients you have early next morning, since you'll be far more focused on not getting arrested.

6. Try herbal potions that are marketed on the Internet that claim to enhance desire, or one of the many lotions that women can put on the private parts of their bodies to heighten erotic response. (I am regularly sent these products with requests to provide endorsements, so I know something about them.) Make sure they're safe and are backed by a competent medical authority. Truth be told, it appears that a great many of these "serums" are placebos. Nevertheless, they give you a new area of erotic focus and a greater sense of physical awareness. It's the experimentation and the novelty they provide that you want to focus on. Even if they don't work, you can *make* them work.

FOURTEENFOURTEENFOURTEENFO
URTEENFOURTEENFOURTEENFOUR
TEENFOURTEENFOURTEENFOURTE
ENFOURTEE fourteen NFOURTEEN
FOURTEENFOURTEENFOURTEENFO
URTEENFOURTEENFOURTEENFOUR
TEENFOURTEENFOURTEENFOURTE

COMMANDMENT EIGHT IN ACTION— HEIGHTENING
Attraction,
MINIMIZING COMPATIBILITY

A man who marries a woman to educate her falls a victim to the same fallacy as the woman who marries a man to reform him.
—ELBERT HUBBARD, AMERICAN WRITER AND EDITOR

It is the things in common that make relationships enjoyable, but it is the little differences that make them interesting.
—TODD RUTHMAN, AMERICAN WRITER AND EDITOR

I have come to the conclusion never again to think of marrying, and for this reason, I can never be satisfied with anyone who would be blockhead enough to have me.
—ABRAHAM LINCOLN,
IN A LETTER TO MRS. O. H. BROWNING, 1838

267

Commandment Eight
Adultery is about attraction.

My friends Jeffrey and Susie Goldstein are happily married. However, he loves football. His wife loves going to foreign art films.

The same thing applies in my own marriage. I used to devote a lot of time to sports (that is, before I grew the overhang that currently passes as a stomach), while Debbie grew up loving to cook and create things around the house and in the garden. I love technology and the latest computers and gadgets. To me, my laptop is my baby. Debbie just wants something that can get her onto the Internet to send e-mail. To her, our actual baby is her baby. (I wonder who is right?) I carry a Palm Pilot with its own satellite receiver that can track incoming nuclear missiles. She loves good pens and quality stationery, and cares nothing for tracking the location of an ICBM.

Now, why would a woman marry a man whose passion is football? Why not marry someone who has the same interests as you do? In other words, why do men and women gravitate toward each other when they are so obviously different? Heterosexuality seems to be an illogical proposition. Why shouldn't men and women be attracted to their own kind? A detailed discussion of gender differences is admittedly beyond the scope of this book. But in all our own lives, that difference is noticeable enough to wonder what on earth it is that draws men and women together at all, if they are so vastly dissimilar? While I cannot provide all the answers, it is worth, at least, posing these questions.

People tell me all the time about someone they are going out with that, although they are in love, they cannot possibly marry because, "We simply don't have enough in common. We'll run out of things to talk about." I usually tell such people that if they are correct—and compatibility is so important—then it should be best to marry someone of the same sex. Women naturally have more in common with women, and men with men. Heterosexuality offers little in the form of natural commonality. Why should you love someone who is your opposite?

Attraction versus Common Interests

Young children tend to gravitate toward members of the same sex, since they innately enjoy the same activities together. Ask any little boy in kindergarten what he thinks about girls and he'll probably stick out his tongue and say, "Yuck."

As they grow older and mature, however, boys begin reaching across the divide.

Sexual attraction begins to supersede common interests during boys' pubescent years, when attraction to the opposite sex becomes predominant. In most cases, it lasts this way for the rest of their lives. Yet what causes boys and girls, men and women, to gravitate toward one another? It's not that they have worlds in common. Indeed, it is precisely what they *lack* in common that causes attraction. But that mysterious thing called *attraction*, which no philosopher has ever fathomed and no scientist has ever explained, is absolutely crucial to sustaining passion.

This is a critical point. In my lectures I usually ask the audience to identify the force that would have a man and a woman remain happily under the same roof together for fifty or sixty years. The first response is usually "love." I then point out that in that case neither man nor woman should leave the parental home. Our parents love us unconditionally. So why marry?

The next response is usually "friendship." But I explain that if this were the force that binds couples, then men should live together with their belching and commitment-phobic male friends, while women should camp out in a giant shopping mall together and go from sale to sale for the duration of their lives.

It is then that I offer the only response that can be verified by empirical testing: attraction. That's right, men and women don't *choose* to live together or to enter into heterosexual relationships. Rather, they are *irresistibly drawn to each other,* despite how irrational the entire enterprise may seem. They *cannot help* but gravitate toward one another. It is an illogical but powerful orientation. It's not something you plan, it's not premeditated. Attraction causes you to fall into a state that we call love. And only attraction—precisely because it is irrational—can last for the duration of a couple's life.

If you love your husband because he's funny, what do you do when he goes through a bad patch at work and becomes bitter? Do you leave him? If you gravitate toward your wife because she's young and beautiful, how do you react when she develops a second or a third chin? Do you send her to a plastic surgeon? Or do you trade her in for a younger version of herself? But when you are attracted inexplicably toward the masculine or feminine energy radiated by your spouse, this serves as a nuclear force that helps you break through all of life's vicissitudes.

One of the fundamental causes of marital breakdown today and the dramatic rise in infidelity is that we call the wrong shots. We draw the wrong conclusions. We make commonality of interests more important than attraction. We mistakenly believe that the more husbands and wives become alike, the more their attraction will grow—when precisely the opposite is true.

All dating patterns today are based on commonality. Studies show that 94 percent of men with a college education will marry only a woman with a college degree. Likewise, 97 percent of American women will not marry a man who earns less money than they do. Adrienne Burgess reported in her book *Will You Still Love Me Tomorrow* that: "When there is genuine choice, most people will pick life partners extremely similar to themselves as regards age, looks, income, education, interests and social class." Men and women today aren't looking to marry their opposites, but their *doubles.*

One woman, when describing what drew her to her husband, catches it exactly, "It was amazing—we were so alike. As soon as we began to talk we found an immediate connection . . . We even looked alike!" (*Sexual Arrangements: Marriage and the Temptation of Infidelity*) But the problem is, what do you do down the road when commonality leads to monotony, when you can no longer enrich or surprise each other, because you have morphed into the same person?

Modern marriage has become aristocratic in nature—the daughter of a duke can marry someone only of similar noble birth—and we are all impoverished as a result. That commonalities are today the determining factor in marriage is captured in the contemporary usage of the word "partner" to connote a spouse. A partner is someone with whom you share nearly everything in common, and with whom you are jointly devoted to a mutual enterprise. Sounds pretty exciting, huh?

Yet, adultery stories are the exact opposite. Studies show that while people marry those similar to themselves, they have affairs with their opposites because it leads to intense attraction.

Adultery stories are replete with references to women suddenly rediscovering their lost feminine side—a renewed desire for flowers; a sudden craving to adorn themselves and show off sexy bras and lacy underwear; a desire to be passively swept off their feet by a risk-taking Prince Charming.

The same is true of men. Husbands who take mistresses suddenly feel masculine. They work out, they become the great planners in romantic trysts, they regain their adventurous side as they slowly crawl out of the TV-watching, couch-potato mode, and they become audacious and exploratory lovers. These are the goodies that no longer exist in their marriage, and note, they are all pursuits that magnify male/female differences. Adultery involves the profound reversal of the homogenizing effects on gender that have become a typical staple of marriage. Whereas marriage is about being unisex for compatibility's sake, adultery is about two different genders whose radically different energies create strong attraction.

Partner or Lover?

One of the principal reasons for the loss of passion in marriage is that, as noted, we look upon our spouse first and foremost as a partner sharing our interests in life, rather than as our lover, sharing our bodies.

A partner is someone with whom we share much in common. Partners in business are selected from those who can match our capital, experience, and business know-how. But we make a mistake when we bring this principal into romantic relationships, where being opposites is crucial and where *attraction* is the force necessary to bind the relationship, rather than *commonality*. Husbands and wives are not friends, partners, or comrades. They are not overthrowing Czarist Russia together or starting a new Internet company. Rather, they are making sparks that ignite a fire. And for that you need two things that rub against each other, not collude. This mistake does not exist in adultery, where lovers treat each other like sweethearts. We must return to the time in our lives when we saw in our spouse a sexual partner, rather than someone with the same political outlook.

The truth is that men and women get married because they are attracted to each other, and this attraction is *not* based on shared interests, but on sexual magnetism. To heighten attraction we need to safeguard the masculine and feminine traits that are intrinsic to men and women. The more we can highlight these differences, the more we can intensify the attraction. In Judaism, the laws that separate the sexes were designed not simply to preserve modesty, but to preserve *the distinctions* between men and women. What woman would be flattered to hear that her male friends are not remotely sexually interested in her, or don't even notice that she is female? Since when is it a compliment for a man and a woman who are best friends to go camping together and share a sleeping bag—yet neither has any sexual thoughts about the other? Yet, in Oxford, I heard male and female students bragging about that sort of thing all the time. And the *New York Times* reported in May 2002 that coed *rooms* are becoming increasingly common on American campuses.

I knew a student at Oxford who was engaged to be married. She invited her closest male friend, who was also soon to be married, to come to visit her from the United States. With her fiancé's permission, they went on a trip to a different city.

They shared a hotel room, but had separate beds.

I said to both of them, "The two of you are engaged. Why did you allow such a stupid thing?"

She replied, "My fiancé trusts me and this man is my closest friend. We weren't going to do anything. It is the greatest compliment to me that my fiancé trusts me that much, and that my friend respects me enough to see me only as a person, rather than as a sex object."

But is this truly flattering? Does one really want to know that a male friend sees her as just another guy? Is it good that in our society, men and women have become immune to each other's sexuality? Without attraction, what will cause men and women to cross the gender divide and spend their lives with the *opposite* sex?

When I was a boy growing up in Miami Beach, almost no one ever put on suntan lotion. That's because the ozone layer had not yet been so completely depleted by greenhouse gases and fossil-fuel emissions. But now, of course, people are terrified of the effects of the sun.

What if the "ozone layer of male/female attraction" has been similarly depleted? What if that magnetism that men and women once carried invisibly has been so decimated that men and women no longer create the necessary polar attraction around one another to cause each others' hearts to start racing?

One member of the L'Chaim Society committee was the kind of girl all of the men would track down in order to talk about their emotional problems. She was every guy's best friend, but never anyone's girlfriend. She walked into my office one day and closed the door, saying she was upset about something. I told her to open the door, for in Jewish law a man and woman who are not married cannot be secluded together in a room. "I'm a married man and you're a single woman," I explained, "so we can't be in a room with the door closed."

She became very emotional. I asked her what was wrong. "It is a law," I told her, "I am certainly not trying to offend you."

She said, "I'm not upset because you 'offended' me. I'm just not accustomed to men treating me like I'm a woman. You've just reminded me of that." Most men who had looked upon her had made her feel as if they were looking at another man instead of a woman.

Many single women who come to my lectures tell me that they wish guys *would* treat them as sexual objects. They are tired of the scores of men who tell them "You're just not my type," by which they mean, "I'm not sufficiently attracted to you." They feel patronized that these same men will go to movies and bookstores with them, but would never contemplate making them into girlfriends. In the words of one woman, "I asked Charles, my best friend, 'If I'm good enough to be your best friend, why can't I be your lover?' But Charles answered that 'the chemistry wasn't right.'"

There is nothing flattering about pretending that your friend of the opposite sex is not attractive, however good a friend he or she is. There are reasons for the centrality of feminine dress in the Jewish religion, specifically women wearing feminine garb as opposed to clothing indistinguishable from a man's. Sure, things like jeans may be comfortable for a woman to wear around the house. But after a while her husband can begin, albeit subconsciously, to look at her as a handyman. Though it is not her intent, she becomes "one of the guys." The key is to never let it reach this stage, and when a woman is walking around all the time dressed in men's clothes and working around the house, it can be easy to overlook her sexual aspects.

Men and women are not supposed to be the same. This doesn't mean women should be subordinate to men. Indeed, as I explained in my book, *Judaism for Everyone,* the ancient Jewish faith has always regarded the feminine as being superior to the masculine and women as being the spiritual elders of men. Rather, my point is that men and women should retain their essential and distinct differences. I believe that husbands should not become extremely close (even platonic) friends with other women, or wives with other men, not only because it may be improper, but also because it is still sending the wrong signals—even if nothing happens. It is the kind of social training that is making this problem within relationships much worse. It means that you are not seeing other people as women and men; instead, everyone becomes "people." But remember, marriage itself thrives on the differences, and hence the attraction, between men and women. Desensitizing ourselves to the other gender, or becoming gender-neutral, robs us of the sexual polarity that draws the opposite gender to us.

When husbands and wives are having difficulties in their marriage, and they are not sexually interested in one another, they rarely address the problem directly. They will go to a cinema, or a concert, together. They will think that they are helping the matter by spending "quality time" together. But is that why they got married in the first place, because they both love music? Is that why they took lifelong vows—so that they would always have someone to see the next Cameron Diaz flick with? Forget the darn film. Do something about your love life. Do as two lovers would: *Go to bed.* If a husband and wife devoted just half as much time to their sexual encounters as they do to their social calendars, they would have a much better chance at achieving the greatest marriage on earth.

Of course, commonality of interests is important. But the differences that separate men and women are essential. You will never be infatuated or in love with someone because you are simply compatible with that person. That's newfangled nonsense. You might do business with the person; you might go on trips with him or her. But you won't share that person's bed every single night because you both love Woody Allen films. You will do so because of attraction: physical, spiritual, and emotional.

Exercises
HEIGHTENING
ATTRACTION

WIVES:

1. Be careful not to walk around the house wearing faded T-shirts and your husband's ripped sweats. Sure, when you're cleaning up and organizing the house you don't have to dress like you would for a cocktail party. But it is possible to appear appropriately feminine in workaday clothes. Dress in a manner in which your respective masculinity and femininity are accented. Men and women are attracted to each other specifically through their differences. Avoid the unisex look at all costs and at all times.

2. Dress differently for your husband than you would for other men. Be conscious of this. If you wear a cap to go to the laundromat, take it off and let your hair down before you have lunch with your husband. Don't wear your ripped up jeans to go out to dinner, even if you are only going to the neighborhood pizza joint. If you resist behaving around your husband like you are just "one of the guys," then he will know not to treat you like one. In Jewish law, married women even cover their hair all the time except when they are with their husbands, *so that their essential femininity is preserved for their marriages.* Thus, their men are afforded another essential erogenous zone that is closed off to the rest of the world. And remember, it's erotic obstacles that create attraction.

3. Never wear anything but sexy undergarments. They need not be unbearable to wear and they can be of cotton rather than silk. But don't allow yourself to wear something that looks like a man's Fruit of the Loom underwear. Put your most feminine foot forward at all times; this means always being ready for a passionate moment, and always being seen by your husband with your femininity accentuated, rather than buried beneath an avalanche of rugged male lumberjack flannels.

4. Light candles around the house to bring in a soft feminine charm rather than harsh and overt light. If you or your husband is working late into the night in the home office, turn off the bright lights in the office and put on some soft candlelight. Do the same thing if the two of you are sitting on the couch and reading. Candle flickering resembles the sparks of love, varying and dancing in the night. And, of course, at least once a week, light candles in your bedroom for softly lit lovemaking. If you're not going to use candles, try those electrical lights with knobs that allow them to be softened. People feel exposed in too strong a light. Make the environment cozy and intimate. Light some incense to increase the sensuality of the environment and your mood.

5. Get your husband to take long baths with you. Go out and buy scented bath oil, and give each other soft sensual massages in the bath. A bath is a uniquely feminine thing, whereas a shower is masculine. Baths are sensual, showers sexual.

Husbands:

1. Learn not to be lazy. Lazing around the house, especially in front of a TV show or video game, reduces your wife's interest in you. Women are heavily turned off by lazy men. Your wife will perceive you more and more as sloth-like— unmotivated and dispassionate—which becomes a major turnoff. Always remember, a woman is turned on to a man with a plan.

2. Exercise with your wife. You will naturally appear more masculine, and your wife will notice your muscles—even if you are only just beginning to work on them. Even sweating in front of your wife can make you appear more masculine (but for goodness sake apply deodorant in heavy quantities). She will see that you are making the effort to improve your muscle tone and body for *her* sake. And there's nothing wrong with seeing your wife in a tight leotard once a week, either.

3. Weather permitting, go swimming with your wife or go to the beach. Seeing each other in male and female bathing suits, and playing together in the water, accentuates gender energy. I know a couple who have a pool at home and who play water basketball several times a week. It's done wonders for their attraction to each other, even though the wife has no clue how to play basketball and the husband usually wins (the winner, of course, gets to massage the loser's sore legs).

4. Take charge in the bedroom. Not *all* the time, but a lot of the time. Women want to be swept off their feet, so do the sweeping. Grab your wife at home and make love on the living room carpet and the breakfast table. Taking charge with strong masculine energy heightens your wife's feminine erotic energy. The more she tells you the neighbors will see or her dress will be ruined, the more you charge ahead. Show that you know exactly what you want to do in bed. Don't stray from your plan. All too many guys let their libidos make them impatient. They go into bed with their wives planning to kiss for half and hour and slowly stroke her body for another hour, only to suddenly run to the finish line, and oops! It's all over and the TV is back on. Big mistake. Doing what comes naturally is just about the worst thing a man can do in bed. Transcend your nature and focus on your wife's pleasure first.

5. Do the occasional manly thing for your wife. Move the furniture when she asks you to. Change the lightbulb. Put up those family photographs on the living room wall. Shower once a week, whether you need to or not.

FIFTEENFIFTEENFIFTEENFIFTEENFI
FTEENFIFTEENFIFTEENFIFTEENFIF
TEENFIFTEENFIFTEENFIFTEENFIFT
EENFIFTEENF fifteen FIFTEENFIFTE
ENFIFTEENFIFTEENFIFTEENFIFTEE
NFIFTEENFIFTEENFIFTEENFIFTEEN
FIFTEENFIFTEENFIFTEENFIFTEENFI

COMMANDMENT NINE IN ACTION— NOURISHING THE Ego

A great poet has seldom sung of lawfully wedded happiness, but of free and secret love.

—ELLEN KEY, SWEDISH AUTHOR

The lure of adultery can be seen in the old saying: "The grass is greener on the other side of the fence." Yet, the grass is greener where you mow it, fertilize it, water it, and take care of it.

—ANONYMOUS

It is the passion that is in a kiss that gives to it its sweetness; it is the affection in a kiss that sanctifies it.

—CHRISTIAN NESTELL BOVEE,
AMERICAN AUTHOR AND LAWYER

Commandment Nine
Adultery boosts the ego; as such, it is an act of re-creation.

All parents know that they have a responsibility to their children not only to bring them to life, but also to *give* them life constantly. We grant them life through constant encouragement and compliments. We praise everything they do. And we know that every act of praise strengthens them and gives them a new lease on life.

Adulterous partners know the same thing, and are constantly complimenting and encouraging one another and telling each other how beautiful the other is. Married couples, on the other hand, exchange compliments about as frequently as Halley's comet passes.

In one of its most significant and famous pronouncements, the Bible maintains that God created man in His own image. From time immemorial, theologians of all denominations have debated what exactly this means. To me the application of this teaching is in everyday life, and its meaning is clear: In the same way that God is a Creator, so is mankind. Just as God creates and takes life, mankind, too, is endowed with that power, and I don't mean literally, by having children or committing murder. Every time we show someone extravagant attention and affection, we make him or her feel important, and in doing so we really and truly "create that person" and bring him or her to life. Those who are ignored or unloved feel as though they are not alive. Our emotions, then, have the power to elicit an identical response. When we love, we create. When we dismiss or reject, we kill and destroy.

When a husband shows his wife that she is the sexiest woman in the world to him, this is what she truly becomes. She thinks of herself as a highly attractive and desirable woman, and she starts to act the part. She dresses with more care; she walks with poise and confidence; and she begins to attract the stares of all the men around her.

The old story goes of an island where the women are exchanged in marriage for cows. A beautiful woman would be exchanged for ten cows from her suitor, whereas an ugly one might only be worth perhaps one or two. There was a father who had a daughter who was so sickly and unsightly that he scarcely thought that he could exchange her for even one miserable heifer. But along came a young man who insisted on marrying her in exchange for ten cows. The father protested that he would settle for far less, but the suitor was adamant. A year later, the father traveled to the other side of the island to visit his daughter and her husband. He could scarcely recognize his daughter. She glowed with an electric beauty that lit up the entire home. The father inquired of his son-in-law what could possibly have brought about such a change in his daughter. "You treated her like a one-cow woman," he told the old man, "so she became what you projected. But I told her that she was a ten-cow woman, so she became what I projected."

It is no wonder, then, that nearly all the studies on adultery point out that one of the initial clues in detecting a partner's infidelity is when he or she dresses much better than ever before and has a renewed sense of confidence.

Here, for example, is a short list based on numerous studies that point to your spouse having an affair.

If he is a man, he might suddenly:

1. Go on a diet, try to trim down his waist, begin exercising, or go to a gym.
2. Wear sexier underwear, stop wearing saggy boxer shorts and trade them in for tight-fitting briefs.
3. Talk of having his teeth fixed, straightened, or whitened.
4. Start sucking mints to have fresh breath.
5. Become much more flirtatious with other women when the two of you go out together.
6. Start reading sex manuals or experimenting with new sexual positions with you (he may be practicing on you for her).
7. Start doing his own laundry.
8. Bleaching his hair and getting rid of the gray.

If she's a woman, she might suddenly:

1. Start dieting, working out, and toning her figure.
2. Switch from cotton undergarments to lacy silk.
3. Wear much more colorful clothing and go on shopping sprees.
4. Show a much greater amount of energy and exuberance, getting up earlier and being more accommodating around the house
5. Show an eagerness to get out of the house.
6. Stop watching TV and begin reading romance novels.
7. Wear much brighter makeup and redder lipstick.
8. Stare at herself in the mirror a lot more.

The studies point out that this increased liveliness applies particularly to women. Their husbands were ignoring them, so they didn't care how they looked or how they carried themselves. Suddenly, they have lovers who find them alluring and attractive and want to have sex with them. They begin to live and act the part. Eventually even their husbands notice, and in turn find them more attractive. Conversely, when a husband fools around with other women—even if his wife is the world's most beautiful woman—her looks will go to pot. Adultery is the quickest form of murder because you show someone that he or she doesn't matter. You kill a person's confidence. You destroy a person's worth. To you, then, it is as if your spouse is dead. And your spouse probably feels dead, too.

The reverse can also work—if you believe and accept that lurking deep within each and every husband and wife is a passionate, sensual, and sexy being. If the person you are married to has a heart in his or her breast that beats, then your spouse also has a hidden, rudimentary fire burning in his or her loins, waiting to be uncovered. For those who do not appear overtly so—and with the passage of time we naturally become bored with even the most beautiful and handsome partner unless we take steps to reverse it—this must be brought to the fore by the incredible love, affection, and desire that only you can show your spouse. When you show your spouse that he or she is sexy and appealing, your partner will dress and act that way.

Love: The Greatest of Saving Graces

Love is the ultimate act of liberation. It frees us from the pathetic life of being obsessed with ourselves. Love releases our greatness, our capacity to reach outside ourselves and leave a permanent imprint on someone else's life. When you love someone, that person's wishes become your wishes, that person's delights become your delights, and his or her pleasures become your pleasures. Anything else is not love but self-interest. Love gives us the ability to put ourselves second to someone else, thereby defying our essential human nature to be selfish. Love allows us to transcend the confines of the ego and experience a one-flesh experience, whereby everything that happens to the person we love is felt by us as well.

Parents love their children enough to give them life for the first time. But husbands and wives do something even more exceptional. They give each other a new burst of life once they have sunk into the morass of mere existence. Real love is when couples come to life, calling their existence into being anew. The enormous power of love is that it has the power to bring forth existence from nothingness; a person giving love plays the role of creator, bringing a partner to life.

By cheating on a spouse and in effect ignoring him or her, we play the role of a creator who has taken away life. Whereas love enhances and uplifts our spouse's existence, adultery degrades and destroys it.

Isn't it ironic that couples in long-lasting relationships often describe themselves as slowly dying? As their married lives fall into routine, they slowly sink under the turbulent waters of domestic pressures, and eventually there is nothing left other than two lifeless corpses who go about their daily lives as automatons in a museum diorama or a life-size advertisement display. How many married couples have allowed themselves to slowly decay until they have become the living dead, or walking corpses? And how many could have avoided it through something as simple as showing each other small displays of daily affection and offering each other a kind word?

Adultery is the opposite: It's the ultimate ego boost that creates people anew and makes them come to life. In her book *Tempted Women,* Carol Botwin quotes a woman in her thirties, married for ten years, who had begun an affair: "My husband and I have had good times, but I feel like there is nothing left for us anymore. We no longer do anything together. We each have different interests, we never agree on anything. We have spent most of our life together arguing about things, sometimes simple things, sometimes about the children. So when I met someone I enjoy being with so much and having someone to talk to, it was great. Seemed like it fitted an empty space in my life."

It's astonishing that people seem to feel this sensation of life-giving love only in an act of unfaithfulness, rather than within the comfort of marriage. The capacity to excite a member of the opposite sex is one of the great pleasures of life. It's not only about coming to life oneself, but it's also about the capacity to give life. When you touch someone, his or her heart rate increases and the pulse quickens. You're giving the other person life, right there before your very eyes. It's no wonder that the majority of male sexual fantasies revolve around touching a woman who is a stranger and making her slowly succumb. But that's the whole problem. When it's a stranger who succumbs, we feel really sexy because this person doesn't know us and wanted to resist us. When we succeed, our sexiness and appeal have been too powerful for the other person. Our masculinity is corroborated as we slowly light her womanly fire. But when a man touches his wife and she succumbs, he doesn't see it as any great achievement because she is already willing to have sex with him.

The Greatest Flaw in Marriage

Upon assuming my responsibilities in Oxford as rabbi in my early twenties, I was convinced that the greatest challenge in marriage was the simple difficulty of two people—both accustomed to their own way of life—now sharing their lives with another person, and somehow accommodating each other's idiosyncrasies. But, as time passed, I began to understand that the real problem was maintaining sexual and emotional desire.

After all, why is it that when people dated before marriage they were far more willing to bend and give in to each other, in order to impress each other? And why is this so much more difficult after marriage? The answer of course is that once people are married, they begin to take each other for granted, and no longer make so much effort to win the love and sexual favors that they once wished to discover.

Why on earth is it that a husband or wife would rather argue over dinner not being ready—and refuse to apologize after an outburst—thereby ending up spending the night in separate bedrooms? Why don't they realize instead that they could fall into each other's embrace and experience an evening of love and bliss? Why would they allow themselves to be incarcerated in the icy prison of wounded pride, rather than be liberated by the warm glow of a loving embrace and live together in the open spaces? The only explanation is that sometimes we just do not value that embrace and that act of love enough. If we desired sex with our spouses badly enough, we would do anything to get it and to keep our spouses' favor—just as adulterous lovers do. Far from being our enemy, sex is our friend—and must be used to our advantage.

Hence, the great lesson that married couples can learn from forbidden lovers is the importance of always making each other feel desirable. Compliments are so easy to give. All you have to do is observe, appreciate, open your lips, and expel air. So why do we find it so difficult? Why don't we feel the desire to compliment each other all the time? After all, the payoffs are great—from better sex to a better chance at a happy marriage!

There is more. Our words have the power to create an outer reality. The more you repeat something, the more it becomes so. When a man compliments his wife's looks, he convinces himself of the beauty that he witnesses. We all know this to be true and the greatest example is anger. The more you talk about something that upsets you, the more upset you become. But the same is true in stoking the fires of physical attraction. Maybe if we could somehow train ourselves to see how each compliment is equivalent to an act of mouth-to-mouth resuscitation reviving an unconscious victim, we would awaken from our own stupor and begin to offer them. That's why the possibility of adultery is such a central alarm clock to marriage. It reminds us to always focus on the four essentials of every thriving relationship:

1. The person we are married to is not just a spouse or a person, but a sexual being. Our spouse is not our partner, but our lover.
2. The person we married has sexual needs and the need to be desired. We all need to be needed, we want to be wanted.
3. Our spouse is sexually attractive to other people who will risk all to have an affair with him or her. Likewise, our spouse is attracted to others, especially those who express an interest in him or her.
4. Finally, bringing all these things together, our spouse is not as much under our spell and control as we might suppose. We must strive hard to retain our spouse's attention and affection, and if we do not—since our spouse is a sexual being—we will lose him or her to someone more attentive.

Great sex doesn't begin when you both close the bedroom door behind you and turn out the lights. It begins in the morning when the sun begins to shine and you offer a compliment that causes the burning embers to glow. Foreplay can happen any time; the day should be spent making each other feel desirable so that your lust and confidence builds up, and naturally makes you want to have sex.

Fulfilling Every Need

Another primary way to create your spouse anew and bathe him or her in attention and affection is to take your spouse's desires seriously. Stop determining which thing he or she asks for is important and which is not. Taking someone's will seriously is the ultimate determiner of whether or not you actually value that person. Just look at how accommodating adulterous couples are with each other. They cater to every need. They will change their schedules—work or otherwise—at a moment's notice to be with each other. They will drop even the needs of their own children to rush to cater to the desires of their lover. Husband and wives, by contrast, ossify in their own little worlds and make a token effort to accommodate each other at all times.

Any husband or wife who loves the person he or she is married to is willing to fulfill every spousal desire. However, sometimes trouble starts when the request doesn't make sense. For example, a wife tells her husband how much she loves flowers and politely asks him to put them at the top of his list of romantic things he buys for her. He replies that flowers die quickly. "I can't understand why you're insisting on my buying things with such a short life span; they're a waste of money!" He agrees to buy her clothing and jewelry instead. She grows angry and insists that he cannot love her unless he does what she has asked. He then demands that at the very least she should explain herself to him, but she cannot.

Is there anyone who can truly explain why women love flowers? To be sure, flowers are delicate and colorful and full of life, just like women. And they perish after a single day, an indication that love must always be renewed. But in the final analysis, it is not about logic or rationale. Rather, a woman's love of flowers is tied to her core and mysterious femininity, and is something utterly transcendent. Yet he insists that he cannot appreciate or respond to her request unless she can rationalize it for him. In the meantime, he continues to buy her even more expensive gifts, and she continues to be miserable.

This husband is making a mistake. He is rejecting the woman in his wife. He insists that she think like a man before she can earn his love. Being in a relationship means being responsive to the needs of your lover and trying your best to please him or her. If you choose to fulfill only those desires of your partner that make sense to you, then your relationship is de facto a relationship with yourself. Being in a relationship doesn't mean doing what you think is best for the other person. In a relationship, you first listen and then you give.

The Woman in Your Wife; the Man in Your Husband

The second mistake that the aforementioned husband makes is far more significant. By saying that he will do whatever she wants as long as she explains herself, he is insisting that he be connected only to her intellectual, rational side. Her deeper, truer self remains a mystery to him—a part of her with which he has no association. This man is not married to all of his wife. In fact, he is not joined to the part of her that is most attractive: her womanhood.

There is an essential femininity in his wife that he will never understand, simply because he is male. There is nothing she can possibly do that can convey to him her intrinsic desire for flowers. It completely transcends male logic and is connected with feminine intuition. But this does not invalidate its importance. On the contrary, it is the very differences between males and females that sustain their attraction. By telling his wife that she doesn't know what she wants, or insisting that her demands are foolish or nonsensical, this husband refuses to acknowledge her independence as a human being. But when he actually fulfills her every wish—whether or not he understands it—he ensures that he is connected with her innermost self. Only now is he married to his wife in her entirety, which also encompasses the part of her that is essentially different from him, that is, the woman in his wife.

Likewise, if a woman denies her husband's right to be different, by refusing to accommodate (what appear to her to be) his irrational desires, like his need to go away fishing for the occasional weekend with the boys, she is forgetting that her husband is not just a breadwinner and father: He is the man she married, and she must cherish him or lose him.

Show your spouse extravagant love. Show your overwhelming interest, and constantly boost his or her confidence. Show through tangible action that amidst your natural attraction to strangers, your spouse has nothing to fear from people outside the marriage so long as he or she is always loving and attentive. Show your spouse how attracted you are to him or her, and emphasize that person's beauty or handsomeness. Prove that you remain fully focused on your spouse. Even if you are forced to go to an extreme for a while in terms of behaving unnaturally and avoiding conversation with other men or women, because of the irrational jealousy we spoke of earlier, do it. Your spouse will feel loved, special, confident, and honored within your relationship.

Marriage is a hungry animal that needs to be fed constantly. But, like every ravenous animal, it is filled with enormous vigor and verve.

Exercises
BOOSTING YOUR
SPOUSE'S EGO

1. Use the power of fantasy to your advantage. First, pretend that a stranger or friend is watching you with your spouse at all times. This will make you into a romantic. You wouldn't yell at your spouse in front of a friend, so don't do it in private either. You would probably always remember to compliment your spouse and speak to her affectionately in front of a friend. So do it at home as well, and be consistent. Remember that marriage is unnatural. Don't fret if you have a period of monotony in your life. It will get better, but only if you create a general ambience of romance and appreciation.

2. Fantasize about your spouse being in very erotic situations that are pleasurable to you. Afford your spouse the quality of newness by mentally placing him or her in novel situations, especially during sex. Husbands should fantasize about their wives as great sexual seductresses who are chased by highly desirable men. Be your own movie director. Every man or woman, put into the right setting, becomes attractive. Visualize your wife as a cheerleader for the Dallas Cowboys. If that doesn't do it for you (and I have to admit that neither the Cowboys or their cheerleaders have ever lit my fire), then imagine her in the locker room of the Los Angeles Lakers, or better yet, on a road trip with them. Never make the terrible mistake of thinking for even one moment that your spouse is not attractive. Second, mentally placing your spouse into inventive situations ensures that he or she appears new to you as you watch your spouse in an erotic situation.

3. Bring a daily surprise that makes your spouse come to life. Buy your spouse little things he or she loves and show your spouse that he or she is always on your mind. One day it could be a colorful key chain with her name on it. The next day bring him a new herbal tea to relax with at the end of the day. It is everyday acts like these that engender and maintain a constant threshold of affection and romance, which in turn lead to long moments of sexual passion. Make your marriage into a fairy tale by constantly animating it with loving acts.

4. FOR HUSBANDS: When having sex, ensure that your wife climaxes first. There are few better ways to make your wife come to life as an exciting sexual object than to watch her in the throes of passion, and there are few better ways of creating her anew as a sexual seductress than to witness her abandoning her complete self to sexual pleasure. Too many husbands just don't take the time to make their wives enjoy the experience. Do this especially in places like darkened movie theaters. Touch your wife dangerously and sinfully in the middle of a crowded theater. (Of course, wait until the lights go out.) Even reticent wives who at first shoo away your hand will, after a few moments, be slinking back in their chairs as their whole body begins to tremble and shudder. This way, even if the movie's awful, you will have had an Academy Award–winning performance.

According to one survey, the ratio of male to female orgasms in marriage is thirty to one, with some women claiming that they can go six months without their husbands giving them pleasure; others say that to date they still have never climaxed. But this is not true in adultery, where women claim to orgasm 83 percent of the time, as opposed to married sex where they climax only 27 percent of the time. According to a recent article in the *Journal of the American Medical Association*, almost a third of the women said they did not regularly experience orgasm, and *Ladies Home Journal* conducted a survey in which over half of the women admitted to faking orgasms. One common joke explains it best. "Mommy, mommy, what's an orgasm?" "I don't know. Ask your father."

The Bible actually mandates that a husband is obligated to provide his wife with several essential items, one of which is sexual and erotic pleasure. In Jewish law, a man must focus on his wife's sexual pleasure before his own. Ensuring that one's wife always enjoys lovemaking is pivotal for the passion of a marriage.

Make your wife into the equivalent of an adulterous woman. Focus on her body and make her sexual pleasure paramount, until she responds to you by abandoning every earthly concern, ascending the heights of sexual passion, pulling you along with her, and in the process becoming your mistress as opposed to your monotonous, everyday partner. As she writhes and gasps in passionate abandonment, she may pull out the last few strands of hair from your balding scalp. But even then it will have been worth it.

5. Abstain from masturbation or other forms of sexual self-gratification. Work your hardest at reducing the vast number of sexual outlets—be they mental, verbal, or otherwise—that have become available to us in the modern age, and channel all your sexual energy toward your spouse. The more you show that you lust after your spouse, the more alive he or she will be. Your lust and your libido have the power to make your spouse into a new person. But when you significantly diminish your hunger for your spouse by repeatedly releasing your sexual steam, that power is greatly reduced.

My objections are not only religious, and I am not trying to return us to a time when boys and girls once again believe that they will go blind if they masturbate. When husbands and wives release their sexual lusts through masturbation, they are almost guaranteed far fewer passionate encounters later on, because they have found an outlet that lessens their hunger. The simple and undeniable fact is that a man and woman who abstain from sex and masturbation for a period of ten to twelve days will lust for one another and grow obsessed with their upcoming night of reunion in the most passionate and powerful way.

6. Stop comparing your spouse mentally to every man or woman who walks down the street. Learn to be subjective, rather than objective, in your attraction. Allow your emotions to color your judgment.

Perhaps one of the strongest deadeners of passion in marriage is the incessant comparison that muddles today's marriages. These days it is so easy to compare one's spouse to others who seem so much more remarkable. Supermodels and film stars, both male and female, parade through our bedroom nightly, making it almost impossible for us not to feel somewhat disappointed as we turn to our bed partner and peer at our less perfect spouse sleeping beside us.

Passion in marriage is predicated on the feeling and conviction that the person we are married to is beautiful and special, and thus worth the extreme exertion of effort to make the marriage work and do all we can to make our marriage passionate and special. People cannot be passionate about things that don't impress them or that they perceive as mundane. Not believing that your spouse is unusually beautiful and attractive leads to tedium in the marriage and a state whereby every exertion of effort at passionate lovemaking feels like an exercise in futility as well as a terrible burden.

So do your spouse a favor. Don't compare him or her to others. It's not fair to your spouse, or to you for that matter. Accept marriage for what it is: an ingenious device on the part of the Creator, whereby each and every one of us would always have someone around us who feels that we are the most attractive and worthwhile person on the globe. To be married is to become a celebrity to one. You may not appear on the cover of *Cosmo* or *Vogue,* and you may not have your own TV show. But there is one person who puts your picture up on the wall. That person saves your silly mementos. That person can remember the first time you kissed him or her on the cheek. That person stares at you when you are both out in public. When you walk into a room that person is totally absorbed by your presence and you immediately become the center of his or her attention, just like a famous movie star.

True enough, this isn't the kind of fame that will get the maitre d' to save you that exclusive table right near the fireplace in the restaurant. And strangers won't come up to you asking for an autograph. What it will give you, however, is someone who is not a fair-weather fan, but a permanent enthusiast.

And every one of us needs to feel that way. It's what makes us impregnable and immune to all the pain of life and the hurt that is to be found in our world.

SIXTEENSIXTEENSIXTEENSIXTEEN
SIXTEENSIXTEENSIXTEENSIXTEEN
SIXTEENSIXTEENSIXTEENSIXTEEN
SIXTEENSIXT sixteen EENSIXTEENS
IXTEENSIXTEENSIXTEENSIXTEENSI
XTEENSIXTEENSIXTEENSIXTEENSI
XTEENSIXTEENSIXTEENSIXTEENSI

COMMANDMENT TEN IN ACTION— EXPERIENCING
Sin

Though I did not miss the pleasures of love, I missed the pain. I thought I was made to love and suffer, but I loved nobody and nothing, and suffered only from my own indifference.

—MADAME RECAMIER,
NINETEENTH-CENTURY FRENCH SOCIALITE

There is a charm about the forbidden that makes it unspeakably desirable.

—MARK TWAIN

Needing to keep an affair secret lends danger to the enterprise. An affair is made all the more thrilling by virtue of its forbiddenness.

—DR. RICHARD TUCH,
THE SINGLE WOMEN-MARRIED MAN SYNDROME

Commandment Ten
Adultery is about danger, forbiddenness,
sinfulness, and excitement.

I saved the most important commandment for last. Adultery, above all else, is about forbiddenness, and nothing is as exciting as something that is forbidden. As the Talmud says, "Forbidden waters taste sweet."

Ellen, a married woman of forty who conducted an affair with a married man, describes it like this: "We did it at least eight times that first night. I couldn't resist him. And I made him come over to my home and make love in my bedroom. My husband could have walked in at any time. But that vastly increased the excitement. We were making love having lost all control, and no danger in the world could stop us. It was beyond anything I could ever have dreamed of."

In story after story of women relating their extramarital experiences, the forbidden quality of the relationship was a principal reason for its excitement. Indeed, committing adultery is one of the few forbidden things that are left to law-abiding men and women. In the stable world that most of us in the West are lucky enough to enjoy, we have lost the sense of danger that adultery seems to provide.

Adultery is taboo—and taboo is exciting. Just think about this for a moment. Nearly every man who has an affair describes the sex as the best he's ever had. Yet, these same men also speak of how different the sex becomes once they have divorced their spouses and moved in together with their mistresses. Once it is no longer forbidden, it becomes stale. Once they marry their mistresses and the relationship becomes lawful, the dangerous and passionate side is lost.

People in adulterous relationships practice what every teenager attracted to drugs knows: Forbidden things have an enticing, erotic quality. Sin is exciting. The more forbidden something is, the more we seem to hunger for it. In no area is this truer than in sex. Sexual attraction is greatly enhanced by the quality of forbiddenness. Desirability and sexuality are not contingent on aesthetic appeal or looks. Rather, it is all in the mind, which gravitates toward forbidden things more than anything else.

The allure of the forbidden and the sinful has to do with the sense of liberation they provide. We all feel somewhat hemmed in by laws, routines, expectations, and responsibilities. What sin says is: to hell with it all. You are the master of your own destiny. You make the rules, and you break others' rules. The exhilaration of emancipation is the soul of sin. This is especially accented in the realm of sexual sin, where the beast within is allowed to roam free.

In addition, real pleasure comes about when you experience a tidal wave of emotion that carries you away to an island of sensual paradise. What sin also provides is a feeling of being swept away. You may be a married man and wish to honor your marital commitments. But there is this goddess in front of you whose body is making yours sweaty and hot. Sinning with her shows that you cannot even stop yourself when you want to. You are being carried away by how good it feels.

Women also love the pleasure of sin because for many it is the only time they cannot help but submit to the ardor of their lust. Their sinful desire for their lovers becomes so strong that neither the battlements of the intellect nor the repercussions of social censure can serve to sever her from the pleasures she knows she must have.

Finally, sin is the apogee of pleasure because it makes a man feel like a man and a woman feel like a woman. When a man seduces a married woman who cannot resist his charms, he feels more masculine than at any other time in his life. Here is a woman who becomes putty in his hands, throws out all her morals and scruples, because she has encountered an Adonis who makes her weak at the knees. Conversely, when a woman snags another woman's husband she is made to feel—through the power of his preparedness to sin—that she is better than that woman, she is more desirable, more beautiful, and much better in bed. Ah, the glories of sin! And I fear that I'm making such a convincing case that I will not lure you back into the lawful confines of marriage. But this is all to demonstrate how important it is that husbands and wives sin with each other.

The Talmud emphasizes the need for forbiddenness in sexual relationships with its amazing pronouncement that: "Since the destruction of the Temple [in 70 C.E.], sexual pleasure has been taken [from those who practice it lawfully] and given to sinners." Rashi, the foremost of all Talmudic commentators, explains: "Because of the power of other worries [since the Temple was destroyed], the spirit does not arise in men to desire their wives, and therefore, the pleasure of intercourse has been taken away."

Men today are harried and harassed to support their families, to battle back against life's constant challenges. Their passion, therefore, is channeled into the functional realm, leaving little for the marital bed. So, if husbands and wives are to eat from the forbidden fruit, they have to become sinners. They have to bring forbiddenness into their marriages by learning to sin with each other.

I was once sitting in a car dealership in Oxford, waiting for two hours for my car to be repaired. All of the employees had to wear a standard uniform consisting of a white top and blue pants or skirt. The women's white tops were slightly see-through. It was amazing to observe how every male customer who walked up to the counter noticed the sheerness of the shirt and their undergarments—the outline of which was visible through their tops.

But here's the interesting thing. Nearly all the women were in their *fifties and sixties,* the kind of women who would normally be overlooked by young men as being unattractive. But that did not stop all of these young, good-looking guys—most of them students—from staring at the outline of these women's bras. When my car was finally finished, I walked up to one of these women who was in her late fifties and said to her, "Be honest with me, do you notice that men are aware of you women and what you are wearing? Let's face it. These uniforms are slightly transparent."

"Of course we notice it," she replied, "You'd have to be blind not to see it. We ask them if they want to pay by check or credit card, and they respond not to our faces but to our busts." When a woman wears a uniform through which her feminine bra straps show through, men are going to look in almost every case. Not because the women are necessarily youthful or beautiful, but rather, because *they are seeing something that they are not supposed to see.*

Most people think that only really pretty young women get stared at or spied on by men. This is not the case. Go on the Internet and you will see that half the women who offer themselves up as WebCam girls are ordinary by objective standards (or at least my friends who have explored this kind of thing tell me so!). By peering voyeuristically into her hidden world and seeing things you are not meant to see, you are entering something extraordinary. Watching an ordinary stranger undress on the Internet is suddenly exciting—even more so than seeing your own spouse do the same. Why? Because the wife is permitted, the WebCam girl is *forbidden.*

Why did the men look at these women with the see-through tops in the car dealership? People look at these attributes—low cut shirts or slits in skirts—because they are *suggestive.* They tell you that you might end up seeing something that you're not intended to see. It's the same reason we all like eavesdropping. It is something that excites a mental attraction. A woman who has a button open in her blouse and doesn't notice seems to be conveying to you that she only wants to get on with her business. She doesn't even know that you're there, which makes it more exciting when she bends over and her bra becomes visible. It's almost like the woman is giving you your own private, forbidden invitation to share something illicit with her—only she pretends not to be extending the invitation. She maintains her mystery and holds up erotic barriers, even as she subconsciously gives you a knowing wink.

Less Is More

Now notice an interesting phenomenon for male readers. If you're on vacation on a tropical island and you meet a woman on the beach in a bikini, you may be impressed with her figure. But just seeing this probably won't sexually stimulate you—especially if you've been exposed to a lot of bikinis over a few days.

Now imagine that at night you see the very same woman in a hotel corridor, walking around in her bra and underwear. No doubt this would excite you far more than the bikini. But why? She is wearing the same amount of clothing she did in the morning when you saw her on the beach. You see just as much of her body! So why is her appearance now so much more erotic?

The reason is that you are not excited simply by seeing her body, but rather, by the signals she is sending by walking around in her intimate attire. It's a forbidden, erotic signal. You're seeing something very private, something you're not supposed to be seeing. You're being invited into a forbidden zone, an invitation for one. *The excitement results from you suddenly finding yourself a guest in her inner, erotic sanctum.* She is sending you a personalized message: "I want you to look at me, even though you're not supposed to look at me." The tension of this double-speak, the friction created by this dual message, is what hooks the guy and makes him wild with desire.

A man who accidentally leaves his zipper open is not seen as sexy by women, but as clumsy and embarrassing. Very few women will get sexually excited at the sight. If anything, they will giggle at his humiliating oversight. But when a man wears jeans with a gaping hole near his bottom, a great many female eyes will gravitate toward the open flesh. It's just different. Here, it is exciting and sexy, rather than clumsy and stupid. In the former case he appears as a buffoon; in the latter he's a hunk. In the former it is an innocent omission where it appears awkward. In the latter, it is a daring gamble that is dangerous. There are countless other examples that demonstrate this point, namely, that sex is all in the mind, and the quickest way to change something ordinary into something erotic is to make it forbidden. That's why people love secrets and gossip. They're hearing something private that they're not meant to hear.

A man or a woman seen through the lens of forbiddenness is transformed into an erotic object. Men can see women walking around the entire day in shorts, and it's no big deal. But if they have a slit in their skirts, the men will already be looking because they might be able to peer into a forbidden zone. Conversely, this is why porn stars are not really erotic. There is nothing forbidden about them. You watch them once and then twice, and, by the third time, you get bored. Their whole bodies are permitted.

Howard Stern likes to portray himself as the horniest man alive. And yet in his book, *Miss America*, where he goes through a long list of attractive women whom he would like to bed, he comes along to Marilyn Chambers, the world's most famous porn star. In determining her availability, he says, "Who knows and who cares." She's way too available.

Occasionally Letting Go

Married couples must learn from adulterous men and women to bring sexual danger into their lives. Like an adulterous couple, husbands and wives have to completely let go and allow their passion to overcome them. In the same way that adulterous lovers cannot help but act on their attraction to each other, married couples are the same. Doing outrageous things together should be a central staple of marriage. Male readers, when was the last time you did something as simple as take your wives out on a warm summer evening—after the kids were asleep—into the backyard and make love to her under the fern tree? When was the last time you made your wives feel that you couldn't keep your hands off them in a public place—even if the police were going to arrest you for indecent behavior? What happened to sin in marriage?

Jerry was married to Donna for three years. They lived in a flashy apartment on Venice Beach in Los Angeles. The passion in their marriage deteriorated quickly. Jerry was an anxious type—a real dealmaker, forever moving about, never feeling settled, always needing a new horizon to retain his interest. Today we would call Jerry an adrenaline junkie. His boredom with everyday life quickly led to his boredom with his own wife, whom he loved, but had tired of. Jerry was on a business trip in New Orleans. Staying in a boutique hotel in the French Quarter, he found himself sitting in the lobby of his hotel at the bar, chatting with an attractive young blonde who seemed to be a regular. The conversation quickly became flirtatious, and Jerry realized where it was headed unless he put a stop to it. Jerry told the woman he had a late-night meeting and had to go, but the woman insisted he take her number so that they could meet later. "You can call me real late," she said.

Jerry went up to his room, confused. Is this what he wanted? Sex with another woman, when he was in the third year of his marriage? He mustered the courage to call his wife back at home. Waking her up, he told her what had happened. He also blamed the whole thing on her: "Our sex life has become so boring, so routine. I'm dying here. My blood is boiling from this woman who practically threw herself at me. Do you know how exciting that is?"

His wife slammed the phone down on him. He called her back. "Okay, I'm sorry. It's not your fault that I'm bored. It's both our fault. Let's do something crazy. Come out here tomorrow. Let's really go wild." He pushed his wife enough that she finally acquiesced. When she arrived the following evening, she was flabbergasted to discover that her husband's intention was to "swing" with another couple. He had bought a local magazine that listed couples who were into foursomes. Disgusted, his wife said that she was going home. They lay in the hotel room very late that night, both in their pajamas, back to back, their faces turned away from each other.

Finally, Jerry spoke up. "Don't you see how important it is for us to do something completely wild? To learn to let go? We've become completely staid—old before our time. We're like a middle-aged couple."

"I do understand that," his wife said, "but your ideas always involve compromising the intimacy of our marriage. I don't want any other man. I want you."

With that, his wife took off her nightgown, ripped off her

husband's pajamas, and started passionately kissing him. When their mutual passion was running out of control, his wife pulled opened the curtains, opened the full-length room window, and began making love to her husband right in the window. I should point out that this hotel was in the center of town in a major thoroughfare, they were on the second floor, and anyone could have seen them. But at last she felt totally free.

It was Jerry who now pulled back and said, "Are you crazy? Somebody will see us." But his wife, consumed by the passion of the moment, totally ignored him, absorbed as she was in the incredible world of bliss she had created. They made love there standing in the window, being fully aware that any passersby could see their silhouettes. (Luckily, in New Orleans that would be par for the course and no one would even notice.)

By the time they finished, they had the best sex of their married life. Caressing his wife lovingly back in bed, he asked her why she did it. But his wife didn't have to answer. Jerry understood the answer. He now knew that his wife was perfectly capable of losing all inhibition, provided that: first, she was not asked to do something that she was totally uncomfortable with, like be with another man; and second, her husband took the time to put her in the mood.

Couples should create more moments like these. They should become forbidden lovers to each other within the context of their marriage. Remember: One of marriage's most important mottos should always be to seduce and sin with your spouse.

Exercises

1. Go out to dinner with friends, choose to sit in the booth side of the restaurant with your friends opposite you. Touch each other under the table. No light stuff either. I mean really fondle each other. Go for the gold. Be adventurous. If your pulse isn't racing from the fear of someone seeing you, you're not doing it right.

2. Make love in public places. Go bicycle riding out in the woods and find a shady tree. One night, go and sleep in your backyard, under the stars, and make love in sleeping bags. The next night, sneak into the neighbor's backyard and do it in their garden. Husbands should sneak into the female lavatories with their wives and make love in one of the stalls. (You need to try this only once.) And while this is said partially tongue-in-cheek, the general idea is to have sexual encounters that are daring, exciting, and push the envelope.

3. Be like Jack, whom I described at the very beginning of this book. Make yourself into your wife's fantasy lover. Pretend to be someone else, seduce her as this mystery man. Be bold, daring, and creative. Never let her suspect it's you. By doing so, you directly make your marriage into something completely forbidden, as your wife slowly gravitates toward a man who is a stranger, without compromising the trust of your marriage, because in the end, that man is you. It really can work.

4. Turn up unannounced at your spouse's office. Take the phone straight out of his or her hands and rip each other's shirts off. Kiss each other all over and make love right there on the desk. Don't worry about getting caught. Heck, you're married, remember. You're allowed to. But don't overdo it either. Keep the noise level to a minimum. In the same way I educated you before about making love in the dark, here make love while coated in silence. The need to be quiet while you pleasure each other in creative ways can greatly enhance the excitement, and it will also ensure that you don't get sued for sexual harassment by distracting the entire office, or sending out sound waves in the direction of those who don't want to hear it because they are jealous of not having been invited to participate. All you need is for the entire office to get wind of what you're doing and soon there'll be a party of onlookers. If your coworkers accuse you and your spouse of "moral turpitude," accuse them of just being jealous. Better yet, deny the whole thing and simply say, "Whatever do you mean? We were just looking at projected forecasts for the fourth quarter."

Important proviso: If you are going to do this, it's best if you or your spouse actually *own the company*. You see, many companies have policies about ripping clothes off or having sex on premises, married or not. We all know how stodgy corporate America can be. They usually would allow you to have sex illicitly with a coworker you're not married to. But it's against the law to ever make love to someone you *are* married to, as the rule seems to have been in the Clinton White House. Therefore, if you are going to take this advice, get permission from your boss to have sex with your spouse on your work desk. In most cases, your boss will grant you permission so long as he is invited to watch. Some are really conservative on this point and may not wish for your office to be converted into a love chamber. If the boss objects to the office use, ask him or her if you can use the conference room. If the boss is still difficult, go out and buy the company. Your marriage is worth it. If you can't afford it right now with the economy being the way it is, then simply start kissing your spouse in the office, and then take him or her to a nearby hotel, which should be a lot cheaper, and for which you can't be fired. Just make sure this all happens during your lunch break. No one said that you can't skip lunch and just have dessert.

5. Learn how to play with each other again. Make a time at least once a week when you can go out and get a little crazy with each other. Run away from the "work" responsibilities of marriage. Go out once a week and have fun. Go play miniature golf, or go bowling or roller-skating. Play practical jokes on one another. Impersonate each other and tease your spouse. Drink a couple of beers and take a taxi home. Laugh out loud at a movie together. All work and no play make Jack and Jane into a dull couple. Make your spouse into your fun playmate instead of your serious partner.

part 4

The
Dawning of the
Kosher Adultery

Revolution

SEVENTEENSEVENTEENSEVENTEE
NSEVENTEENSEVENTEENSEVENTE
ENSEVENTEENSEVENTEENSEVENT
EENSEVEN seventeen EENSEVEN
TEENSEVENTEENSEVENTEENSEVE
NTEENSEVENTEENSEVENTEENSEV
ENTEENSEVENTEENSEVENTEENSE

PARENTS ARE Lovers, TOO

A single man has not nearly the value he would have in that State of Union. He is an incomplete animal. He resembles the odd half of a pair of scissors.

—BENJAMIN FRANKLIN

Life is the struggle for position and the search for love.

—HERMAN HESSE

The trouble with some women is that they get all excited about nothing—and then marry him.

—CHER

Adulterous couples are unencumbered by children. Of course, this doesn't mean that they don't have children, only that they don't really think much about them while they are in the throes of passion. The intensity of the affair is such that everything is subordinated to it—even those things that in normal, everyday life would be the most precious in the world to us.

Countless women who have lovers describe how shocked they are that the needs of their own children are being neglected, but they admit to being powerless to do anything about it. Indeed, one of the principal giveaways to a husband that his wife is having an affair is that the children are much more irritable. They sense the natural tension in the home, the depletion of love between husband and wife, and the distraction of either or both of the parents. They are being neglected, they lack supervision, and they sense the tension in the air.

Here is an example of what happens. Bob's wife Carol started having an affair in the eleventh year of their marriage. At first, he had no idea what his wife was up to and he never caught her with her lover. Over a four-month period, however, their eight-year-old son and six-year-old daughter started exhibiting behavioral problems that they had never exhibited before. They were always exceptionally well-behaved children. Bob was used to seeing the kids in bed at seven. Now, he would come home at night at nine, and they would still be running around the house. Carol seemed to have lost all discipline with her children. In addition, the once orderly home had descended into chaos. Things were lying around and Carol seemed to be sinking under the mountain of work—only, she didn't seem to care.

Bob noticed how spacey Carol had become. She bumbled around the home as if on another planet. He thought his wife was depressed. They talked about it, but Carol dismissed it as "a phase." One day Bob's mother came to visit from San Francisco. She immediately understood what was going on. She informed her son that she was positive that Carol was having an affair. Bob refused to believe it. Only when Bob's mother confronted Carol did she come clean.

In another instance, I knew a young and married woman who had fallen in love with a younger man from the Middle East, who was a student at Oxford where she taught. They carried on an affair for a year. When the student returned to his native country, she was devastated. She could not explain to her husband what had happened. She thought she would die without her exciting lover. So she arranged to do three months of field research in the desert, conveniently choosing the Middle Eastern country to be with her lover. The father, a banker, traveled constantly, so she even took her two-year-old daughter with her for the duration, exposing the child to the hardships of living out in the open in the field, with no schooling. Worse, the mother left her daughter with her lover's family for many days at a time, as the two of them went off on romantic journeys.

And the amazing thing about this story is that the woman, as I knew her, was the most punctilious mother, always afraid of exposing her daughter to the wet cold of Britain in the winter months. But once she had an affair, she had no compunctions about making her daughter live in a tent in the horrible heat or abandon her to strangers.

Then there was Francis, a religious Jewish woman raised in a strictly religious home. She married young and had four children in quick succession. The household she ran was extremely conservative, and the children went to a highly religious school. Before marrying, Francis had trained as a nurse, and when her eldest child turned ten, she decided to return to her profession. Two years later, she fell in love with a married surgeon. Six months into the affair, she decided to leave her husband, the surgeon left his wife, and they moved in together. The community was scandalized. Her furious husband told her that he would prevent her from seeing the children. He told her that the children were ashamed of her and didn't want to see her again. She went to court and obtained visitation rights, but not once did she think of leaving her lover so that she could have her children. The court awarded sole custody to the father, with whom the children remain till this day. What surprised everyone who knew Francis was that she was viewed as a wonderful mother who would do anything for her kids.

No one is advocating that parents become so irresponsible as to neglect or, God forbid, harm their children. Our children are our glorious treasures and, along with our spouse, the greatest blessings in our lives. But neither should we go to the opposite extreme and place our children first to the detriment of our marriages. There is something to be learned from the passionate intensity of the unfaithful couple who are so focused on each other that everything else is drowned out. Sadly, far too many marriages suffer from a loss of intensity precisely *because* of the responsibilities of parenthood. The conflict between being lovers and parents is ancient, and requires a studied remedy.

When a couple weds, they do so in the hopes of building an entire life filled with the same intimacy and affection that they experienced throughout their dating lives. And usually, the romance lasts for several years while the couple remains a couple. But somehow, as the children proliferate and the couple adds three . . . four . . . or *seven* (yes, it can happen, I am a witness) the children become the first priority. Then they become the only priority. The relationship is put on hold.

Here are three typical scenarios parents face:

- A young mother in Chicago lies in bed with her insomniac three-year-old, leaving her husband alone in the living room with the remote control.
- A couple in Miami feels out of place when they enter a restaurant that does not offer crayons and paper placemats as premeal fun.
- A husband and wife in New York City cancel their anniversary trip to Paris—their first child-free vacation in eight years—because little Janet has the sniffles.

Romance has met its foe: the beloved child. When a baby is born, everything changes in the landscape of a couple's life. Where there were once hours of intimate sharing and meandering conversation, there are now hours of diaper changing and meandering the halls with a crying infant.

Research from the Masters and Johnson Institute in

Chesterfield, Missouri, shows that the incidence of sexual intercourse between new parents drops by more than 40 percent in the first year following childbirth. As I've stated earlier, the average amount of time married couples take to make love is slightly more than fourteen minutes. (When I mention this to some of my fellow husbands, they look at me in disbelief and say, "Who *are* these supermen?")

This is truly ironic. A newborn child is both the living embodiment of her parents' passion and the one thing capable of extinguishing the fire that lit her existence. I hear the same story time and again from married couples: "After the kids were born, we just couldn't find the time . . . energy . . . passion . . . desire. Our sex life imploded."

I hear mothers complaining all the time that at the end of day they simply have no strength left for sex. "When the day's done, I just want to go to sleep. Sex? I can barely keep my eyes open, let alone feel passionate."

We become parents and we think that our life as lovers has ended. "The kids must always come first!" we declare. We mistakenly believe that above and beyond all else the gift we should give our children is unconditional love. But this behavior is unhealthy for parents and their children. Children should be the natural and organic outgrowth of a couple's love for each other. And that should be true not only for their conception, but for their upbringing as well. The love between parents should never be in conflict with the love we show our children. On the contrary, the love a man and a woman have for each other should be the wellspring that feeds the river of love that nourishes the children.

The most important gift that we can pass along to our sons and daughters isn't unconditional love—it's hope. It's the hope that love works and that the world is composed of pieces of a puzzle that ultimately fit together. When children witness their parents arguing, they become cynical about the prospects of love and they become reticent about opening their hearts. They learn instead to look out for number one. Indeed, they become cynical about their prospects in life. They conclude that life is a puzzle consisting of incongruent pieces that ultimately never fit. After all, the two people responsible for their very existence can't even seem to get along. This is what the kids think: "You're telling me that if I make an effort I can get along with my classmates at school, when I come home and watch you guys argue all the time?" And, indeed, there is something hypocritical about it. The greatest gift a man can give his children is to love their mother, and the greatest gift a woman can give her kids is to love their father.

Lessons from Your Marriage

No matter how immense your love for your children, it will never be enough to sustain them through adulthood. When they are young, your love for them is all-important, but as they become teenagers, they begin cherishing the hope of romantic love and they want the love of a significant other. Parental love, once *omnipotent,* suddenly becomes *impotent* as our children grow older and begin to crave romantic love instead. No matter how much smothering love you give your children, it will never be enough to sustain them through adulthood.

When they were little kids they were chained to your skirt. When they're teenagers, all the chains in the world can't keep them home on a Saturday night. They now want the love of an affectionate *stranger.* And that is the way that it should be.

Success in life comes from mastering the vertical, as well as the horizontal. Vertical is being good parents; horizontal is getting along well with each other. But in many American families, failure in the horizontal leads to an obsession with the vertical. You don't connect as husband and wife anymore, so instead you obsess over the children. They become your sole emotional outlet.

In her trendsetting book *Sex and the City,* Candace Bushnell maintains that in that strange planet called Manhattan, all the mothers obsess over their sons because they are far more in love with them than with their husbands. The son, in effect, becomes the man in her life. In an environment where husbands and wives are sorely lacking in passion and intimacy, spouses find passion in being parents and they establish intimacy in their relationships with their children—all at the expense of their marriages. And although Bushnell writes this largely tongue in cheek, there is much truth in what she says.

In life there is practical love and theoretical love, and to a child, the job of a parent is designed to convey both. They must show their children love in action—and love in theory. The former is shown by loving your kids; the latter by loving your spouse. By loving our children, our kids *experience* love. By loving our spouse, our children *witness* love. Thus parents must teach their children how to make this theoretical love work, by giving them the chance to witness it in action. They should provide their offspring with the ability to love, the belief in love, and the example of love, so that when the time comes they, too, will be able to love.

By doing so, parents convey to their children that life can be lifted by the purely functional (or, in the case of many modern families, the *dys*functional) and embedded with deep meaning. The proof is that every one of us has a significant other preordained from before creation.

An unhappy—and all too common—alternative is for children to grow up as children of divorce, as I did. In these instances, the very relationship responsible for your existence has dissolved before your eyes. You end up a cynic for whom vulnerability is a sign of weakness. Better to close off your heart rather than believe in myths about love that lasts forever.

Is it any wonder that the odds are higher that children whose parents have divorced will end their own marriages? Studies on the percentage of divorce among children of divorce have vacillated between one-and-a-half and two-and-a-half times more likely over the past ten years, according to a 1999 University of Utah study by Nicholas H. Wolfinger.

Recharging Your Love Life

Fortunately, parents can learn to be better spouses from interactions with their children. And the parent/child relationship can be mutually reciprocal. Parents and children can teach

each other about the way love works.

Adults can learn to love like children—full of abandon, free of expectation, filled with surprises, and with a child's sense of play. For what is sex but two adults at play, filled with passion and giddy anticipation? It's about two adults laughing and giggling, teasing and flirting, unafraid of stains on their clothing, and focusing on the pleasure they are capable of gifting one another.

Recharging your love life is not a luxury, but a necessity, and it can wean both of you off all the far less satisfying and mundane pursuits of marriage. Parents must take active steps to halt the incidence of sexual drought that often accompanies parenthood. The following suggestions are practical changes that can be made to remind a married couple with children that they were a couple first, then a married couple, and only in the final stretch did they become parents.

1. Put a lock on your bedroom door.

Never allow the kids to sleep in your bedroom, except under very extraordinary circumstances. Your bedroom is a love chamber, not a family sitting room. So lock the door. A child must understand these boundaries. So many parents are afraid of making love, fearing that their kids will run in and find Mommy hovering in mid-air in transfixed pleasure, and Daddy climbing the hills and valleys, leaving little Susie traumatized for life. Well then, let Susie know that once she is put to bed, your bedroom is like security in the White House. And all the crying in the world will not influence the sentinels to grant her entry. Because what will most certainly traumatize your child as he or she gets older is having to guess whether or not his or her parents still make love.

And what if the kids are screaming at night and they want to come to Mommy? Stand your ground. Take them back to their beds and soothe them to sleep. Soon they will get the message they stand a better chance in their own nice warm bed than on the cold hard floor outside their parents' bedroom.

2. Never talk "business" during lovemaking.

A husband starts making love to his wife and she suddenly jolts upright in bed and asks, "Mark, what was that noise?"

No, it's not a burglar carrying off Johnnie Jr. It's the sound of her imagination carrying off her love life. Don't let your mind wander to whether you left the oven on or whether you remembered to sign Bobby's homework assignment. Your brain can be an enemy to restoring your sex life. It gets stuck in "function mode"—and it worries about everything else that's going on in the house. But remember, function is not romantic; function is not liberating; function reminds us of dysfunction, and that brings up all sorts of frightening ideas about broken homes and loveless marriages.

3. Honeymoon together at least twice a year.

One of the happiest memories of my childhood was when I was six years old and my parents went away to Israel together to try to save their marriage. Sure, I missed them. Worse, they left me with my two disciplinarian uncles who made me exercise and eat things like spinach. But I realized that my parents went away for the sake of our family, and that brought me comfort and happiness.

Make arrangements for your children to stay with relatives or close friends, then book a vacation and act like newlyweds. Make love, take long walks, giggle, and have meaningful conversations so that you can rediscover that you're not just a mother of someone with a runny nose, but a woman with a beating heart. Treat the financial burden of these retreats as wise investments in your marriage and your children's future. If this is something you can't afford, then at least try to get the kids out of the house. You can perhaps send them to their grandparents so that you and your spouse have time together at home. Start dating again.

4. Set aside a regular night for couple time, at least once a week.

It's okay to meet friends, but save at least the first hour or so for just the two of you. Don't blow the evening on a movie. Get emotionally naked. Discuss your anxieties and fears, and comfort each other in a way that allows you to really connect. What's more, do everything you can to break the monotony and bring surprises into your relationship, whether that means a night out at a hotel, sexy lingerie, or scented candles to heighten the mood.

5. Make kid conversation off limits for at least fifteen minutes a day.

This means a total of a few hours a week when you're not allowed to talk about the children or their needs. You are people, too, and you have your own needs. An empty vessel will not be empowered to nurture children. Instead, use the time to talk about each other, but avoid perfunctory topics like finances, work, and domestic affairs.

6. Get physical.

When you come home, hug your spouse. When you wake up, kiss each other. Nothing creates better communication and closeness than experiencing love through touch. The more you feel with your hands, the more you'll feel with your heart. Many studies have shown that children need to experience physical affection. Children who are not held or hugged by their parents grow up with deep insecurities. Now if that's true for the little kids, do you think it is any different for the big kids we call adults? Hugging each other is the *experience* of love, as opposed to merely declaring your affection, which is only the language of love.

7. When it comes to housework, get less physical.

Spend less money on new clothes or even family vacations, and put it instead on more household help so that the two of you aren't so tired. If you have hours of housework even after you come home from a full day's work at the office, how will you have any energy left for fiery sex?

8. Declare family time over at 9 P.M. every night.

From 6 to 9 P.M., have dinner with your family, bathe the children, read them stories, help them with their homework, and allow them time to talk to you about any subject they choose. This advice follows the recommendation of Prof.

Stanley Greenspan of George Washington University, both in his books and in my many conversations with him, that children need three hours of their parents' attention per day. But at 9 P.M., make sure all the young children are in bed with the lights out and that teenagers understand you are not to be disturbed. Don't let them stay up. If they say they're not tired, let them read in bed. This gives you time to unwind, cuddle, and, hopefully, make love. (No, could it really be?!)

A Love Quiz for Parents

How does your relationship rate? Take this quiz to find out whether your love life is on snooze or in high gear. Then read on for some tailor-made advice.

1. Which of the following openers most closely resembles the start of your last conversation with your spouse?
   a. You'll never believe what Johnny's teacher told me he's been doing in class.
   b. Honey, I'm a little bit concerned about the strange odor that's coming from the refrigerator where you stuffed that moose head.
   c. To continue the discussion we were having about Marxist influence on French films of the 1950s, I did have another thought.
   d. I've been thinking a lot about what you said about your father's workaholism and the influence it's had on your view of your career.

2. How often do you and your spouse discuss subjects that have nothing to do with your kids, car, or house?
   a. Once a week, as long as there isn't an emergency involving one of the kids.
   b. Two to three times a week, but it's usually about work.
   c. At least once a day, before we go to sleep.
   d. Several times a day. We can't help it.

3. Married couples say that the average amount of time they spend making love is about fourteen minutes. This:
   a. Makes me jealous. Fourteen whole minutes?
   b. Sounds just about right. Ours is probably closer to fifteen minutes.
   c. Seems rather low. We usually break half an hour, at least.
   d. Is that possible? Eleven minutes? The last time we took less than an hour, we were on an airplane.

4. The purpose served by sexual activity in my marriage is:
   a. To satisfy my spouse—so that I can sleep.
   b. To satisfy both of us—so that I can sleep.
   c. To satisfy both of us—so that I can sleep and feel more emotionally connected to my spouse the next day.
   d. Purpose? Who needs a purpose when you love someone as much as I love my husband/wife? I can't keep my hands off my spouse.

5. You've just had a fabulous/horrible/amazing/fascinating experience. Who's the first person you share this with?
   a. My best friend Gail.
   b. My mother. She'd kill me if I called anyone else!
   c. My family at dinner. They'd want to know.
   d. My husband. Right away.

6. How often do you wake up and find the children sleeping at the foot or side of your bed?
   a. Every other night. They have nightmares. We even go to sleep together in the corner of the bed, anticipating his/her arrival.
   b. Once a week or so. We bought the little one a nightlight and now she brings it into our room.
   c. Maybe once every few months and only during thunderstorms.
   d. Never. When they started to do that, we would walk them back to their rooms every night.

7. Vacation means:
  a. Disney World with all the kids.
  b. Historical sights with the older kids. The younger ones can stay with grandma.
  c. The beach with the kids. But we'll bring along a baby-sitter so we get at least two nights out as a couple.
  d. Once-a-year trip for the family. Twice a year we make it to a bed and breakfast or some other getaway just for us.

8. What makes you laugh?
  a. When the kids do something amusing.
  b. When we watch a funny movie with the kids.
  c. When we watch a grown-up movie without the kids.
  d. My spouse always makes me laugh. That's why we got married!

To score:
For every A answer, give yourself 3 points.
For every B answer give yourself 2 points.
For every C answer give yourself 1 point.
For every D answer give yourself no points.
Add up your points for the total.

If you scored:
18 TO 24 POINTS: *Get a life.* A *love life,* that is. Okay, I don't mean to be mean. But *come on.* Did you guys get married in order to be camp counselors? And this isn't good for your kids. Take an emergency kid-free vacation this month. Rediscover who you are as an individual and, more important, who you and your spouse are as a couple. Call an absolute moratorium on kid talk while you're away. Drink mimosas in the morning and sleep until 11 A.M. Talk about the things that really matter to you as human beings, not as parents. If you can't afford a vacation right now, send the kids to grandma's and make each other breakfast in bed. Then stay in bed all day. The time and money you spend now healing your marriage will save your kids hours of therapy later on when they have to figure out why they don't believe in love—or worse, they've witnessed their parents divorce.

12 TO 17 POINTS: *Date your spouse.* You and your partner probably love each other very much, but you've strayed from the path of a healthy marriage. You think you're doing the right thing by dedicating all your time and energy to your kids. You're actually doing them a disservice. Go to a romantic French bistro this weekend. Get dressed as if this were a second date. Find out what your spouse's most precious childhood memory is and what he or she hopes to achieve in the next ten years. Rediscover the person behind the parent.

6 TO 11 POINTS: *Keep on kissing.* You're on the right track. The love and appreciation of your spouse are there, but at times you lose sight of the romance. Keeping the flame alive takes a bit of effort, but it's worth it. So concentrate on the little things: Send a love note, fill the bed with roses, have a candlelight dinner, wear something silky underneath, always remember to compliment each other and show appreciation. Remember, the little things count as much—if not more—than the big ones.

0 TO 5 POINTS: *Congratulations!* You've revealed your marriage to be one filled with love and romance. May you pass along the ability to love from one generation to the next. May your child learn to love and teach his or her future spouse to do the same. Boy, you guys ought to write a book.

EIGHTEENEIGHTEENEIGHTEENEIGH
TEENEIGHTEENEIGHTEENEIGHTEE
NEIGHTEENEIGHTEENEIGHTEENEIG
HTEENEIGH **eighteen** EENEIGHTE
ENEIGHTEENEIGHTEENEIGHTEENEI
GHTEENEIGHTEENEIGHTEENEIGHT
EENEIGHTEENEIGHTEENEIGHTEEN

THE REBIRTH OF
Lust AND
Love
IN MARRIAGE

*MARRIAGE, n. The state or condition of a community con-
sisting of a master, a mistress and two slaves, making in all, two.*
—AMBROSE BIERCE, THE DEVIL'S DICTIONARY, 1911

*George Bush never noticed. So why had I gone through those
years of agony?*
—BARBARA BUSH, EXPLAINING WHY SHE
STOPPED DYEING HER GRAY HAIR IN 1970

*Your acquaintance, D. Rodriguez, has had a small accident
befallen him. Mr. Annesely found him in bed with his wife . . .
and brought a bill of divorce into Parliament. Those things grow
more fashionable every day, and in a little time won't be at all
scandalous. The best expedient for the public, and to prevent the
expense of private families, would be a general act of divorcing
all the people of England. You know those that pleased might
marry again; and it would save the reputations of several ladies
that are now in peril of being exposed every day.*
—LADY MARY WORTLEY MONTAGU,
LETTER TO THE COUNTESS OF MAR, 1725
(QUOTED IN THE *Penguin Book of Infidelities,*
by Stephen Brook)

323

Is the Marriage Libido Destined to Die?

Can passion *really* be maintained within a monogamous relationship, or are the Ten Commandments I wrote about earlier merely an exercise in futility? All too many people think that the jury is already in with a definite settlement. While marriage can provide support and security, it cannot maintain its excitement.

Every week when I was the rabbi at Oxford I held a debate on some important social, political, or religious issue, in front of a large student audience. When I once made the case for marriage, the audience conceded that my arguments had been convincing, and one student stood up and said, "Yeah, I guess it is worthwhile to sacrifice passion for the sake of stability."

Everyone else agreed. And that shocked me. *Sacrifice what for what?* What was he talking about? Why is there an assumption that having many sexual partners is more passionate and more exciting than having a single sexual partner with whom one is really and truly in love, and with whom one can explore the full gamut of sexual possibilities?

This is one of the greatest relationship fallacies and must be refuted. Rediscovering passion in sexual relations involves a change in attitude, not partners. We equate passion with newness, and finding a new partner might result in very passionate sex. But it is a shortcut that has no permanence—how long can a new partner remain new? For a long-term solution to the problem of monotony through familiarity, we must search for something new in our partner, on a regular basis.

The Dullness of the Marriage Bed

Is having sex with the same partner over a long time a preordained ticket to erotic boredom? Here are comments from three married men:

"I've been married sixteen years now and been completely faithful to my wife. I'd have to say, in all candor, that our sexual relationship now is much better than it was when we were first married. To me, the trick has been to be creative about our sex lives—not with whips and chains, or gymnastic positions—but with keeping away from routines; and staying attuned to each other's needs. For instance, we've learned to spend a lot of time giving each other sensual massages as part of our foreplay. It's an almost incredible, tantalizing delight. . . ."

Less encouraging, a forty-four-year-old man says: "Let's face it, my wife isn't as attractive as she once was; she's let her body go to pot, and her idea of good sex is [coitus] twice a week. It's like she's doing me a favor. Is it any wonder I say our sex life is boring? . . . So I go to a classy hooker once a month as my way of getting even."

Finally, a forty-nine-year-old man: "Although I've been happily married for twenty-seven years, I've certainly noticed a definite deterioration in our sex life. We get along really well, we do more together now than we ever did, but sex is the one area in our lives where we seem in such a rut. I'm not sure who's to blame for it, since I think we're both involved, but I guess we've both given up too easily, accepting a lousy sex life as a given. I'm not proud to admit it, but the way I've coped with this for years is by having occasional affairs. At least that way I feel like I can still turn someone on."

The last two accounts surely seem damaging, for they portray an all too common scenario. But is it inevitable? Well, was it inevitable that IBM would lose out to Microsoft as the world's premier computer-technology company? Or was it a lack of vision and effort? Is it inevitable that a lawyer who has worked years to build up a client base will lose all his clients to the new firm that opened across the street? Or can he retain their loyalty by showing exceptional courteousness matched by a top-notch professional service? And, if that same lawyer can make all his clients feel like kings, then what makes him so impotent when it comes to coming home and making his wife feel like a queen? Only lazy and uncreative people lose passion in their marriages and take the easy way out by finding excitement with someone else, until they get bored with that partner, too.

Creativity and Romance

Even the most pessimistic sex therapists agree that capitulating to monotony in marriage is wholly unnecessary and avoids the central issue. Their advice is not to vary your partner, but to vary your routine.

Other practical suggestions include introducing new options into your sexual interactions, such as experimenting with sensual massage; new types of sexual activity that you have never tried before; different positions and foreplay; changing venues; and so on. To be sure, all this is wonderful advice and we all should endeavor our utmost to bring any and all creative suggestions—with the absurd exceptions of those, like ménage a trois, which compromise intimacy—into the parched earth of our marriage.

But from researching this book I can tell you that this advice alone will not suffice. The reason is simple: They all presuppose that you have the inclination to implement them in the first place. They all take it for granted that you have the motivation to re-energize your marriage, that you are erotically attracted to your spouse, and it's only the new techniques that are required. In essence, then, they are all fatally flawed because they teach technique without imparting the inspiration needed to carry out those techniques. They teach you how to make love with your body rather than with your mind. But we all know that precisely the opposite is true. We're not missing the creative ideas to try once we have developed a lusty interest in a member of the opposite sex. It's *creating and maintaining the erotic interest in the first place* that presents the greatest challenge.

My own personal immediate advice is this: Do unto your wife as you would do unto your secretary, business assistant, or airline stewardess. Do unto your husband what you would do to that sexy fellow lawyer if you wanted him to think of you as a sex goddess. Surely, you have ideas how you would win someone over to you, and how you would pleasure that person.

Let your own sexual creativity run riot. Make your marriage into an illicit affair. Your wife's opinion of your sexual virility is no less important than the woman's next door. Make your wife new, and make her forbidden. Create the erotic excitement in your mind by implementing all the eroticism-inducing techniques outlined throughout this book. Make love to her in the most forbidden places. Sin outrageously with your spouse. Break through routine once and for all and make your marriage into a daily bag of magic tricks. Experiment with your spouse in new sexual positions and in public places, just as you would if the two of you were illicit lovers. You *can* make your marriage into an affair, and you'll have the greatest thrill doing it. Get your spouse to tell you all the people that he or she is lusting after and then you'll see if your spouse is still the man or woman you thought you married.

Another important point that should not be forgotten: Sexuality is not an entity on its own, but is a natural outcome of a loving and romantic relationship. So the best way of enhancing one's sexual life is not *only* to implement new sexual positions and techniques, however important that may be, but to bring greater romance into everyday life. Make marriage one big act of foreplay. Preserving romance is an ongoing challenge, which bids us to focus on those small, nonsexual interactions of affection, which sadly have become all too rare. How many people today write love letters to their spouses? And how many buy flowers even when it's not a special occasion, but just as a sign of affection for the person they love? These gestures aren't just ceremonial. They make a recipient feel loved and appreciated—and can have a direct bearing on the passionate feelings that ensue at bedtime. As Masters and Johnson say in their study, *Human Sexual Response*, "It is no surprise that as we fall into nonromantic complacency in our relationships, our sexual interests and passions are apt to dwindle, too."

If married couples focus purely on their sexual lives out-side a romantic framework, if they see nothing in each other but their flesh, they will undoubtedly get bored with each other quickly. If they cannot enjoy conversation and do not see the magic of sharing a life with another human being—a crea-ture of limitless depth—then their partner presents nothing new to discover. How many inches of flesh does a person have? Are we really going to be excited by seeing the same thing day in and day out? But when we peer into each other's souls, when we are inspired by each other's infinite beauty, and are inspired enough to write and sing to each other about that process of discovery, then how can we possibly become bored? Our marriage then becomes a journey, embarked upon with the express purpose of reaching new heights together.

Bringing Back Vulnerability and Strength

Another way to jumpstart a dying marriage and avoid the possi-bility of infidelity is for men to be more vulnerable and for women to show greater independence and strength. Studies show that affairs bring out the masculine and feminine qualities in the opposite gender that have remained dormant until now. In other words, one of the things that women most complain about is a husband who is not emotionally vulnerable, who doesn't lean on them, or show any profound need. She can't pierce his outer shell.

Yet, research show that when men have affairs they often open up to their mistresses in a way that they would never do with their wives. In fact, as we all know, the stereotypical state-ment that a married man makes to a woman as he tries to ini-tiate an affair with her is, "My wife doesn't understand me," implying that he wishes to open up and become emotionally dependent on this new woman. And women absolutely love being needed by a man. That's one of the main reasons that so many virtuous women gravitate toward bad boys. They love rescuing bad boys. She feels that only she—in the guise of redeemer—really appreciates the bad boy's true potential and virtue. He's a rough diamond, but only she sees it. And only she can polish and restore his lustre and shine. In the same vein, one of the reasons men have affairs is to be pampered. That's why many of them choose profoundly feminine mistresses, women who are often far different from their own wives. So adultery seems to bring out the vulnerable qualities of an otherwise emotionally closed man.

Conversely, women who normally marry highly educated men who tend to be good providers, emphasize a different quality altogether when taking a lover. Studies show that whereas women require the husband to be at least in the sixty-first percentile of education, a lover need not be higher than the forty-seventh percentile. Similarly, whereas women don't require their husbands to be higher than the fifty-eighth percentile in manly sexiness, when it comes to taking a lover, he has to be at least in the seventy-sixth percentile. When it comes to choosing a lover, looks, appearance, and muscles become much more important to a woman than a man's personality or character.

The same is true of how women often brag about being in control of their affairs. Rather than becoming more vulnerable, as their husbands do, many women revel in being the one in the driver's seat when they have affairs. It's not about opening up to a man, but rather, about a man desiring them sexually. It is the woman who controls how often her lover will see her. And he better earn a next appointment by being outstanding in bed. As author Lynn Atwater writes about adulterous wives in *The Extramarital Connection*: "Most of the change in self-confidence was rooted in a sense of being more physically appealing because they knew other men were interested in them."

But for heaven's sake, why can't we do the same thing in marriage? Forget the *Men Are from Mars, Women Are from Venus* approach which justifies a husband's emotional retardation by explaining how men are Martians who retreat into their caves rather than unburdening themselves emotionally to their wives. If they can do it with their mistresses, why can't they do the same with their wives? Why does a wife have a harder time pulling information out of her husband than a dentist does yanking a tooth?

Husbands who open up to their wives and are unafraid to need them, know how to turn their wives on. Look at the example of Christopher Reeve. In the make-believe world of Hollywood, he portrayed Superman, the ultimate man of steel. But in real life, as everyone knows, he later had a terrible riding accident that left him paralyzed and his wife supported him through the trauma. As Reeve describes in *I Like Being Married*:

> *Dana came into the room. She stood beside me, and we made eye contact. I mouthed my first lucid words to her: "Maybe we should let me go." Dana started crying. She said, "I am only going to say this once: I will support whatever you want to do, because this is your life, and your decision. But I want you to know that I'll be with you for the long haul, no matter what." Then she added the words that saved my life: "You're still you. And I love you." If she had looked away or paused or hesitated even slightly, or if I had felt there was a sense of her being—being what? noble, or fulfilling some obligation to me, I don't know if I could have pulled through. Because it had dawned on me that I was going to be a huge burden to everybody, that I had ruined my life and everybody else's. Not fair to anybody. The best thing would be to slip away. But what Dana said made living seem possible, because I felt the depth of her love and commitment . . . I knew then that she was going to be with me forever."*

What you have here is a classic case of a husband courageous enough to be vulnerable in front of his wife, and thereby eliciting her everlasting love. What a far cry from those more shallow husbands who are afraid to show that they are made of flesh rather than steel.

I remember witnessing the same thing with Ariel Sharon, a man seen around the world as a battle-hardened warrior. Yet, when I hosted him for a lecture at Oxford University, he held the hand of his wife, Lilly, throughout his daylong trip. Even while hundreds of Palestinian protestors chanted against him, he held her hand. He wasn't afraid to show his emotional dependence on his wife in front of his sworn enemies. And why not? This was the woman who had comforted him after his first wife—who happened to be Lilly's sister—died in a terrible car accident.

Another famous example is U.S. President Woodrow Wilson, whose wife Ellen died while he was in office. Shortly thereafter, he began courting Edith Galt. One of the things that most cemented their quickly blossoming relationship was that Wilson, even as commander in chief of the United States during World War I, had no apprehension in showing the woman in his life that he deeply needed her. In one letter, he wrote to her: "Here stands your friend, a longing man, in the midst of a world's affairs—a world that knows nothing of the heart he has shown you. . . . Will you come to him sometime without reserve and make his strength complete?"

Edith later responded to him: "I am a woman—and the thought that you have need of me is sweet."

Now, compare this to Richard Nixon, who once told journalist Steward Alsop, "I can't let my hair down with anyone, not even with my family." Nixon's inability to show emotion led to a cold and emotionally bankrupt marriage. His inability to trust led to worse problems, like Watergate. He also told Alsop, as recounted by Kati Marton in *Hidden Power: Presidential Marriages That Shaped Our Recent History*, "A major public figure is a lonely man. . . . You can't confide absolutely in anyone."

In fact, it seems that Nixon did not even confide in his wife his decision to resign as president of the United States. As their daughter Tricia Nixon wrote later in her diary: "Julie and I talked some more and I learned that Mama had not been told of Daddy's tentative decision [to resign] . . . It is strange how you try to spare those you love from worry."

Nixon was a closed man, incapable of showing affection or vulnerability. As he himself once said, "My mother never said, 'I love you' because she considered that to be very private and very sacred. And I feel the same way . . . I don't say . . . 'I love you' and the rest . . . that's just not the way I was raised . . . In my family we considered affection and love to be very private" (*Hidden Power,* by Kati Marton).

And yet, at his wife Pat's funeral in 1993, Nixon wept publicly and uncontrollably for the very first time. Isn't it amazing how we often learn how to show emotion when it is a little too late?

Conversely, wives who occasionally display that they are strong and free spirited do much to entice their husbands. They fire up their husband's desire—and desire is what it is all about.

The Future of Love

I am convinced that one of the principal causes in the breakdown of relationships today is that we have become *objective* about the people we love. We've become objective about things that we were never meant to be objective about.

In various seminars, I asked the members of the audience to posit a one-word synonym for love. These are the most common responses: "devotion," "respect," "admiration," "a longing," and finally "selflessness." These are all insightful responses—and the opposite words, such as disrespect and selfishness would *never* be acceptable—but they somehow miss the essence of love. To me the best synonym for love is *subjectivity.* Being in love with someone means not seeing that person's faults, or being aware of a person's faults but relegating them to the realm of insignificance. Your love for someone colors your perception of that person, and *to you* he or she appears beautiful and glorious, irrespective of what the objective facts really are. You should be thinking: "This person is so important; I know this person has faults, but it does not matter. To me, this person is the most special person in the world."

Conversely, falling out of love is objectifying your partner so that you are in a constant state of appraisal, always comparing him or her with the people around you. The breakdown in relationships is due to the fact that we have become objective about our partner in love. We are constantly re-evaluating our spouse as if to decide whether he or she is still attractive and worthwhile, or whether perhaps we made a mistake in marrying that person.

A woman came to me to complain about her husband. She said, "To be honest, Rabbi, Jonathan, whom I know from work, seems as though he would have been a lot more suitable as a lifelong partner. He's funnier, more patient, loves kids, and is far more affectionate than my husband. It's a pity that I didn't meet him five years ago before I married."

It's easy to see how this kind of attitude can lead directly to an adulterous affair. Even after marriage, this woman is still comparing her husband with everyone around her. She is still objective about her husband. So where is the love?

The Most Beautiful Woman in the World

Contrast this woman's attitude with the following story. When I was a student in a rabbinical seminary, I was once invited by their grandson to the home of an elderly couple for dinner. During the meal, I dropped a fork under the table and bent down to pick it up. When I did, I noticed that this couple— both in their late seventies—were holding hands under the table. Coming as I did from a broken home, I was impressed; I got choked up with emotion.

As I was leaving, I couldn't help but mention how happy I was to have witnessed this display of romantic love between the couple, and how their feelings for each other had not diminished through time. "You are the world's greatest romantics," I said. "It's amazing!"

The wife blushed at my words, but the husband did not. He just looked at me with a quizzical stare, as if he had not really understood me. "You sound surprised that we can remain in love for all these years. Why, for me it's very easy. After all, my wife is the most beautiful woman in the whole wide world."

Then he kissed her.

What amazed me was that his sincerity was beyond question. Why was I surprised? Because his statement about her beauty was blatantly not true! Surely, however attractive his wife was, I didn't expect to wake up the next morning and find her face on the cover of *Vogue!* She was in her seventies and most men might have described her as matronly, but not beautiful.

And yet, not only did he mean every word, but also he was accurate. Here's what he was really saying: "She is the most attractive woman in the world *to me.* I love her and therefore I am subjective in my evaluation of her. I don't want anyone else. Just her. My emotions dress her up. In *my* eyes, she blooms in the full blossom of youth."

If this does not happen between two people, then there is something missing, something inadequate, in their love. If you disagree and feel that this is too high a standard, then consider how you would feel about a father who says his child is ugly or stupid—even if it were true. Would you applaud that father for his honesty? No, you would probably be horrified. And yet, husbands and wives make hurtful statements along these lines to one another all the time.

Has it ever happened that you are patiently sitting in a doctor's waiting room, and someone's kid won't stop crying, sneezing on you, staring at the inside of your nostrils, and generally making you wish that you could strangle him and put everyone in the waiting room out of their misery? Then, as you visualize tying the noose to do the dirty deed, you see the child's mother looking starry-eyed at her son, as she says, looking right at you: "Isn't he adorable? He's so sweet!"

Of course, it's blatantly untrue. The kid's a monster. But the love that a mother has for her child is capable of transforming a monster into an angel, at least in her own eyes.

Now, we seem to accept that this should be true of children. Why don't we accept that the same should be true of our partners in relationships and marriage? Why aren't we as subjective? Every one of us is perfectly capable of cheating on our spouses in a way that we would never betray our children. The reason: Whereas we might compare our children with other children, we still never find ourselves seriously dissatisfied with them and longing for different ones. This is not true of a spouse. Husbands and wives are evaluating each other constantly, with adultery and divorce the unfortunate outcomes.

A husband may look upon his aging wife and compare her with a younger woman in much the same way that he compares his 1993 Toshiba laptop with the newer, more feature-laden edition. And, just as he sells the old laptop to buy the new model, he can trade his wife in for a newer model—either through divorce, or by an apparently far less messy solution, having an affair.

Searching for "the Best"

In marriage, each one of us is not interested in someone who is good enough, and suits all of our needs and desires. What we want today is *the best*. I cannot begin to relate how many times I have heard young successful people justify breaking off relationships with men and women with whom they were once very serious, not because of any real problem, but simply because, in their estimation, this man or woman they were dating did not reach their high standards. Moreover, if they held out just a little while longer, something "better" might come along. What they want is the best, so they will keep looking.

What we forget is that, while we can speak of the plushest house, the fanciest car, or the finest cigar, because people aren't superficial, three-dimensional, material objects, we cannot speak of "the best" person because every human being has infinite depth and is special in his or her own way. It is no wonder, then, that singles often go out with the wrong person since they do not seek someone who suits them so much as someone who is judged to be "the best" according to values that are transient, arbitrary, and shallow.

But there is no such thing as "the best" in marriage; there is nothing better than *good enough*. We should treat marriage like a glove that fits. The person to whom we are attracted, and who makes us happy, whom we miss when he or she is not around, and who seeks to make us happy and to fulfill all of our needs, is the one who is usually perfectly suited to us. But people often refrain from marrying such a person, especially if that person is one of the first people they date, since they feel they *must* first shop around to see who else is available, because maybe it will turn out that while this person is *good,* he or she is not *the best.*

The woman I married was, thank God, the very first girl I dated, and when I tell this to our students at Oxford they look very surprised. "Look, Debbie is a great wife," they admit, "but could you have been sure that she was the right girl for you if you had no one to compare her with?" And armed with this philosophy, the students date and date in search of the very best possible partner for life, and in the process ensure that no one will make them happy since it is not human warmth they seek, but accolades. Dating has been reduced to the search for bells and whistles.

If this approach to relationships were confined to the time before marriage, it would be bad enough, but at least forgivable. The problem is that once you teach yourself to objectify people, it won't stop even after you marry: You will fail to find satisfaction with your spouse since you will still be scrutinizing your other acquaintances to see if you could have done better. Marriage means choosing one partner for life, and closing off all other possibilities. The search has now been terminated. Now go and make *this* relationship work.

The Ghosts of Lovers Past

What makes something special is that it is distinct and unique. In Jewish thought the very word "holy" means "separate, distinct, and different." The Sabbath day is holy because it is different from the other days of the week, and it is treated differently. If one treats it in exactly the same way as one treats Tuesday, if one goes to work and drives the car, then it stops being special.

The same applies to intimacy. What makes a sexual moment exciting and special is that it is only the two of you who experience it. But when the ghosts of former lovers enter your minds, the whole experience suffers. This is especially true because of the very physical nature of human sexuality. Memories are strong enough when they involve a conversation, a laugh, and an emotional exchange. But they are positively stifling when they involve intense physical pleasure, excitement, and fulfillment. Inevitably, if one brings such memories into the bedroom, one will be tempted to judge the performance of one's current partner by comparison.

I strongly advise against informing your fiancé, or your spouse, of sexual liaisons—boyfriends, girlfriends, one-night stands, and so on—that took place before you met your current partner, if your partner is in any way threatened by them. (If your partner feels excited by it, that's a different story altogether.)

You have to allow those previous images, however powerful, to fade. Memories might lead you to compare your current happiness and satisfaction with that experienced in a previous relationship. So why allow this to become a subject of conversation? It is imperative that a husband and wife begin life anew. They should not bring the ghosts of relationships past into their marriage. They need not be haunted by disembodied emotional spirits. Love means the ability to lose objectivity, to forget the insignificant, ancillary, and shallow details of your partner, instead choosing to embrace his or her core. A person's infinite soul, when allowed to shine forth through all its transient coverings, becomes truly fulfilling and powerful enough to sustain everlasting human excitement and commitment.

NINETEENNINETEENNINETEENNINE
TEENNINETEENNINETEENNINETEE
NNINETEENNINETEENNINETEENNI
NETEENNIN   nineteen   TEENNINET
EENNINETEENNINETEENNINETEEN
NINETEENNINETEENNINETEENNINE
TEENNINETEENNINETEENNINETEE

Spirituality
Mysticism·AND·
AS OUR
EROTIC GUIDES

*I entered the Ma'aras Hamachpela (the cave in Hebron where
the Biblical matriarchs and Patriarchs are buried in Hebron),
and saw Abraham sleeping in Sara's arms.*

—RABBI YEHUDAH LOWE OF PRAGUE,
KNOWN AS MAHARAL, CHIDDUSHEI AGGADOS 3:82

*The matter is not as Rabbi Moses Maimonides thought and sup-
posed in his* Guide to the Perplexed, *where he praises Aristotle for
saying that the sense of touch is despicable to us. G-d forbid! . . . For
if he believed that the world was created intentionally [by G-d], he
would not have said this. But we who have the Torah and believe
that G-d created all in His wisdom [do not believe that He] created
anything inherently ugly or unseemly. If we were to say that intercourse is repulsive, then we blaspheme G-d who made the genitals
. . . Marital intercourse, under proper circumstances, is an exalted
matter . . . Now you can understand what our rabbis meant when
they declared that when a husband unites with his wife in holiness,
the divine presence abides with them.*

—NACHMANIDES, IGGERET HAKODESH

No society with a 60-percent divorce rate can call itself civilized.
—RABBI SHMULEY BOTEACH

Sex: The Loftiest of Pursuits

When I published my book *Kosher Sex*, I never expected it to become an international phenomenon. That was the pleasant part. Less so did I expect it to be so sharply criticized by many religious men and women who argued that any open discussion of sex was unholy, unGodly, and breaches the boundaries of decency. That was the *less* pleasant part.

The misguided view that religion and spirituality have nothing insightful or redeeming to say about love and sex is terribly destructive. It has consigned an entire generation of men and women to having to look to unwholesome sources for advice on their relationships. This is doubly tragic because Judaism, since its inception, has offered expert and explicit advice on achieving passionate sex with one's spouse.

In fact, the Jews have survived millennia of unspeakable persecution, the loss of their ancestral homeland, and dispersion to the far corners of the earth in no small measure due to the rock-solid and passionate marriages constructed out of the religion's fiery advice on love and sex. While a Jewish man may have lived in constant degradation among his Gentile neighbors, he would come home at night to a woman who treated him like a prince. At the same time, a Jewish woman—consigned to a life of poverty—might have been robbed of her dignity, but she came home every night to a husband who made her feel like a queen.

As mentioned earlier, the Bible contains no word for sex other than "knowledge." This fact reflects the belief in Judaism that sex is the most Godly and lofty of all human pursuits. The powerful pull of sexual craving, rather than being seen as a sinful desire to indulge the flesh, is rather seen as an irresistible urge pulling us outside of ourselves, thereby guaranteeing that we do not remain selfish and self-absorbed. Sex is about transcending the confines of the ego and reaching out to another.

Sex is the most pleasurable of all human experiences because it is the most liberating. All of us know that freedom is life's greatest blessing and pleasure.

I remember watching the joy of the Oxford students when they would complete their final exams, which tested them on three years of material. The partying would go on for weeks. The students had finally been relieved of all the pressure that had built up over those thirty-six months.

Of course, sex is an even greater release. It's the only area of life where we get as much pleasure in giving as we do in receiving. A man who really gets caught up in the erotic moment feels much greater pleasure stoking the fires of his wife's erotic lust than simply and stupidly focusing on his own boring pleasure while his wife remains cold. As Rabbi Reuven Bulka, a leading contemporary Jewish thinker, writes in *Judaism on Pleasure*, "The sexual encounter is the ultimate exhilarating and meaningful expression of love, the type of pleasure that carries with it a tidal wave of positive emotion, enough to cement a relationship in everlasting affection."

Spicing Up Married Sex

Beyond the everyday need for sexual passion in a marriage in order to sew husband and wife together as one flesh, Judaism recognizes the importance of changing sexual norms. If talk of sex runs rampant in the media and entertainment worlds (which it does), and married couples are watching how everyone is having a nightly circus in the bedroom except them (which it does often sound like), then the married couple is bound to feel dispirited and left out. Hence, there has to be a greater emphasis from religious teachers about what married couples can do to bring greater excitement into their lives.

This view was expressly made by Rabbi Moshe Feinstein, arguably the foremost Jewish legal authority of the twentieth century, who wrote: "As to the innovation of recent authorities in our day, that students of the law should perform the duty of *onah* (conjugal relations) twice a week, I too support this view . . . Because of the promiscuity of this generation and jealousy for another woman's lot, a woman feels desire and erotic passion more often than once a week. Therefore, her husband is obligated in this respect" (Iggrot Moshe, Even Haezer, 3:28).

That religion must reckon with the shift in erotic energy within the generations is an astonishing statement by one of the greatest Jewish sages. The background to his ruling is this: A husband has an express Biblical obligation to provide his wife with food, shelter, clothes, and conjugal pleasure. But how frequently must the conjugal act take place? In ancient times, the students of the law, the rabbis, were *required* to make love to their wives only once a week, preferably on the Sabbath. The Talmud says that they were not expected to do more because "their constant Torah study weakened them." (Back then, it was the husbands who had the headaches!) But here Rabbi Feinstein says that in modern times, even married rabbis have to be responsive to their wives' lust and thus increase the frequency of marital lovemaking. (Remember what I wrote earlier about how Judaism conceives of women as being far more sexually charged than men?) Sex is holy. It is the principal glue that brings two souls together as one flesh. The more love you make, the more loving you feel.

Nor was Rabbi Feinstein's opinion an isolated one. He based his views on those of Jonah Landsofer, an eminent eighteenth-century rabbinical authority, who said that Judaism must respond to, and accommodate, the changes in sexual mores of the day. Part of this accommodation involved the need for greater "sinfulness" in marital relations. Husbands and wives needed to recapture the risky side of sex, which their unfaithful counterparts seemed to have in such great abundance.

Men are pressured to support their families, to battle life's constant financial challenges and social demands. Their passion is therefore channeled into the functional realm, into keeping their heads above the water, leaving little energy for the marital bed. The cure for this would be to enhance erotic interest by emulating the forbidden ways of "the sinners." This is a sure way to reawaken male desire and keep men going even after a long and exhaustive day. Hence the need for "the possibility of adultery" in governing our relationships. As the Talmud says, "Since the destruction of the Temple, sexual pleasure has been taken [from those who practice it lawfully] and given to sinners."

One of Europe's greatest rabbis, Yaakov Emden, relates many of the intimate details of his life in his autobiography, including his sexual problems with his first wife whom he could barely get along with. He also speaks of the powerful erotic attraction he felt for his cousin, who apparently tried to seduce him. This does not mean that he believed in succumbing to the forbidden sexual instinct. Indeed, in a latter incident he boasts of his ability to overcome his powerful "evil impulse," but he also speaks of his own sexuality in less externalized terms: "I was very hungry for a woman. . . . I was a man with all of my powers and impulses."

For Rabbi Emden, sexuality is not something dirty and attraction to strangers does not make us repulsive. It simply makes us human. He took an extremely positive position on conjugal relations. Quoting at length from the Iggeret Hakodesh (Holy Letter, a famous twelfth-century Jewish epistle on the sacred quality of married sex written by Nachmanides, and which I quote from at length in my book *Kosher Sex*), Rabbi Emden goes into great detail about erotic foreplay and concludes, "To us the sexual act is worthy, good, and beneficial, even to the soul. No other human activity compares with it."

A Word from the Mystics

Indeed, the mystical sages of the Kabbalah emphasized that the holy nature of sex was owed to the fact that it brought about the unification of the masculine and feminine energies of the Godhead. God possesses both a masculine and feminine quality. In the sexual union of man and woman, those two dimensions are brought together as one, reestablishing the single, indivisible nature of God. When men and women make love, they create an equation that defies all mathematics: One plus one equals one. Two bodies enter the marital bed, but they emerge as one flesh. That men and women can coalesce together to become bone of one bone and flesh of one flesh has profound implications for the metaphysical unity of God in the universe. It means that although they appear to be fragmented, heaven and earth are really one. There is no dualism operating in the universe. God is not opposed by any equally powerful devil or a fallen angel like Lucifer. Rather, "God is one and His name [the created Universe] is one."

Throughout the empirical world we see these two different energies in operation in a variety of forms: donor and developer, provider and recipient, heaven and earth, mind and matter. The Chinese called it *yin* and *yang,* the Tibetans *yab* and *yum.* For Hindus it was *shiva* and *shakti,* while in Buddhism the masculine and feminine are known as *samsara* and *nirvana.* There are other expressions that symbolize the masculine and feminine, such as justice and love; prose and poetry; form and substance; and, of course, body and soul. In other words, God is capable of incorporating within Himself all these opposing forces.

The masculine and the feminine energies desire to harmonize. Like the number 10, which is the first number to encompass two digits, all relationships of pairs require a line and a circle—the masculine and feminine components. Notice that the principle anatomical characteristic separating men and women is that men are lines, and women are circles. When you put a line and a circle together, you get "10," perfection and wholesomeness. The number 10 is the first number consisting of two digits, representing, not only the basic binary code, the classic mathematical language of unit-opposites that runs all of modern technology like computers, but especially the masculine and feminine models. The Kabbalah calls this the unity of *memalei kol almin* and *soveiv kol almin,* and the amalgamation of *za* and *nukva.*

The medieval Christian scholar Nicholas of Cusa called it *coincidental oppositorum* (union of opposites). The Hindu *jivan-mukta,* the liberated individual, is he who orchestrates together the masculine and feminine and is thereby liberated from duality. And the liberated couple would be the man and the woman who are orchestrated together as an intimate and indivisible organism.

But the union of the masculine and feminine reached its apogee in the mystical discipline of the Jewish Kabbalah, where the coming together of the masculine and feminine is the principal theme. The *Zohar*, the Bible of the Kabbalah, says of sex: *Zivug* (sexual intercourse) is the fulfillment of the ultimate goal of marriage, which is to unite two bodies who share two half-souls, so that they become "one body, one soul." The ancient rabbis further demonstrate the relationship between human love and the divine unity by pointing out that the Hebrew words *ahavah* (love) and *echad* (oneness, connoting the divine unity) have the same numerical equivalent of 13 (in Hebrew every letter has a numerical quotient), because in the act of physical congress between husband and wife, God Himself becomes one.

Sex—The Ultimate Binder

The harmony in the divine being is channeled down as a profound act of unity between husband and wife. As Tehilla Abramov, a leading female Jewish religious writer, says of sex, "This extreme closeness has the power to help a couple overcome their differences. It gives them the strength which emanates from a one body, one soul unification. They become one person handling their different challenges together."

That's why communication and talking can never equal the profound oneness generated by sex. God decreed that sex be the profound step that always brings husband and wife together as one. As Abramov continues, "The key to a couple's unity is in the bedroom, which is compared to the Holy of Holies chamber in the [Holy Temple in Jerusalem]."

Just as a desire for food connects our bodies with our souls, so, too, does the lust for lovemaking with our spouse connect two individual bodies—as well as the two half-souls of which they were comprised before they were united in marriage. The physical aspect is absolutely necessary to achieve the spiritual goal. But this idea that the body and its processes are essential to the soul shocks the natural religious sensibilities that are accustomed to denigrating the physical and embracing the spiritual. But in Judaism it is a central idea that the needs of the body are placed before the needs of the soul. As

Abramov says, "We attain the greatest spirituality via our physical bodies. This is the basis of Judaism, which shows us how
physical pleasures are uplifted and sanctified."

Indeed, anyone who has ever read any Jewish mystical text
knows that sex is the loftiest of human endeavors. The Kabbalah
repeatedly uses sexual imagery as a metaphor for the *yichudim
elyonim*—the higher celestial unions of the masculine and feminine energies of the Godhead. The Jewish mystics rejected the
philosopher's hostility to the material world and sought to restore
the integrated relationship between body and soul that had pre-
vailed in Biblical and rabbinic culture. The mystics celebrated
human sexuality as a requirement for divine harmony, which was
usually portrayed in sexual terms. In fact, the Kabbalists held the
very opposite view of many medieval Christian writers who
believed that the holy spirit could not be present while human
beings were engaged in carnal intercourse. On the contrary, in
Kabbalah, intercourse between man and wife brings the *Shekhina*,
the divine presence, into the conjugal bed.

This is a far cry from those misguided religious individuals
who downgrade the centrality of sex in marriage and instead
emphasize spiritual qualities like a shared faith. To be sure,
Judaism desires that couples have strong religious convictions,
and that a woman admires her husband's righteousness and a
man feels attracted to his wife's piety. Yet, the attraction that a
man, for example, has to his wife's body and personality is
even more important. As Rashi says, "It is specifically in the
intimate area of their lives that a woman most desires that her
husband love her" (Bereishis 3:16). A woman wants to be sexually desirable to her husband. She wants him to *want* to make
love to her. And that desire is holy.

This all-important fact was an axiom of faith to the ancient
rabbis. Possessing keen psychological insight, they understood
that a wife wants to be physically and erotically desirable to her
husband. The *Zohar* writes very movingly that the Sabbath candles, which are lit every week by Jewish wives the world over
on Friday afternoons as the sun sets, are a symbol of a wife's
ability to rekindle her husband's lust and ardor for her.

The various aspects of physical love were always imbued by

Judaism with deep spiritual meaning. The *Zohar* says of kissing: "When a married couple kiss, their life breaths (*ruchos*) come together. When they embrace, then their spirits (*nefashos*) come together. And when they have marital relations, their bodies (*gufim*) come together." This leads to a profound three-pronged unity, where life breath, spirit, and body come together to close a powerful circle of unity.

It is during a face-to-face sexual encounter in which man and woman achieve a deep and lasting intimacy induced by this triangular harmony. First, husband and wife kiss, exchanging life breaths and thereby becoming one life force. Second, they peer deeply into each other's eyes, the windows of the soul, thereby becoming one spirit. Finally, they are completely intertwined limb by limb, thereby becoming one flesh. Sex has the power to sew us together so that two strangers become one indivisible organism: one life, one spirit, one flesh.

Anything Goes . . . ?

Aside from three things I discussed in *Kosher Sex*—having sex during the menstrual period, having sex in a way that compromises intimacy (such as a ménage à trois or watching pornography), and thinking about another person while making love to one's spouse—Judaism has adopted a no-holds-barred attitude toward marital sex. Anything goes in sex with one's wife; the sky is the limit. The more adventurous, the better. The more imaginative, the more holy. God wants a man and a woman to love each other deeply, and stoking the fires of sexual lust in marriage is the surest way. The ancient rabbis of the Talmud expressly declared that a husband may do as he pleases with his wife in the sexual arena (of course, always with her consent) (Nedarim 20b). That means that Jewish law permitted any kind of intercourse.

So emphatic is the Talmud on this point that it even tells an incredible story of a woman who came to Rabbi Judah the Prince to complain to him. She told him that she had "set a table" for her husband in bed, who then proceeded to "overturn it," a pretty clear reference to anal intercourse. Her complaint was not that she was personally opposed to this new sexual repertoire, but rather that she was convinced that there was something religiously wrong with it—that it was somehow dirty and immoral. It just felt wrong to her, even if she may have enjoyed it. (The Talmud doesn't actually say whether she did or did not.) Thus this wife visited the greatest rabbi alive to confirm her intuitive censure and pass his condemnation on to her adventurous husband. Yet, Rabbi Yehuda responded to her, "My daughter, the Torah has permitted you to him and him to you. Therefore, there is nothing that I can do for you" (Nedarim 20b). So long as the wife was agreeable, the Torah was agreeable. But Rabbi Judah the Prince could not object to what her husband had done on Jewish legal grounds. Indeed, while oral and anal sex are considered unnatural sex in the Jewish religious literature, Talmudic sources address these issues without reserve and occasionally permit "unnatural" sex if the purpose is to create passion and bring husband and wife closer together. "If it is occasional, and the desire of his heart is to come upon his wife in an unnatural way, it is permitted" (Tosefot Yevamot 34b, Gold, 1992). This is quite a change from other religious traditions that saw sex as being strictly for procreation.

Indeed, passion and experimentation in a marriage are so important that one is even allowed to compromise the need for modesty. This is demonstrated in the Talmudic law that states that sex should take place at night so that husband and wife are making love to a personality and not just a body. During the day when everything can be seen, husband and wife might get too preoccupied with individual body parts to the exclusion of the total personality. This is also the reason that the rabbis advised husbands against *staring* and becoming visually obsessed with their wives' genitalia. One must always be on guard so as not to objectify one's spouse. Yet, Talmudic opinion held that one might have intercourse during the day, since otherwise the husband, overcome by sleep, might perform perfunctorily and end up displeasing his wife (Niddah 17a). The need for passion pre-empted the need for modesty.

In this vein Rabbi Saadia Gaon, one of the leading Jewish

thinkers of all time, wrote in the tenth century that "sexual intercourse holds the most remarkable of pleasures. It increases the soul's gladness and gaiety. It drives gloomy thoughts from the mind and serves as an antidote to melancholy. And there cannot be anything reprehensible about the sex act since God's holy men in the Bible engaged in it with His approval."

Notice that there is not one word of procreation mentioned here and that the word used in the Bible to describe the sexual interaction between Isaac and Rebecca is *metzachek,* rejoicing, celebrating. As Rabbi Menachem Meiri said in the thirteenth century: "Had relations been only physical, the Bible would not have referred to them as *yediah,* knowledge."

The Privileges of Marriage

According to Biblical law, a wife enjoys three fundamental rights in marriage: food and shelter, clothing, and conjugal rights. Rabbi Norman Lamm, a leading contemporary Orthodox Jewish thinker, adds in *Contemporary Jewish Ethics* that only a refusal of the last one, conjugal rights, dubs the husband or wife a *mored,* a rebellious spouse deserving of divorce. Lamm writes, "That surely is because *onah* is the essence of marriage. Food and clothing can be handled in court, but a withdrawal from *onah* is a functional termination of married life."

That the rabbis viewed sex as inherently holy is perhaps best demonstrated by the explicit sexual advice given by the ancient sages in order to enhance intimacy and passion. Whole libraries could be filled with this advice, but a classic example in the Iggeret Hakodesh is that given by Nachmanides to his son, and designed to be read by all married men: "Therefore engage her first in conversation that puts her heart and mind at ease and gladden her . . . Speak words that arouse her to passion, union, love, desire, and Eros [agavim] . . . Never may you force her . . . Rather win her over with words of graciousness and seduction . . . Do not hasten to arouse passion until her mood is ready; enter her with love and willingness so that she 'seminates' [that is, has an orgasm] first."

The rabbis also stressed the centrality of sexual aids, like lingerie, in order to arouse lust. Maimonides, considered by many to be the greatest Jewish thinker of all time, even says that of the four requirements that a husband must provide for his wife, as discussed earlier, there is also an obligation to provide her with clothing appropriate to sexual activity. He adds, however, that this obligation to provide things like lingerie and lacy underwear is not part of the *clothing* obligation, but part of the *onah*, or sexual, obligation. In other words, a husband's obligation to have sex with his wife must be accompanied by passion and desire.

Honor for a wife presupposes that the husband shows his interest in her desirability by expending time and resources to work on their passion. Buying intimate garments is one of the principal ways that this is achieved. So the Torah's mandate to a husband to make love to his wife includes the need to make the lovemaking sessions erotic, rather than perfunctory or degrading acts of insemination. In the Torah, the procreative side and pleasurable side of sex are clearly delineated, such that a married man is obligated to sexually pleasure his wife— even while she is pregnant.

Judaism views the need for a husband and wife to always remain physically attractive to each other as so essential, that the Talmud actually declares that together with the *mannah* (the heavenly bread that rained down and sustained the Jews for forty years in the Sinai desert) God also sent down many different kinds of perfumes for the forty years they were there (Yoma 65a). Thus, God equated the need for perfume with the need for the basic staples of survival, like bread. And all this in a barren desert! This proves that passion between husband and wife was viewed not as a luxury, but a necessity.

Indeed, lusting after your own spouse is a holy commandment. As Rabbi Lamm observantly notes, the Tenth Commandment expressly says, "Do not covet *another* man's wife."

It says nothing to limit the desire for one's *own* spouse, which should be infinite and eternal, never subsiding in any stage of life.

EPILOGUEEPILOGUEEPILOGUEEPIL
OGUEEPILOGUEEPILOGUEEPILOGU
EEPILOGUEEPILOGUEEPILOGUEEPI
LOGUEEPIL epilogue GUEEPILOG
UEEPILOGUEEPILOGUEEPILOGUEEP
ILOGUEEPILOGUEEPILOGUEEPILOG
UEEPILOGUEEPILOGUEEPILOGUEEP

A FINAL NOTE
FROM
THE Author

A Rabbi Writing a Sex Book?

Finally, for those who would say, as many have, that a book of this nature is inappropriate for a rabbi to have written, or that an intense discussion of sex is outside a religious man's remit, I draw their attention to one of the most remarkable stories of the Talmud (Berachot 62a):

> *Rav Kahana lay under the bed of Rav [his illustrious teacher] who was carousing and speaking frivolously with his wife of sexual matters; afterward, the teacher had intercourse with her. Kahana made his presence known and said to his teacher: "You appear to me to be like a hungry man who has never had sex before, for you act with great fervor in your lust."*

The teacher said to Kahana: "Are you here? Get out! It is improper for you to lie under my bed!"

Kahana said to him: "This is a matter of Torah and I must study."

Whoa! What a tale. Rav Kahana, a great sage, lies under the marital bed of his master, Rav, in order to learn the holy art of lovemaking. And why? Because he is a pious man who wishes to serve God with all his faculties. And he does so primarily by learning how to love his wife.

Books of this nature are not only important, they possess holiness. In fact, any advice that leads to husbands and wives falling more deeply in love with each other serves a divine purpose.

Likewise, I have written this book in the hope we can all regain the love of our early marital years and become precious and desirable to each other once again. A beautiful story in the Midrash relates how an Israelite in Sidon in the second century came to the great Rabbi Shimon Bar Yochai to seek a divorce from his wife. The man told Rabbi Shimon that he had been married to his wife for ten years, and in all that time they had had no children. Although he loved her, since his wife was barren, he wished to invoke the Jewish law that said that a husband may divorce his wife after ten years if the couple has not had any offspring.

Rabbi Shimon Bar Yochai told the man that indeed he was right. He may divorce his wife. But the learned old rabbi had something else up his sleeve. He told the couple that now that they had finally achieved clarity as to their future, they should celebrate even though they had made the sad decision to divorce. They should throw a party.

The couple did as they were told. At the feast, the husband drank a great deal of wine and got drunk. He looked at his wife, whom he still loved, and told her that he was sad to have to leave her, but he wished to have children. But since she had been a loving wife, she could choose any item in his home as a permanent possession. The wife thanked her husband and said that on the morrow she would take him up on his kind offer.

Shortly thereafter, the husband fell asleep. The wife instructed the servants to move her drunken spouse to the new home that she was moving into after their divorce. The next morning, the husband was surprised to awaken at his wife's new abode.

"What I am doing here?" he asked her.

"Recollect," she said to her husband, "did you not tell me last night that I might take out of your house whatever I valued most? Now, believe me, my beloved husband, among all your treasures there is not one I value so much as I do you; no, there is not a possession in this world that could possibly mean more to me than you."

So the husband and wife chose each other. The story does not tell us if they were ever blessed with children. But what we do know is that, even without offspring, their love for each other made them into one flesh.

REFERENCESREFERENCESREFEREN
CESREFERENCESREFERENCESREFE
RENCESREFERENCESREFERENCESR
EFERENCES references SREFERENC
ESREFERENCESREFERENCESREFER
ENCESREFERENCESREFERENCESRE
FERENCESREFERENCESREFERENCE

Chapter One: Trust, the Destroyer of Marriage

Boteach, Shmuley. 1999. *Kosher Sex: A Recipe for Passion and Intimacy.* New York: Doubleday.

DeSalvo, Louise. 2000. *Adultery: An Intimate Look at Why People Cheat.* Boston: Beacon Press.

Gottman, John M. 1994. *Why Marriages Succeed or Fail . . . And How You Can Make Yours Last.* New York: Fireside.

Lawson, Annette. 1988. *Adultery: An Analysis of Love and Betrayal.* New York: Basic Books.

Chapter Three: Curiosity— The Single Most Important Ingredient

Boteach, Shmuley. 1999. *Kosher Sex: A Recipe for Passion and Intimacy.* New York: Doubleday.

Botwin, Carol. 1994. *Tempted Women: The Passions, Perils and Agonies of Female Infidelity.* New York: William Morrow.

Heyn, Dalma. 1997. *The Erotic Silence of the American Wife.* New York: Plume.

Janus, Samuel S., and Cynthia L. Janus. 1993. *Janus Report on Sexual Behavior.* New York: Wiley.

Noonan, Peggy. 1990. *What I Saw at the Revolution: A Political Life in the Reagan Era.* New York: Random House.

Chapter Four: The Insatiable Woman and the Male Animal

Boteach, Shmuley. 1999. *Kosher Sex: A Recipe for Passion and Intimacy*. New York: Doubleday.

Boteach, Shmuley. 2001. *Why Can't I Fall in Love? A 12-Step Program*. New York: HarperCollins.

Michael, Robert T., et al. 1995. *Sex in America: A Definitive Study*. Boston: Little Brown.

Then, Debbie. 1999. *Women Who Stay with Men Who Stray: What Every Women Needs to Know about Men and Infidelity*. New York: Hyperion.

Wright, Robert. 1994. *The Moral Animal: Why We Are the Way We Are: The New Science of Evolutionary Psychology*. New York: Vintage.

Chapter Five: Adultery 101: What Makes Adultery Hot?

Cleland, John. 2001. *Fanny Hill: Or, Memoirs of a Woman of Pleasure*. New York: Random House.

Hite, Shere. 1976. *The Hite Report: A Nationwide Study of Female Sexuality*. New York: Macmillan.

Lawrence, D. H. 1976. *Lady Chatterley's Lover*. New York: Bantam Books.

Lawson, Annette. 1988. *Adultery: An Analysis of Love and Betrayal*. New York: Basic Books.

Popenoe, David, and Barbara Dafoe Whitehead. 2000. *The State of Our Unions: The Social Health of Marriage in America*. Piscataway, NJ: Rutgers, the State University of New Jersey.

Chapter Six: Monogamy and the Sin of Adultery

Botwin, Carol. 1994. *Tempted Women: The Passions, Perils and Agonies of Female Infidelity*. New York: William Morrow.

Buss, David M. 2000. *The Dangerous Passion: Why Jealousy Is As Necessary As Love and Sex*. New York: The Free Press.

Glass, Shirley. July/August 1998. "Shattered Vows: Getting Beyond Betrayal." *Psychology Today*.

Gottman, John M. 1995. *Why Marriages Succeed or Fail: And How You Can Make Yours Last*. New York: Simon & Schuster.

Hite, Shere. 1976. *The Hite Report: A Nationwide Study of Female Sexuality*. New York: Macmillan.

Hite, Shere. 1981. *The Hite Report on Male Sexuality*. New York: Knopf.

Janus, Samuel S., and Cynthia L. Janus. 1993. *Janus Report on Sexual Behavior.* New York: Wiley.

Laumann, Edward O., et al. 1992. *The National Health and Social Life Survey.* Chicago: NORC (National Opinion Research Center), University of Chicago.

Lawson, Annette. 1988. *Adultery: An Analysis of Love and Betrayal.* New York: Basic Books.

Staheli, Lana. 1997. *Triangles: Understanding, Preventing, and Surviving an Affair.* New York: HarperCollins.

Then, Debbie. 1999. *Women Who Stay with Men Who Stray: What Every Women Needs to Know about Men and Infidelity.* New York: Hyperion.

Chapter Seven: Seducing and Sinning
with Your Spouse

Alese, Janet, and Martin Reibstein. 1993. *Sexual Arrangements: Marriage and the Temptation of Infidelity.* New York: Scribner.

Barash, Susan. 2001. *A Passion for More: Wives Reveal the Affairs That Make or Break Their Marriages.* Berkeley, CA: Berkeley Hills Books.

Boteach, Shmuley. 1999. *Kosher Sex: A Recipe for Passion and Intimacy.* New York: Doubleday.

Botwin, Carol. 1994. *Tempted Women: The Passions, Perils and Agonies of Female Infidelity.* New York: William Morrow.

Buss, David M. 2000. *The Dangerous Passion: Why Jealousy Is As Necessary As Love and Sex.* New York: The Free Press.

Cott, Nancy. 2001. *Public Vows: A History of Marriage and the Nation.* New Haven, CT: Harvard University Press.

Deida, David. 1995. *Intimate Communion: Awakening Your Sexual Essence.* Deerfield Beach, FL: Health Communications.

Glass, Shirley. July/August 1998. "Shattered Vows: Getting Beyond Betrayal." *Psychology Today.*

Hayden, Naura. 1999. *How to Satisfy a Woman Every Time . . . and Have Her Beg for More.* New York: St. Martin's Press.

Lawson, Annette. 1988. *Adultery: An Analysis of Love and Betrayal.* New York: Basic Books.

Moore, Thomas. 1992. *Care of the Soul: A Guide for Cultivation Depth and Sacredness in Everyday Life.* New York: HarperCollins.

Tolstoy, Leo. 1993. *The Kreutzer Sonata and Other Short Stories [1828–1910].* New York: Dover Publications.

Vaughn, Peggy. 1998. *The Monogamy Myth: A Personal Handbook for Recovering from Affairs.* New York: Newmarket Press.

Chapter Eight: Commandment One in Action— Becoming a **Total** Sexual Partner

Boteach, Shmuley. 1999. *Kosher Sex: A Recipe for Passion and Intimacy.* New York: Doubleday.

Hite, Shere. 1976. *The Hite Report: A Nationwide Study of Female Sexuality.* New York: Macmillan.

Jong, Erica. 1994. *Fear of Fifty: A Midlife Memoir.* New York: HarperCollins.

Lawson, Annette. 1988. *Adultery: An Analysis of Love and Betrayal.* New York: Basic Books.

Phillips, Adam. 1997. *Monogamy.* New York: Pantheon Books.

Pittman, Frank S. 1990. *Private Lives: Infidelity and the Betrayal of Intimacy.* New York: Norton.

Then, Debbie. 1999. *Women Who Stay with Men Who Stray: What Every Women Needs to Know about Men and Infidelity.* New York: Hyperion.

Chapter Nine: Commandment Two in Action— Erotic Obstacles That Lead to **Desire**

Boteach, Shmuley. 1999. *Kosher Sex: A Recipe for Passion and Intimacy.* New York: Doubleday.

Hardy, Thomas. 1998. *The Mayor of Casterbridge [1886].* New York: Penguin.

Kaplan, Aryeh. 1976. *Waters of Eden.* New York: NCSY Orthodox Union.

Lamm, Norman. 1987. *A Hedge of Roses: Jewish Insights into Marriage and Married Life.* New York: Feldheim.

Morin, Jack. 1995. *The Erotic Mind: Unlocking the Inner Sources of Sexual Passion and Fulfillment.* New York: HarperCollins.

Talese, Gay. 1980. *Thy Neighbor's Wife.* Garden City, NY: Doubleday.

Tripp, C.A. 1975. *The Homosexual Matrix.* New York: McGraw-Hill.

Chapter Ten: Commandments Three and Four in Action—Creating **Friction**

Amsel, Rabbi Nachum. 1994. *The Jewish Encyclopedia of Moral and Ethical Issues.* Northvale, NJ: J. Aronson.

Friedman, Manis. 1990. *Doesn't Anyone Blush Anymore?* New York: HarperCollins.

Madonna. 1992. *The Sex Book.* New York: Warner Books.

Marton, Kati. 2001. *Hidden Power: Presidential Marriages That Shaped Our Recent History.* New York: Pantheon Books.

Morris, Desmond. 1977. *Manwatching: A Field Guide to Human Behavior.* London: Cape.

Chapter Eleven: Commandment Five in Action—Attraction to **Strangers**

Bandura, Albert. 1969. *Principles of Behavior Modification.* New York: Holt, Rinehart & Winston.

Jong, Erica. 1973. *Fear of Flying.* New York: Holt, Rinehart & Winston.

Lucian. 1961. *Dialogues of the Courtesans.* Harvard Classics Shelf of Fiction, Vol. VII, translated by M.D. Macleod. Cambridge, MA: Harvard University Press.

Tolstoy, Leo. 2001. *Anna Karenina: A Novel in Eight Parts [1877].* New York: Viking.

Chapter Twelve: Commandment Six in Action—**Jealousy** Is Essential

Boteach, Shmuley. 1999. *Kosher Emotions.* London: Hodder & Stoughton.

Buss, David M. 2000. *The Dangerous Passion: Why Jealousy Is As Necessary As Love and Sex.* New York: The Free Press.

Buss, David M., Todd K. Shackelford, Lee A. Kirkpatrick, Randy J. Larsen. 2001. "A Half Century of Mate Preferences: The Cultural Evolution of Values." *Journal of Marriage and Family*: Vol. 63, No. 2, pp. 491–503.

Lagache, Daniel. 1947. *La Jalousie Amoureuse.* Paris: Presses universitaires de France.

Landy, Eugene. 1971. *The Underground Dictionary.* New York: Simon & Schuster.

Lawson, Annette. 1988. *Adultery: An Analysis of Love and Betrayal.* New York: Basic Books.

Ondaatje, Michael. 1993. *The English Patient.* New York: Vintage Books.

Russell, Bertrand. 1967. *The Autobiography of Bertrand Russell.* 3 vols. London: George Allen & Unwin.

Twain, Mark. 1974. *Letters from the Earth* (1909). New York: Harper & Row.

Chapter Thirteen: Commandment Seven in Action— Intense Focus

Barash, Susan Shapiro. 2001. *A Passion for More: Wives Reveal the Affairs That Make or Break Their Marriages.* Berkeley, CA: Berkeley Hills Books.

Botwin, Carol. 1994. *Tempted Women: The Passions, Perils and Agonies of Female Infidelity.* New York: William Morrow.

Desalvo, Louise. 2000. *Adultery: An Intimate Look at Why People Cheat.* Boston: Beacon Press.

Chapter Fourteen: Commandment Eight in Action— Heightening Attraction, Minimizing Compatibility

Alese, Janet, and Martin Reibstein. 1993. *Sexual Arrangements: Marriage and the Temptation of Infidelity.* New York: Scribner.

Boteach, Shmuley. 2002. *Judaism for Everyone.* New York: Basic Books.

Burgess, Adrienne. 2001. *Will You Still Love Me Tomorrow?* Minneapolis: Vermilion.

Lewin, Tamar. May 11, 2002. "No Big Deal, but Some Dorm Rooms Have Gone Coed." *New York Times.*

Chapter Fifteen: Commandment Nine in Action— Nourishing the Ego

Botwin, Carol. 1994. *Tempted Women: The Passions, Perils and Agonies of Female Infidelity.* New York: William Morrow.

Chapter Sixteen: Commandment Ten in Action— Experiencing Sin

Stern, Howard. 1996. *Miss America.* New York: Harper.

Tuch, Richard. 2000. *The Single Women-Married Man Syndrome.* North Vale, NJ: Jason Aronson.

Chapter Seventeen: Parents Are Lovers, Too

Bushnell, Candace. 1997. *Sex and the City.* New York: Warner Books.

Wolfinger, Nicholas H. 1999. "Coupling and Uncoupling: Changing Marriage Patterns and the Intergenerational Transmission of Divorce." Presented at the annual meeting of the American Sociological Association. Chicago.

Chapter Eighteen: The Rebirth of Lust
and Love in Marriage

Atwater, Lynn. *The Extramarital Connection: Sex, Intimacy, and Identity.* 1982. New York: Irvington Publishers.

Bierce, Ambrose Gwinnett. 1998. *The Devil's Dictionary.* Oxford: Oxford University Press.

Brook, Stephen. 1996. *The Penguin Book of Infidelities.* New York: Penguin.

Gray, John. 1992. *Men Are from Mars, Women Are from Venus.* New York: HarperCollins.

Leach, Michael, and Therese J. Borchard (Editors). 2002. *I Like Being Married: Treasured Traditions, Rituals, and Stories.* New York: Doubleday.

Marton, Kati. 2001. *Hidden Power: Presidential Marriages That Shaped Our Recent History.* New York: Pantheon Books.

Masters, William H., and Virginia E. Johnson. 1966. *Human Sexual Response.* Hagerstown, MD: Lippincott, Williams, and Wilkins.

Chapter Nineteen: Spirituality and Mysticism
As Our Erotic Guides

Abramov, Tehilla. 1988. *The Secret of Jewish Femininity.* New York: Targum.

Boteach, Shmuley. 1999. *Kosher Sex: A Recipe for Passion and Intimacy.* New York: Doubleday.

Bulka, Reuven P. 1995. *Judaism on Pleasure.* New York: Jason Aronson.

Kellner, M. M. (Editor). 1978. *Contemporary Jewish Ethics.* New York: Sanhedrin Press.

Maimonides, Moses. 1963. *The Guide to the Perplexed,* translated by Shlomo Pines. Chicago: University of Chicago Press.